Technology- and Innovation-management: Comprehensive Perspectives

Sönke Albers (Ed.)
Cross-functional Innovation Management
Perspectives from Different Disciplines
2004. xiv, 518 pp. With 72 Fig. and 50 Tab. Hardc.
EUR 59,90 ISBN 978-3-409-12627-4

International authors of very different fields look at technology and innovation management from several perspectives: they discuss in 27 articles aspects of their disciplines focussing on innovation management, ultimately presenting an interdisciplinary crossing-over into all other functional areas within the realm of business. Furthermore, some authors devote themselves to new topics such as venture capital, virtual stock markets, and futurology.

The Editor
Professor Dr. Sönke Albers is Head of the Department of Innovation, New Media and Marketing at the Institute of Business Administration and Innovation Management Research at the Christian-Albrechts-University at Kiel (Germany).

Einfach bestellen: kerstin.kuchta@gwv-fachverlage.de Telefon +49(0)611. 7878-626

KOMPETENZ IN SACHEN WIRTSCHAFT

Zeitschrift für Betriebswirtschaft

Special Issue 1/2008

Economics and Management of Education

ZfB-Special Issues

1/2005 Revenue Management
Herausgeber: Günter Fandel/Hans Botho von Portatius
136 Seiten. ISBN 3 8439 0050 8

2/2005 Perspektiven der Kommunikationspolitik
Herausgeber: Manfred Krafft
128 Seiten. ISBN 3 8349 0108 3

3/2005 Reverse Logistics I
Herausgeber: Günter Fandel/Joachim Reese
128 Seiten. ISBN 3 8349 0109 1

4/2005 Reverse Logistics II
Herausgeber: Günter Fandel/Joachim Reese
112 Seiten. ISBN 3 8349 0134 2

5/2005 Unternehmensethik und Unternehmenspraxis
Herausgeber: Horst Albach
132 Seiten. ISBN 3 8349 0228 4

1/2006 Unternehmensethik und globale Märkte
Herausgeber: Horst Albach
116 Seiten. ISBN 3 8349 0239 X

2/2006 E-Learning Geschäftsmodelle und Einsatzkonzepte
Herausgeber: Michael H. Breitner/Günter Fandel
136 Seiten. ISBN 3 8349 0249 7

3/2006 Herausforderung Ostasien
Herausgeber: Werner Pascha
144 Seiten. ISBN 3 8349 0315 9

4/2006 Entrepreneurship
Herausgeber: Thomas Ehrmann/Peter Witt
195 Seiten. ISBN 3 8349 0363 9

5/2006 Governance Innovations and Strategies
Herausgeber: Oliver Fabel/Egon Franck
176 Seiten. ISBN 3 8349 0426 3

6/2006 Rechnungslegung nach internationalen Grundsätzen
Herausgeber: Norbert Krawitz
180 Seiten. ISBN 3 8349 0425 6

1/2007 Der Ehrbare Kaufmann: Modernes Leitbild für Unternehmer?
Herausgeber: Joachim Schwalbach/Günter Fandel
140 Seiten. ISBN 3 8349 0659 X

2/2007 Innovation, Orientation, Innovativeness and Innovation Success
Herausgeber: Holger Ernst/Hans Georg Gemünden
156 Seiten. ISBN 3 8349 0698 0

3/2007 Direct Marketing
Herausgeber: Manfred Krafft/Jürgen Gerdes
192 Seiten. ISBN 3 8349 0728 6

4/2007 Open Innovation between and within Organizations
Herausgeber: Holger Ernst/Hans Georg Gemünden
140 Seiten. ISBN 3 8349 0731 6

5/2007 Hochschulrechnung und Hochschulcontrolling
Herausgeber: Hans-Ulrich Küpper
188 Seiten. ISBN 3 8349 0778 2

6/2007 Empirische Studien zum Management in mittelständischen Unternehmen
Herausgeber: Horst Albach/Peter Letmathe
140 Seiten. ISBN 3 8349 0799 5

Economics and Management of Education

Herausgeber
Prof. Dominique Demougin, Ph.D.
Prof. Dr. Oliver Fabel

Die Deutsche Bibliothek – CIP-Einheitsaufnahme

> **Zeitschrift für Betriebswirtschaft** : ZfB. – Wiesbaden :
> Betriebswirtschaftlicher Verl. Gabler
> Erscheint monatl. – Aufnahme nach Jg. 67, H. 3 (1997)
> Reihe Ergänzungsheft: Zeitschrift für Betriebswirtschaft /
> Ergänzungsheft. Fortlaufende Beil.: Betriebswirtschaftliches
> Repetitorium. – Danach bis 1979: ZfB-Repetitorium
> ISSN 0044-2372
> 2008, Special Issue 1. Economics and Management of Education
> Herausgeber: Dominique Demougin, Oliver Fabel – Wiesbaden: Gabler, 2008
> (Zeitschrift für Betriebswirtschaft; 2008, Special Issue 1)
>
> ISBN 978-3-8349-0904-6

Alle Rechte vorbehalten

© Betriebswirtschaftlicher Verlag Dr. Th. Gabler GmbH, Wiesbaden 2008
Lektorat: Susanne Kramer/Annelie Meisenheimer

Der Gabler Verlag ist ein Unternehmen von Springer Science+Business Media.

Das Werk einschließlich aller seiner Teile ist urheberrechtlich geschützt. Jede Verwertung außerhalb der engen Grenzen des Urheberrechtsgesetzes ist ohne Zustimmung des Verlags unzulässig und strafbar. Das gilt insbesondere für Vervielfältigungen, Übersetzungen, Mikroverfilmungen und die Einspeicherung und Verarbeitung in elektronischen Systemen.

http://www.gabler.de
http://www.zfb-online.de

Höchste inhaltliche und technische Qualität unserer Produkte ist unser Ziel. Bei der Produktion und Verbreitung unserer Bücher wollen wir die Umwelt schonen: Dieses Buch ist auf säurefreiem und chlorfrei gebleichtem Papier gedruckt. Die Einschweißfolie besteht aus Polyäthylen und damit aus organischen Grundstoffen, die weder bei der Herstellung noch bei der Verbrennung Schadstoffe freisetzen.

Die Wiedergabe von Gebrauchsnamen, Handelsnamen, Warenbezeichnungen usw. in diesem Werk berechtigt auch ohne besondere Kennzeichnung nicht zu der Annahme, dass solche Namen im Sinne der Warenzeichen- und Markenschutz-Gesetzgebung als frei zu betrachten wären und daher von jedermann benutzt werden dürften.

Satz: Fotosatz-Service Köhler GmbH, Würzburg

ISBN 978-3-8349-0904-6

INHALTSVERZEICHNIS

VII   Editorial

1   **Early Childhood Education and Care in Germany:
The Status Quo and Reform Proposals**
Prof. Dr. C. Katharina Spieß, Berlin

23   **The Economics of Tracking and Non-Tracking**
PD Dr. Volker Meier, Munich, and Dipl.-Vw. Gabriela Schütz, Munich

45   **How Equal Are Educational Opportunities? Family Background
and Student Achievement in Europe and the United States**
Prof. Dr. Ludger Wößmann, Munich

71   **Public Universities, Tuition and Competition – A Tiebout Model**
Prof. Dr. Robert Schwager, Göttingen

91   **Young Researchers in the Field of Management: Assessing the Relation
between the Work Environment for Creativity and Job Satisfaction,
Self-Confidence, and Publication Productivity**
Dr. Marina Fiedler, Munich, Dr. Isabell M. Welpe, Munich, and
Prof. Dr. Dres. h.c. Arnold Picot, Munich

115   **Further Education: The Role of School Type**
Prof. Dr. Klaus Harney, Bochum, and Dr. Susanne Warning, Trier

137   **Works Councils and the Productivity Effects of Different Continuing
Training Measures**
PD Dr. Thomas Zwick, Mannheim

151   **Public Employment Services and Employers:
How Important are Networks with Firms?**
Dipl.-Vw. Stefanie Behncke, St. Gallen, Dr. Markus Frölich, Mannheim,
and Prof. Dr. Michael Lechner, St. Gallen

IX   GRUNDSÄTZE UND ZIELE
XI   HERAUSGEBER/EDITORIAL BOARD
XII   IMPRESSUM/HINWEISE FÜR AUTOREN

WWW.GABLER.DE

Dynamic perspectives for international management

Thomas Borghoff
**Evolutionary Theory
of the Globalisation of Firms**
2005. xxiv, 481 pp. (mir-Edition, ed. by
Klaus Macharzina | Martin K. Welge |
Michael Kutschker | Johann Engelhard)
Softc. EUR 65,90
ISBN 978-3-8349-0013-5

The author develops an evolutionary theory of the globalisation of firms using a thorough historical analysis to identify the basic globalisation processes. The identification of the underlying mechanisms allows managers to perceive these mechanisms in their influence on the evolutionary dynamics of the firms and to use these dynamics actively.

The Author
Thomas Borghoff is Senior Lecturer and Scientific Assistant at the Faculty of Economics and Social Sciences, University of Dortmund, and Senior Lecturer at the School of Marketing and International Business (SMIB), Victoria University of Wellington, New Zealand

Order your copy now: kerstin.kuchta@gwv-fachverlage.de
Telefon +49(0)611. 7878-626

KOMPETENZ IN SACHEN WIRTSCHAFT

Editorial

In the knowledge society of the 21st century, general education, training, and further education have been recognized to be major determinants for the economic success of entire regions, countries, and continents. Recent international comparisons like the PISA study point out that, despite its glorious past, the German education system appears in an alarming state and in dire need of reforms. Similarly, the research output of German universities as measured by the number of publications in the SCI and in the SSCI per capita suggests that the system is underperforming. But of course, looking at an education system requires more than comparing one or two links in the education chain of a country. In that respect, the contributions collected in this issue attempt to look at the main building blocks of the German education system.

The first paper by Spieß examines the predominant issues facing the German Early Childhood Education and Care (ECEC) system. The paper provides comparisons with other European countries with respect to a number of important variables like governance, funding, attendance – in particular with regard to children with immigration backgrounds –, rationing, quality, the use of vouchers etc. The next two papers focus on secondary schools. Meier and Schütz survey the recent theoretical and empirical literature on tracking in schools, i.e. the performance-contingent sorting of children in different classes or schools. The paper examines whether tracking improves the average performance and analyzes its effect on children of socially disfavored background. The latter question is also at the center of the analysis by Woessmann. Specifically, that paper uses a large international comparative student achievement test in mathematics and sciences to estimate the impact of parental education on children's test scores. Family background proves to have a strong impact that is remarkably similar in size across countries and education systems. There are, however, a few outliers such as Germany. In Germany the education system performs poorly at equalizing chances on the backdrop of the respective milieu.

The subsequent two papers focus on current reform agendas for the German university system. Schwager uses a theoretical framework à la Tiebout to investigate the impact of tuition fees for public universities and its ensuing effect on the quality of education. The paper tackles two pertinent subject matters of the current discussion: Should universities get more decision power with respect to budget and enrolment? And should all competence regarding higher education be transferred from the federal government to the federal states? The next paper by Fiedler, Picot and Welpe considers working conditions of junior faculties in German-speaking Europe. The paper develops a catalogue of hypotheses and uses survey data and publication records to evaluate confidence, job satisfaction, and publication productivity of young academics. Hence, the paper provides one of the first evaluations of the introduction of the junior professorship which expressly aimed at increasing the productivity of young researchers in the German university system.

The last three papers deal with the organization of adult education. Harney and Warning look at the second-chance education generally leading to a qualification for university entrance. In particular, they compare full-time day schools with part-time evening schools. The main argument is based on signalling: high ability students credibly signal their type by choosing day schools. The model is then confronted with empirical data of adult schools in the state of Hesse. Zwick proceeds by studying the impact of different types of continuing training on the productivity of firms with a special emphasis on the role of work councils. Intuitively, the latter should matter; the presence of a work council should increase investment in general human capital. Moreover, a work council may help select appropriate employees and motivate them. The paper reviews these hypotheses and confronts them with panel data. Finally and rounding up this issue, Behncke, Frölich and Lechner post a clear warning concerning the limits of formal training for unemployed individuals. Their analysis shows that over all educational levels, qualification groups, and ages the re-employment chances are significantly affected by the Unemployment Agency's case workers' integration into the business environment. Thus, the tacit knowledge of the case-worker concerning the demand side must match with supply side's efforts to produce integration success.

Of course, no special issue could exhaustively inform about the *Economics and Management of Education*. However, as editors we are very proud to offer a line of contributions covering every step in an individual's educational career – from early childhood all the way up to adult further education. We sincerely hope that the readership will endorse this somewhat "alternative" structure – also, combining the variety of methods available in theoretical, empirical, and managerial economics. We sincerely thank the contributors and our referees for the inspiring discussions across the border lines of academic disciplines and research topics. Special thanks go the DFG Research Group 454 "Heterogeneous Labor" for organizing a workshop to exchange our ideas.

Prof. Dominique Demougin, Ph.D.
Prof. Dr. Oliver Fabel

Early Childhood Education and Care in Germany: The Status Quo and Reform Proposals

C. Katharina Spieß*

Abstract

- The high returns of early childhood education and care (ECEC) services, especially for disadvantaged children, are receiving more and more attention in economic research. The viewpoint of educational economics may be expected to contribute particularly important findings on these services. The present paper offers an overview of the most important issues currently facing the German ECEC system. First, with regard to specific German governance and funding issues, it outlines public organizations and authorities responsible for this aspect of education and illustrates the supply and demand sides of the ECEC market using the most recent official statistics and comparing these findings with other European countries. Second, it discusses the specific issue of rationing and the problem that attendance rates only provide information on the group of parents who received one of the limited spots available in the German system. Furthermore, while quality issues are not a major focus of this paper, they are mentioned here as well. Third, the paper summarizes studies on the utilization of ECEC services in Germany based on representative national data sets, also referring to empirical studies that have focused on the correlation between school outcomes and ECEC attendance. Finally, some important issues at the top of the political agenda are highlighted, and the use of a federal voucher approach is discussed from an economic perspective.

Keywords Child care · early education · demand and supply · public funding

JEL: I2, H4, H3

Prof. Dr. C. Katharina Spieß (✉)
is Professor of Economics of Family and Education at the Freie Universität Berlin, in cooperation with DIW Berlin (Deutsches Institut für Wirtschaftsforschung). Research interests: various topics in the field of early childhood. DIW Berlin, Mohrenstr. 58, 10117 Berlin, Germany, E-mail: kspiess@diw.de

A. Early childhood education and care – an often-forgotten part of the educational system

Early childhood education and care (ECEC)[1] is a component of the broader educational system that economists often forget when discussing educational issues. Many studies on the educational system, in fact, simply begin with primary school. Yet given the importance of this early phase in the lives of learners, such a narrow perspective appears clearly inadequate. While psychologists and educational researchers have emphasized the importance of this stage for some time, only in recent years has a trend emerged among economists to investigate the high returns of early childhood education. One prominent example is the recent study by Heckman and co-authors (for instance, Heckman/Masterov 2007), who emphasise that the returns on educational investments – particularly for disadvantaged children – are much higher in earlier life stages than in later ones.[2]

The high returns on investments in ECEC services, in particular, has been corroborated by cost-benefit analyses conducted mainly in Anglo-American contexts. Ideally, a solid and carefully conducted cost-benefit analysis of ECEC programs should be based on data covering the individual's entire lifespan. However, this kind of data is extremely rare, and when detailed information is available on ECEC programs at all, it is usually not representative for a broader population. The Perry Preschool Project is probably the best known example of such a study, since it succeeded in observing individuals from the point of entering an ECEC program to the age of 40 (for a recent reference, see Belfield et al. 2006). For each dollar invested, the program returned $12.90 to the public and $4.10 to participants, for a total return of $17.07. The sources of the return were savings in welfare and education due to less need for special education classes, greater earnings of participants, higher taxes paid on greater earnings, and, in particular, reduced criminal justice system costs and victim costs of crime. Positive return rates have been established by other cost-benefit studies as well. However, high return rates are driven mainly by the beneficial effects of high-quality early childhood education on children from low-income families with a low socio-economic status. The effects are much smaller for children from families with a higher socio-economic status (for an overview, see Cleveland/Krashinsky 1998, Lynch 2004, Karoly et al. 2006, and OECD 2006, pp. 249-264)[3]. In addition it is important to highlight that cost-benefit ratios are heavily influenced by the quality of services provided as well (see, for instance, Lamb 1998).

ECEC also has other implications which relate more to the care effect of these services than to the purely educational aspect. ECEC services allow parents, in particular mothers, to combine family and work. Society also benefits from this second dimension of early education programs in several ways: the better women with children are able to combine work and family life, the higher their income and the greater the tax benefits and other benefits to social security systems. For an estimation of these effects due to an increase of ECEC services based on German data, see Spiess et al. (2002a) or Rauschenbach/ Schilling (2007)[4]. Moreover, a society benefits from investing in the human capital of women at an earlier stage if those women are able to make use of their human capital by joining the highly educated labour force. If we take the current and increasing labour shortage resulting from widespread demographic change throughout the Western world into account, this benefit increases even further. ECEC services can help to reduce this labour shortage indirectly, since they help to increase the number of qualified mothers entering the workforce (see, for instance, Spiess et al. 2002a or OECD 2006).

This paper is structured as follows. The second chapter discusses governance and funding issues. It gives an overview of the various public players and authorities responsible for ECEC. The third chapter illustrates the demand and supply sides of the ECEC market using the most recent official statistics, comparing these findings with other European countries. A short fourth chapter provides a few remarks on quality issues. The fifth chapter summarizes empirical studies on the use of ECEC services in Germany and refers to some other studies that have focused on the correlation between school outcomes and ECEC attendance. The last two chapters point out some important issues at the top of the political agenda, mainly of the federal government, and evaluate these from an economic perspective. The option of a federal voucher is discussed in particular.

B. The German institutions governing ECEC programs[5]

In Germany, the educational aspects of ECEC programs have been the subject of public discourse on *Kindergarten* education for some time. In the early 1970s, *Kindergarten* (for a definition, see below) officially became the first step in the German educational system. It was created for children starting at the age of three and thus not intended to help parents combine work and family duties. Only recently has the economic aspect gained prominence in the political discourse, along with the educational benefits of ECEC programs for children below the age of three (see for instance, BMFSFJ 2007). Although it is sometimes argued that care options for this age group should not actually be conceived of as preschool education in the sense of preparing children for school, a broader understanding of education as lifelong learning should include these care and learning options, which are crucial for the development of diverse cognitive and non-cognitive skills.

Today, the German ECEC system encompasses three main groups of programs: *Krippen* or nurseries for children under the age of three; *Kindergärten* or day-care centers for children between the ages of three and six; and a combination of the two, offering day care for all children up to school age. The broader term for all these ECEC services, *Kindertageseinrichtungen*, includes all of these programs.

ECEC programs in Germany are part of the child and youth welfare system. In contrast to the primary and secondary schools, which are run at the state level (Germany's 16 *Länder*), the federal government has legislative and organizational authority over the area of child and youth welfare, including children's services. The federal government's legislative authority over ECEC services is rooted in its responsibility for the public welfare. It has set out the framework for the ECEC system in the "Child and Youth Welfare Act" of the Social Code VIII (*Kinder- und Jugendhilfegesetz*, KJHG). With the enactment of this law, the federal government has exercised its legislative authority for child and youth welfare by requiring that equivalent living conditions be achieved throughout the country.

The actual implementation of the KJHG, including the financing of programs designed to achieve the aforementioned stipulations, are a state (*Länder*) responsibility. The states normally regulate, fund, and direct children's services both through the ministry responsible–usually child and youth services, or education–and through the independent state-level Youth Welfare Offices (*Landesjugendämter*).

The municipality level must plan and ensure the provision of ECEC services, but should do so under the principle of subsidiarity, which requires that societal tasks be undertaken by the smallest possible social unit. Thus, in principle, municipalities should not take direct charge of providing ECEC services if other providers offer them as well. Municipalities share responsibility with the states for the funding of ECEC services, and do so through local tax revenues and funds allocated by state governments. Overall, the ECEC system is complex and highly decentralised, with responsibilities shared by three different government levels and numerous non-profit providers (see figure 1). It is characterized by constant debates and negotiations about the roles and responsibilities of different levels of government for ECEC, particularly regarding the application of the subsidiarity principle.

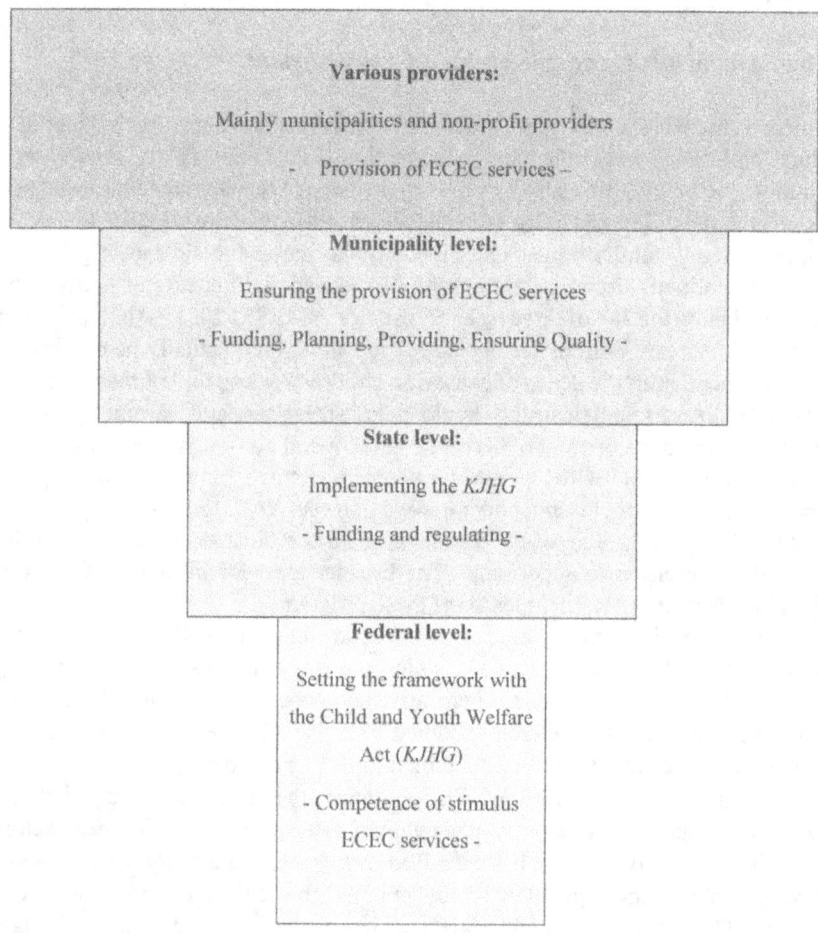

Fig. 1. The governance of ECEC services in Germany: Stylized Facts
Source: Authors.

Nevertheless, municipalities have a particularly important role in the overall system. In addition to fulfilling the responsibilities described above, it is the municipality that decides where the public funds provided by state and municipal governments actually go. The municipality also decides how many slots should be provided in ECEC centers based on demographic forecasts and in some municipalities based on surveys of the child care needs of parents. Nevertheless this planning process is up to the individual municipality (see Kreyenfeld et al. 2001).

Besides operating their own ECEC centers and given the principle of subsidiarity, the municipalities give public money to other, mainly non-profit providers. To obtain public funding, an ECEC center must both be licensed by the state youth welfare office as meeting the state's standards for ECEC services and be accepted as part of the plan for local services. On average, 75-80% of the costs of non-profit providers are covered by public funds, about 10% by the providers themselves, and the rest by parents. In Germany, these parental fees are relatively low compared to other countries (Immervoll/Barber 2005): they are estimated to lie between zero and 30 percent of total costs. Unlike most other countries, Germany's federal government has no direct role in the basic funding of ECEC services, so each state or even each municipality has its own funding system.

Furthermore, the municipalities are in charge of ensuring the quality of the ECEC centers. There is no free entry to the ECEC "market": all providers have to be licensed, as described above. Given this constellation of responsibilities, one can argue that fair competition among providers does not exist: the municipalities have a particular strong position, as they decide on the funding, the regulation, and "market entrance" and are themselves providers of the same services (see Spiess 1998, Spiess et al. 2000 and below).

Long time, in most states, the funding systems have a supply-side orientation, meaning that the providers themselves get the money rather than the parents on the demand side. Since, in principle, this supply-side funding system does not provide adequate incentives for providers to design their services according parental needs, some states have changed to a funding system more oriented toward the demand side. The most prominent examples are Hamburg and Berlin, where municipalities have been providing day care vouchers to parents since 2003 and 2007 respectively (for Hamburg, see for instance, Falck 2004). These vouchers allow parents to choose among ECEC services according to their preferences. Other states have moved in a similar direction toward a demand-side-oriented funding system (DJI 2005, chapter 2.4, and BMFSFJ 2003).

C. Supply and demand of ECEC services in Germany

From the perspective of the supply/demand framework described above, the German ECEC market can be described as follows: on the supply side the market is dominated mainly by non-profit providers and the municipalities themselves. The main non-profit providers are the two major churches in Germany (Catholic and Protestant) and large welfare associations such as the *Paritätische Wohlfahrsverband* and the *Arbeiterwohlfahrt*. The current official statistics on the different provider groups in the ECEC system show that approximately 43% of all child-care slots are provided by municipal facilities and 57% by non-profit organizations[6]. However, these numbers vary widely among the states, with only 5% municipal vs. 88% non-profit providers in Hamburg and as much as 52% municipal vs. 48% non-profit providers in Saxony (see Table 1).

For-profit providers are almost nonexistent on this "market", offering only about 1% of all child-care slots covered in the current official statistics.[7] This small percentage has to do with the fact that up to 2005, when the *Tagesbetreuungsausbaugesetz (TAG 2004)* went into effect, for-profit providers were generally not considered for subsidies. Thus, in general, they were not able to compete. Since 2005 it has been up to the German states to find new regulations on this issue. To date, no thorough overview has been done on how this is being regulated in municipalities throughout Germany. Nevertheless, some empirical evidence exists: for-profit providers hold a significantly higher market share in states where they are subsidized, such as Hamburg, than in states where they are not, such as Berlin. Employer-based ECEC does not play a major role in Germany (see table 1).

The demand side of the German ECEC system – using the term "demand" in a strict sense – is difficult to describe since the official statistics report ECEC attendance rates only. This is true for representative surveys as well, such as the *Mikrozensus*, the German Socio-Economic Panel *(SOEP)*, *DJI Kinderpanel* or *DJI Kinderbetreuungsstudie*. In these surveys, too, only the attendance of ECEC programs is observed. If there were no rationing in the German "ECEC market", these attendance rates would represent the actual demand. However, as is shown by special surveys that ask parents directly about

Tab. 1. Slots in ECEC centers by group of provider and state, 2006

State	Total	Municipality provided		Non-profit provided		Employer provided		For-profit provided	
		Number of slots	%*	Number of slots	%*	Number of slots	%*	Number of slots	%*
Schleswig-Holstein	95 110	25 966	27	68 330	72	293	0	521	1
Hamburg	71 508	3 925	5	63 284	88	2 783	4	1 516	2
Bremen	23 177	10 363	45	12 658	55	0	0	156	1
Hesse	243 586	130 655	54	112 187	46	470	0	274	0
Rhineland-Palatinate	159 507	71 137	45	88 212	55	26	0	132	0
Saarland	35 755	10 544	29	25 151	70	0	0	60	0
Berlin	124 136	41 527	33	81 570	66	426	0	613	0
Mecklenburg-Western Pomerania	85 261	23 849	28	58 581	69	46	0	2 785	3
Saxony	236 757	122 498	52	113 538	48	143	0	578	0
Saxony-Anhalt	135 143	82 259	61	52 424	39	185	0	275	0
Thuringia	93 159	32 141	35	60 531	65	369	0	118	0
Total	**1 303 099**	**554 864**	**43**	**736 466**	**57**	**4 741**	**0**	**7 028**	**1**

* Share provided by this group of provider on all slots provided.

Source: data from the Child and Youth Services Statistics 2006 provided by *the Dortmunder Arbeitsstelle Kinder- und Jugendhilfestatistik* 2006, author's calculations.

their preferences for higher provision of ECEC services (for a more recent survey, see Perspektive Deutschland 2006), there is an over-demand for ECEC services in particular for children up to three years. In economic terms this means the demand side is rationed. To our knowledge, there is only one study based on microdata that estimates a demand probability for ECEC services and not an attendance probability (see Wrohlich 2005 and Spiess/Wrohlich 2005).

Before discussing this study, we first describe the attendance rates in ECEC programs reported by official statistics. First of all, the attendance rates still differ widely between West and East Germany. This difference still stems from the fact that the former GDR provided a universal ECEC system for all children from birth on. The most recent numbers based on the official statistics concerning ECEC attendance are shown in Table 2: 11% of all children in Germany under the age of three currently attend ECEC programs, while this percentage is much smaller in West Germany with 6%, and much higher in East Germany with almost 37%.

As attendance rates show, there are major differences between states[8]. The state of Saxony-Anhalt is at the top with a rate of almost 48% of all children in the age group attending ECEC, while Lower Saxony is at the bottom with a rate of only 4%[8]. Concerning the hours spent in ECEC programs, only 32% of all children up to the age of three in West Germany attend full-time day care (defined as more than seven hours a day), while the percentage for East Germany is 63% (DJI 2007).

Since family day care is being discussed increasingly as a formal care option for children up to the age of three, the numbers for these facilities are presented in Table 2 as well. It remains open to debate whether such care arrangements should be considered part of the educational system, but there is no doubt that they make an important contribution to child development and learning. Since this care option is being promoted heavily at the moment it may play a more prominent role in the future. At present, only about 2% of all children up to the age of three are in this type of care (Table 2).

The differences between East and West Germany are much smaller when analyzing attendance of ECEC programs by children from age three up to compulsory school age. In West Germany, 89% of these children attend ECEC programs and in East Germany, 93%. These figures reflect the fact that all children three years of age and older are entitled to a part-time slot in a *Kindertageseinrichtung*. Nevertheless the state-specific numbers show some variety. In Bavaria 98% of the children in this age group attend ECEC programs, while in Hamburg only 79% attend. More age-specific usage rates show that the differences between the states are much wider if only three-year-old children are considered. Once the children have reached age four, the differences between the states decrease, particularly with regard to hours spent in the different ECEC programs for this age group: 40% of West German children are in part-time day care (defined as five hours a day or less) compared to 15% in the East, where most attend full-time ECEC programs (DJI, 2007).

These varying attendance rates reflect the differing state-specific provision of day care services, which is primarily the result of variations in the amount of funding allotted to ECEC programs. Table 3 shows the public funds spent on ECEC programs by state. The state of Rhineland Palatinate spent 91% of its budget for child and youth welfare issues on ECEC programs, while Baden-Württemberg spent only 76%. When the public expenditures for day care centres – standardized to 8 hours care per day – are broken down by

Tab. 2. Attendance rates for ECEC services and family day care by state and age group*, 2006

State	Children below the age of three, ECEC services	Children below the age of three, family day care	Children between 3 and 5 years of age, ECEC services and family day care together
Baden-Württemberg	6.8	1.5	93.8
Bavaria	5.6	0.9	98.4
Berlin	33.9	3.5	88.0
Brandenburg	36.5	4.7	92.0
Bremen	7.0	1.8	85.1
Hamburg	16.7	4.5	79.1
Hesse	7.3	1.3	89.1
Mecklenburg-Western Pomerania	33.7	9.3	91.8
Lower Saxony	4.1	0.6	79.5
North Rhine-Westphalia	5.3	1.2	83.3
Rhineland-Palatinate	8.1	0.6	93.8
Saarland	9.1	0.4	94.1
Saxony	31.9	2.2	92.8
Saxony-Anhalt	47.6	0.3	91.3
Schleswig-Holstein	5.4	1.7	81.2
Thuringia	36.2	1.1	94.9
Germany	**11.3**	**1.6**	**89.1**
West Germany	6.2	1.3	88.6
East Germany	36.6	3.1	92.6

* Percentage of children who attend ECEC services or family day care out of all children in the relevant age group.
a) Results for Bavaria, Berlin and North Rhine – Westphalia are provisional.
Source: data from the Child and Youth Services Statistics 2006, DJI (2007) and Statistisches Bundesamt (2007a), author's calculations.

the number of children in such ECEC programs, it is shown that Berlin spent about €7 562 per child while Saxony spent only €3 727 per child.

Given all these figures, it is obvious that the educational opportunities for children before compulsory school age vary from state to state. Apart from this, they share much in common, which is again related to the differences in demand and attendance. There is a shortage of slots for children below the age of three in all states of West Germany as well as in some of East Germany if the demand probability is compared with the probability that a slot will be provided. This rationing is shown by the estimations of Wrohlich (2005) based on microdata (see also Spiess/Wrohlich 2005). Based on representative microdata for Germany, Wrohlich has shown that 57% of all children below the age of three in East Germany and 61% in West Germany received rationed childcare slots. At first glance the relatively high percentage in East Germany seems implausible given the much higher provision rate there (see DJI 2005). However, the percentage of children whose parents seek an ECEC slot for their child is much higher in East Germany than in West Germany: 83% versus 65%. The probability of being rationed is much lower for children aged three up to compulsory school age. In West Germany, only 10% of these children and in East Germany only 3% were rationed. It could be that rationing is taking place for this age group with respect to full-time slots, but this is not taken into account in the study to which we refer (see Wrohlich 2005, for more details).

A comparison of the overall attendance rates in Germany with other European countries supports the thesis of an undersupply in the German ECEC systems for children up to the age of three. As shown in Table 4, the attendance rates in ECEC programs are much higher in the Scandinavian countries, France, and Belgium. Furthermore, including family day care, the attendance rates are also higher in the Southern European and Anglo-Saxon countries. With respect to the hours included in ECEC services, Germany is in the middle for this age group (without table, OECD, 2006), offering primarily full-time care for younger children. The results for older children allow a number of different conclusions to be drawn. Germany is at the middle among other European countries in provision rates for the age group of 3 to 6 year-olds. Concerning the hours in ECEC services, Germany offers six hours per day on average, while the Scandinavian countries and France offer

Tab. 3. Public Expenditures for ECEC services by state, 2005*

	Total Expenditures in €1000	Percent over all expenditures on child and youth issues	Expenditures per child in ECEC centres in €1000 (standardized to 8 hrs/day)
Baden-Württemberg	1 319 909	75.8	4 589
Berlin	742 846	87.8	7 562
Brandenburg	394 113	86.5	3 802
Bremen	93 858	80.4	6 364
Hamburg	322 657	85.9	6 917
Hesse	829 948	84.8	5 157
Mecklenburg-Western Pomerania	214 098	83.3	4 218
Lower Saxony	753 407	82.7	4 568
North Rhine-Westphalia	2 188 615	79.8	4 851
Rhineland-Palatinate	743 452	90.7	6 789
Saarland	119 885	80.3	5 214
Saxony	612 339	87.0	3 727
Saxony-Anhalt	335 087	87.1	3 755
Schleswig-Holstein	269 932	77.2	4 500
Thuringia	320 101	86.5	4 099
Germany	**9 729 325**	**82.0**	**4 854**

* For all children (including school children) in childcare in 2006, final data from the Child and Youth Services Statistics provided by the *Dortmund Arbeitsstelle Kinder- und Jugendhilfestatistik* in August 2007. Expenditures reported by Bavaria are not complete.
Source: Statistisches Bundesamt (2007b), *Dortmunder Arbeitsstelle Kinder- und Jugendhilfestatistik*, author's calculations.

more (without table, OECD, 2006). These provision rates generally reflect the level of priority given to these kinds of services. A further indicator is the percentage of ECEC expenditures per GDP. This percentage is about 0.5% of GDP in Germany but much higher in countries such as Denmark, with more than 1.7%, and Sweden, with more than 1.3% (Eichhorst et al. 2007).

D. Quality Control

Apart from these quantity-related issues, quality-related issues play a major role in the debate on ECEC programs. In Germany, basically, each state has its own set of quality standards. Standards generally cover number of slots, opening hours, parent fees, building requirements and maintenance, group size, staff-child ratios, and space. However, the post-PISA debate has called attention to earlier German studies showing that the quality of ECEC programs in Germany overall does not adequately reflect the crucial role of quality in education (see for instance Tietze et al. 1998). This debate has resulted in national consensus on the idea that unified guidelines are needed. Thus, all states are currently developing or have already developed education plans (*Bildungspläne*) for *Kindertageseinrichtungen*. However, these plans vary by state. Apart from this, beginning in the late 1990s there was an attempt on the federal level to agree on universal standards. Nevertheless the National Quality Initiative (*Nationale Qualitätsinitiative*) produced sev-

Tab. 4. ECEC services in European countries, percentage rates of children in ECEC programs in the appropriate age group

	Licensed ECEC services[1]	Regulated ECEC and pre-primary education[2]			
	0-3 years	3 years	4 years	5 years	6 years
Denmark	83	83	93	92	99
Sweden	66	79	83	85	97
France	27	101	103	101	1.2
Belgium	28	99	99	99	5
Finland	36	36	45	53	97
Germany	9	72	86	87	45
Portugal	25	61	81	91	3
Austria	10	20	62	18	0
Italy	19	100	102	99	1.3
Ireland	15	2.3	1.5	0.8	0
Netherlands	29	0	73	100.2	0
Great Britain	26	50	95	0	0

[1] using licensed child care arrangements
[2] Lower attendance rates in some countries might be due to attendance of primay education which starts at age 5 or age 6 in some countries.
Source: OECD (2006: Figure 4.1 and 4.2).

eral reports but no universal agreement on quality standards[9]. One can therefore conclude that Germany places high value on decentralisation and diversity, not only with respect to governance and funding issues, but also in the area of quality standards. Since child care markets do not work as markets are meant to in theory–that is, they do not guarantee quality (see Ball and Vincent 2005 for a recent study on this argument)–and given the results of empirical studies showing that parents are unable to adequately judge the quality of ECEC centers (see Tietze et al. 1998 or Spiess 1998), this situation is certainly less than ideal. Given these information asymmetries regarding the quality of ECEC services on the consumer side[10], an efficient solution would be to set minimum quality standards at the federal level ensuring that all children are guaranteed a minimum quality level in educational facilities, independent of where they are located (see, for instance, Spiess and Tietze 2002).

E. ECEC services and distribution

I. Attendance of ECEC services in Germany

The attendance of ECEC programs in Germany shows wide differences in the degree of state and municipal provision of ECEC services (see chapter C for the state level and DJI 2005 for the municipality level). Apart from these differences, attendance of ECEC programs is dominated by other demographic and socio-economic factors. This has been shown in a variety of studies analyzing the attendance of ECEC services in Germany. Although these studies are based on differing data sets such as the *German Socio-Economic Panel Study (SOEP)* (see Merkle 1994; Büchel/Spiess 2002; Spiess et al. 2002b and Wrohlich 2007), the *Mikrozensus* (see DJI 2005, Fuchs 2006, Kreyenfeld 2004 and 2007; and Konsortium Bildungsberichterstattung 2006) and the *DJI Kinderbetreuungsstudie* (Bien et al. 2006), some results are common to all of them. With respect to ECEC programs for children up to the age of three, it is shown that the probability of attending an ECEC program is significantly related to the child's age, the mother's employment, the education of the mother, and family status. Consequently, older children and children with more highly educated and employed mothers have a higher probability of attending ECEC. The results of Fuchs (2006) also show that it is solely the fact of being employed and not the working volume that influences the probability of using ECEC services. This is true for children of single mothers as well. It may be that children of single mothers are given a higher priority when the slots in such programs are rationed out. For children in West Germany from age three up to school age, the child's age increases the probability of attending an ECEC program. The same is true for children with fewer siblings or for children in higher-income households whose mothers work part-time or who live in urban areas. Nevertheless the income effect is not significant in all empirical studies. For children in East Germany household income and single-mother effects are the main significant influences on the probability of attending full-time rather than part-time care[11]. A recent study by Buechner/Spiess (2007) analyzing the duration of ECEC attendance over the entire early childhood period presents the following picture: only 3% of all children never attend any kind of ECEC, while the vast majority attend ECEC for a period of three years. About 4% of all children use these programs throughout almost their entire early childhood. Number of siblings and household income are statistically significant in determining the probability of ever attending ECEC. Years of ECEC attendance, or ECEC duration, are highly correlated with the number of siblings, the migration status of a child, the mother's education, the years the mother was employed during early childhood, and the household income.

From a methodological point of view, it is important to point out that none of these studies intend to measure causal effects between the attendance of ECEC services and other socio-economic variables. This is particularly important with respect to the employment decision of the mother. Apart from this, in the German case, the endogeneity problem between the child-care and employment decision is less significant. Given the structure of the German ECEC system, particularly the way in which the municipalities plan the provision of ECEC services, this provision is exogenous to a mother's employment decision. Moreover, ECEC services are not the only care alternative for children: there are other, informal care alternatives. Last but not least, it is important to keep in mind that German ECEC services, especially those for children three years and over, are often attended for educational reasons and not for care reasons only, since the German Kindergarten is the first step in the educational system.

To summarize, independent of the data sources used, the different studies on the attendance of ECEC services show that for the age groups below the age of five, children from families with a higher socio-economic status are more frequently enrolled in ECEC programs, while children in the same age group from migration backgrounds are less frequently enrolled in ECEC programs. It is important to note that this is not the case for children at the age of five and six: here, almost all children in Germany attend some kind of ECEC program. This is true even for children with a migration background, 92% of whom attend ECEC at the age of five compared to an only slightly higher 96% of those without a migration background. In the group of younger children (one to three years of age), the difference is significant: 10% of these children with a migration background attend ECEC programs, while 27% of those without such a background attend these programs (author's calculations based on the SOEP, for similar results see Bien et al. 2006). Apart from this, when interpreting the results one should not forget that these studies only look at the group of parents and children who received one of the few spots available in the German system, which is particularly true for the highly rationed segment of ECEC services for younger children. These studies do not intend to measure the actual demand for ECEC services. As mentioned earlier, to our knowledge, there is only the study by Wrohlich (2005), which estimates the demand probability and not the attendance probability. The results of this study show that the demand for ECEC services is significantly related to the age of the child, the number of siblings, the household income, the presence of other adults than the parents in the household, and regular church attendance by the mother, which is considered a proxy for educational values.

Given the high return rates on ECEC programs for children from lower socio-economic backgrounds, the various findings on the attendance rates lead to the policy question of what can be done to encourage more low-income, less-educated parents to enroll their children in ECEC programs at an early stage. The importance of solving this question is illustrated in Chapter A[12], and its answer must be sought in the reasons for the lower attendance rates of this particular group. To our knowledge, however, little if any systematic empirical research has been conducted on this question to date (see OECD 2004 for support to this conclusion). We therefore summarize the reasons on a more speculative level. One explanation might be that these parents have to pay too high costs for ECEC programs. The study by Wrohlich (2007) shows that the price elasticity of the demand for day care is greater than zero. Thus a decrease in the parental fees increases the demand for ECEC services. Nevertheless taking into account the fact that almost all states have fees dependent on income (and family size, see OECD 2004) resulting in almost zero costs for families at the bottom end of the income distribution, it is difficult to say whether lower fees would really result in a higher percentage of the target group attending ECEC programs. Another explanation for the relatively low attendance rates for this group might be that these parents are disadvantaged in the rationing process. If this is the case, it would make sense to increase the overall number of slots in ECEC programs. A third explanation might be that these families simply have different preferences and do not value ECEC programs as highly as parents from higher socio-economic backgrounds[13]. One solution to this latter problem might be to increase measures raising public awareness of the positive effects of ECEC programs. A more restrictive solution might be to make ECEC services mandatory for every child, as is done from elementary school on in Germany and starting from an even earlier age in countries such as France (for instance, BMFSFJ 2006). From an economic point of view, this alternative would result in various welfare losses, however, since it fails to take individual preferences into account. Moreover, the use of ECEC services among older below-school-age children indicate that high attendance rates can be reached even without a mandatory system (see chapter C.).

II. Attendance of ECEC services and school outcome

In the empirical literature on the relation between school outcomes and ECEC programs, not much research has been done on this topic in Germany based on nationwide representative microdata sets (see Biedinger/Becker, 2006, who reach the same conclusions)[14]. However, in the literature on early education, there are a number of studies based on smaller sample sizes as well as quantitative studies analyzing the effects of ECEC programs which show a positive effect of these programs if they provide good quality (for a recent summary from an educational science perspective, see for instance, Tietze 2007). This lack of empirical research is mainly due to the lack of appropriate data. Among the few studies based on nationwide data sets, there is the study by Spiess et al. (2003) using the SOEP data, which shows that attendance of ECEC programs in early childhood decreases the probability of attending a *Hauptschule* at the age of 14 years for children with migrant backgrounds only. Becker/Lauterbach (2004), however, who conducted a similar study based on the SOEP, do not corroborate these findings. In the new study by Buechner/Spiess (2007), it is shown that the probability of attending a *Hauptschule* at the age of 14 is significantly influenced by the duration in ECEC, which is true for a sample of Germans and migrants. The IGLU study is another example of empirical research demonstrating that the duration of ECEC attendance increases children's reading, math, and other skills (Bos et al. 2003, pp. 127ff). These results are confirmed by a more recent study by Anger et al. (2007) based on the data from the PISA study.[15]

F. Current issues on the political agenda

Given these findings on supply and attendance of ECEC services in Germany, the following chapter gives a brief overview on the current political debate of these services in Germany. First of all it should be stated that never before have ECEC programs taken such a central place in the public debate as they do today. This is due not only to the educational benefits of such programs but to other factors as well: first, Germany's relatively low birth rates; second, the relatively low but increasing number of working women with young children; and third, the relatively high rate of child poverty in Germany (for a summary of these issues, see, for instance, OECD 2006). ECEC programs are now being discussed as means of fostering higher birth rates in Germany, promoting higher employment of mothers, and thus indirectly reducing the number of children in poverty. Although the present study cannot deal with the complex causal links among these problems, they do show that the educational objectives of ECEC services have to compete with other objectives in the context of family-friendly policies, labor market policies, and welfare policies. This makes things more complicated, since these different agendas are only partially complementary (see Ball/Vincent 2005, for the same argument).

The current debate goes back to a first attempt undertaken by the federal government under the Schröder administration. The aim was to promote ECEC programs for children up to three years in particular. With the *Tagesbetreuungsausbaugesetz (TAG 2004)* in 2005, a law intending to expand the provision of daycare services, the federal government attempted to provide more incentives to municipalities to increase their ECEC services. It foresaw the provision of an annual 1.5 billion euros for the development of ECEC service for children below the age of three to the municipalities from savings generated through the consolidation of unemployment and social welfare benefits. But these funds were not actually earmarked and thus no solution could be reached to directly support ECEC services.

The current Minister for Family Affairs, Senior Citizens, Women and Youth has publicly stated the goal of providing 30% of all children two years and younger with access to ECEC services by the year 2013 (BMFSFJ 2007). By doing so, Germany would meet the benchmark set by the EU governments at their 2002 summit in Barcelona. To reach this aim, the federal government has for the first time pledged extra federal funds to promote the system. But given Germany's federal structure and Basic Law, this cannot be carried out through direct subsidies, so other options have to be considered. During the early summer of 2007, the idea was discussed of providing a federal voucher for ECEC programs for children up to the age of three (Emundts 2007), which would be supplementary to the existing state and municipal funding. Although the various political actors in Germany have not been able to agree on this system, the proposal appears both effective and efficient from an economic point of view (see Spiess 1998, Spiess 2002, and Kreyenfeld et al. 2001, in a German context; Stutzer/Reto 2005, and Levin/Schwartz 2007, for recent international references). Given these advantages, the following chapter focuses in more detail on the various arguments for such a voucher system.

I. A federal voucher for ECEC services?

There are a variety of arguments for a federal voucher system. The first set of arguments is based on the advantages of providing *additional funding* to the ECEC segment. This increase in public resources to this part of the educational system would not only help to diminish the rationing in the ECEC segment, but also contribute to a more equal partnership between ECEC programs and schools. Up to now, the vast majority of public educational resources have been spent on schools and only a fraction on the ECEC sector.[16]

A second set of arguments in favor of such an approach is based on the advantages of the *federal government providing the additional funding* to the ECEC sector. The idea behind this argument is that if providing equivalent living conditions for each child independent of his/her region is a task shared by the federal government (see article 106 of the German Basic Law), then the federal government could effectively help in diminishing the differences in provision rates. Another argument is related to the benefits of ECEC programs on the municipal, state, and federal levels. Rauschenbach/Schilling (2007) estimated that an increase in ECEC provision rates will result in savings of several million euros by the year 2013. Of this, 26% will be at the federal level. Under the current funding system, however, expenditures are covered exclusively by the states and municipalities. To eliminate this discrepancy it would be necessary for the federal government to carry part of the expenditures as well; not for the states and municipalities to stop providing financial resources for ECEC programs (for a general discussion of this misalignment in costs and benefits of ECEC programs, see also Karoly et al. 2006, pp. 97).

A third set of arguments is based on the advantages of the *voucher approach itself*. Economists argue that a voucher system would be effective and efficient because of its demand-side orientation, and thus identify the benefits of such a system above all in the fact that parental preferences determine which ECEC programs are chosen. They expect that parental purchase of services will bring private entrepreneurs, new funding, and greater dynamism into the provision of services (see Besharov/Samari 2000; OECD 2006; Levin/Schwartz 2007). This would stimulate competition between the ECEC providers if the vouchers could be used for any licensed ECEC program.[17] This kind of stimulus could be highly beneficial to the German ECEC segment, which is now heavily dominated by municipal care providers and five major non-profit organizations. Furthermore, various surveys show that the parents are not satisfied with the ECEC services provided (see, for instance, Perspektive Deutschland 2006).

However, comparative analyses of various European countries in studies by the OECD (OECD 2006) and Cleveland/Krashinsky (2003) claim that the direct funding of services brings more effective control, advantages of sale, better national quality, and a higher degree of equity in access and participation than consumer subsidy models such as vouchers systems. Nevertheless, these conclusions do not adequately address the issue that the existing demand-side funding systems in comparison to supply-side funding systems have so far failed to achieve adequate regulation, monitoring structures and quality standards in the childcare sector. Thus the "ECEC outputs" described in the OECD (2006) review might be more related to these issues and not so much to the funding system itself. If a demand-side funding system is combined with better regulatory and monitoring structures and quality standards, then the advantages of a voucher system are combined with those of a regulated ECEC market. The success of a voucher system work thus depends crucially on how the regulatory structure is defined and not on the voucher itself.

Moreover, a voucher-based system could potentially increase attendance rates among children from disadvantaged socio-economic backgrounds. One argument for providing vouchers directly to the parents is that it should make them fully aware of their responsibility for enrolling their children and their market power in doing so. Proponents of the voucher system expect that by giving tangible vouchers with a specific monetary value to each eligible family, this will stimulate higher enrolment (see Levine/Schwartz 2007). There is some empirical evidence from the US that day care voucher programs do indeed increase the probability of the target group using ECEC programs to an increased degree (see Besharov/Samari 2000).

A fourth set of arguments is related to the specific *German funding system*. For Germany in particular, a federal voucher would offer a sustainable solution to funding not only providers' capital costs but also their operation costs. Thus in contrast to an earlier attempt by the federal government in 2003 to promote full-day schooling through a federal government program limited to four years and covering capital costs only (see http://www.ganztagsschulen.org/, download July 10th 2007), a federal voucher for ECEC programs would provide a sustainable funding alternative covering both capital and operation costs. Apart from that, a federal voucher might produce signaling effects, triggering reforms of state funding systems in a similar, more demand-oriented direction. Once ECEC vouchers become available for children below the age of three, this might also lead to a more demand-side oriented funding of ECEC services for older preschoolers. If all ECEC services independent of age group are funded with a demand-side orientation, such as through a voucher system, the different providers of ECEC services will have more incentives to design their services according to the demand-side preferences.

A final argument brings together the arguments already mentioned. If additional funding is available through a voucher system, and thus the amount of public money spent on ECEC services increases further, this again increases the freedom of choice and productive efficiency by stimulating a greater market supply of competitors (see Levin/Schwarz 2007 for such an argument in the US context). The experience of Australia provides additional empirical evidence undergirding this expectation. It suggests that if sufficient voucher and subsidy money is made available, independent family day careers and commercial providers will respond to the business opportunity and quickly expand provision (OECD 2006). Also the Finnish voucher experiment suggests that sufficient funding increases demand and the diversity of supply (Viitanen 2003). However, it is obvious that the adequacy of the amount of funding cannot be predicted in advance, but can only be answered ex post.

II. Other important issues

Apart from these funding issues, universal minimum quality standards are needed for ECEC programs in Germany (see Chapter D). From an economic perspective and in particular from a cost-benefit perspective it is important that the quality of services offered is high. Nevertheless, it does not have to be the municipality itself that controls the quality. To balance the asymmetric information on the demand side, minimum quality standards that must be met by all providers would guarantee at least a basic quality level in all programs; in addition an instrument, such as a federal seal of quality for day care centers could inform parents about differences in the quality of programs above the minimum quality standards (see Spiess/Tietze, 2002).

Future reforms should therefore not aim at deregulation. Instead they should re-regulate the system from the perspective of the demand side. This is true for funding issues, but for quality issues as well. Thus the reforms outlined in this contribution intend to promote an "ECEC market" with a mixed provision in which choice and innovation exists, while maintaining a sense of national, state, and municipal responsibility for services.

Endnotes

* *Acknowledgments*: I appreciate the hospitality of the Department for Policy Analysis and Management (PAM) at the Cornell University, USA and travel funds from the German Science Foundation (Project no. SP 1091/1-1), which allowed me to finalize most of this paper.
1 The term early childhood education and care has been adopted from the OECD's thematic reviews. This term combines the two aspects of childcare for children below compulsory school age: development and learning on the one hand, and the labour market conception of children's services on the other.
2 For a recent special issue on the economics of early childhood education, see Belfield (2007) or the article by Currie (2001).
3 See Barnett (1995) for a systematic but older overview on cost-benefit studies.
4 For a discussion of this in an US context see Karoly et al. (2006: 116 onwards), Karoly and Bigelow (2005) or OECD (2006).
5 For a detailed overview of regulations concerning the German ECEC system in English, see OECD (2004) or (2006: 333-341). For a specific focus on the public-private partnership in this sector, see Bode (2003).
6 Up to now these figures cover the results for 11 out of 16 states.
7 Based on survey data such as the SOEP covering all states, it can be estimated that 3% of all children in the ECEC system have a childcare slot with a for-profit provider (author's calculation based on the SOEP).
8 This partly reflects entitlements by various states, where children up to the age of three are entitled to ECEC programs (DJI, 2005)
9 For more information see: http://www.bildungsserver.de/zeigen.html?seite=3768 (Download September 10th 2007).
10 Ball and Vincent (2005: 564) describe this asymmetry as follows: "The consumer is often in a position of relative ignorance in relation to forms of expertise which are part of the purchase of services".
11 Since most children in this age group attend an ECEC it does not make sense to estimate the probability of attendance at all.
12 For this argument in an international context see the references given in the first chapter of this contribution.
13 For some empirical hints on this, see the findings of Wrohlich (2005), who showed that the higher income parents have a higher probability of demanding ECEC services than the reference group.
14 For one of the few examples of a regionally restricted but solid study, see for instance Becker (2006), who analyses the school outcome of migrant children and controls for the duration of Kindergarten attendance using a sample from the city of Osnabrück. Furthermore, the new BIKS project at the University of Bamberg creates long term data that will be of particular interest for this research question, see http://www.uni-bamberg.de/index.php?id=2713 (download: June 10, 2007).
15 One drawback of all these empirical studies is that they do not control for the quality of the ECEC programs. This is due mainly to the lack of survey data linked with quality data on institutions.
16 In Germany in the year 2002, 4 999 equivalent US dollars were spent for pre-primary education and 7 025 equivalent US dollars for all secondary education (OECD, 2005, Table B1.1).
17 In the strict sense of evaluation, there is no evaluation up to now of a real voucher system, although various US states and some other countries have introduced such systems (for the few studies that could be considered evaluation studies, see Parker 1989, Levin and Schwartz 2007, and Viitanen 2003).

References

Anger, C., Plünnecke, A., Tröger, M. (2007): Renditen der Bildungsinvestitionen in den frühkindlichen Bereich, Studie des Instituts der deutschen Wirtschaft Köln, Köln 2007

Ball, S. J., Vincent, C. (2005): The 'childcare champion'? New Labour, social justice and the childcare market, in: British Educational Research Journal, Vol. 31 (2005), pp. 557–570.

Barnett, S. (1995): Long-Term Effects of Early Childhood Programs on Cognitive and School Outcomes, in: The Future of Children, Long-Term outcomes of Early Childhood Programs, Vol. 5 (3) (1995), pp. 25–50

Becker, B. (2006): Der Einfluss des Kindergartens als Kontext zum Erwerb der deutschen Sprache bei Migrantenkindern, in: Zeitschrift für Soziologie, Vol. 35 (2006), pp. 449–464

Becker, R., Lauterbach, W. (2004): Vom Nutzen vorschulischer Kinderbetreuung für Bildungschancen, in: Becker, R., W. Lauterbach (eds.) (2007): Bildung als Privileg? Erklärungen und Befunde zu den Ursachen der Bildungsungleichheit. VS Verlag für Sozialwissenschaften, Wiesbaden 2007, pp. 127–159.

Belfield, C. (2007): Introduction to the special issue "The economics of early childhood education", in: Economics of Education Review, Vol. 26 (2007), pp. 1–2

Belfield, C. R., Nores, M., Barnett, S., Schweinhart, L. (2006): The High/Scope Perry Preschool Program: Cost-Benefit Analysis Using Data from the Age-40 Followup, in: Journal of Human Resources, Vol. 41(1) (2006), pp. 162–190

Besharov, D. J., Samari, N. (2000): Child-Care Vouchers and Cash Payments, in: Steuerle, E. C., van Dooren, O., Petersen, G., Reischauer, R. D. (eds.): Vouchers and the Provision of Public Services, Washington D. C. 2000, pp. 195–223

Biedinger, N., Becker, B. (2006): Der Einfluss des Vorschulbesuchs auf die Entwicklung und den langfristigen Bildungserfolg von Kindern, Working Paper des Mannheimer Zentrums für Europäische Sozialforschung, Mannheim 2006

Bien, W., T. Rauschenbach, T., Riedel, B. (eds.) (2006): Wer betreut Deutschlands Kinder?, Beltz Verlag, Weinheim and Basel 2006

BMFSFJ – Bundesministerium für Familie, Senioren, Frauen und Jugend (2003): Auf den Anfang kommt es an!, Beltz Verlag, Weinheim and Basel 2003

BMFSFJ – Bundesministerium für Familie, Senioren, Frauen und Jugend (2007): Kinderbetreuung, Pressemitteilung vom 18.April 2007.

BMFSFJ – Bundesministerium für Familie, Jugend, Frauen und Senioren (ed.) (2006): 7. Familienbericht: Familie zwischen Flexibilität und Verlässlichkeit, Berlin.

Bode, I. (2003): The organisational evolution of the childcare regime in Germany: Issues and dynamics of a public-private partnership, in: Annals of Public and Cooperative Economics, Vol. 74 (2003), pp. 631–657

Bos, W., Lankes, E., Prenzel, M., Schwippert, K., Walther, G., Valtin, R. (eds.) (2003): Erste Ergebnisse aus IGLU. Waxmann. Münster, New York, München and Berlin 2003

Büchel, F., Spiess, C. K. (2002): Form der Kinderbetreuung und Arbeitsmarktverhalten von Müttern in West- und Ostdeutschland, Kohlhammer, Stuttgart 2002

Büchner, C., Spiess, C. K. (2007): Die Dauer vorschulischer Betreuungs- und Bildungserfahrungen: Ergebnisse auf der Basis von Paneldaten, DIW Discussion Papers Number 687, Berlin 2007

Cleveland, G., Krashinsky, M. (1998): The Benefits and Costs of Good Child Care, The Economic Rationale for Public Investment in Young Children – A Policy Study, University of Toronto at Scarborough 1998

Currie, J. (2001): Early childhood education programs, in: Journal of Economic Perspectives, Vol. 15 (2) (2001), pp. 213–238

DJI – Deutsches Jugendinstitut and Universität Dortmund (eds.) (2005): Zahlenspiegel 2005. Kindertagesbetreuung im Spiegel der Statistik, München 2005

DJI – Deutsches Jugendinstitut (2007): Kinder, Kosten – Fakten zur Kinderbetreuungsdebatte, DJI Thema 2007/04, München 2007

Eichhorst, W., Kaiser, L. C., Thode, E., Tobsch, V. (2007): Vereinbarkeit von Familie und Beruf im internationalen Vergleich, Verlag Bertelsmann Stiftung, Gütersloh 2007

Emundts, C. (2007): Geld macht nicht schlau, in: Die Zeit, 6. Juni 2007, Nummer 24.

Falck, O. (2004): Das Hamburger „Kita-Gutscheinsystem" besser als sein Ruf?, in: Sozialer Fortschritt, (3/2004), pp. 68–74

Fuchs, K. (2006): Wovon der Besuch einer Kindertageseinrichtung abhängt...!, in: Rauschenbach, T., Schilling, M. (eds.): Kinder- und Jugendhilfereport 2. Analysen, Befunde und Perspektiven. Juventa, Weinheim 2006, pp. 157–173

Heckman, J. J., Masterov, D.V. (2007): The Productivity Argument for Investing in Young Children, IZA Discussion Paper Number 2725, April 2007
Immervoll, H., Barber, D.(2005): Can parents afford to work? Childcare Costs, Tax Benefit Policies and Work Incentives, OECD Social, Employment and Migration Working Papers Number 31, Paris 2005
Karoly, L. A., Bigelow, J. H. (2005): The economics of Investing in Universal Pre-School Education in California, RAND Cooperation, Santa Monica 2005
Karoly, L. A., Kilburn, R. M., Cannon, J. S. (2006): Early Childhood Interventions: Proven Results, Future Promise, RAND Cooperation, Santa Monica 2006
Konsortium Bildungsberichterstattung (eds.) (2006): "Bildung in Deutschland. Ein indikatorengestützter Bericht mit einer Analyse zu Bildung und Migration" im Auftrag der Ständigen Konferenz der Kultusminister der Länder in der Bundesrepublik Deutschland und des Bundesministeriums für Bildung und Forschung, W. Bertelsmann Verlag, Bielefeld 2006
Kreyenfeld, M., Spiess, C. K., Wagner, G. G. (2001): Finanzierungs- und Organisationsmodelle institutioneller Kinderbetreuung. Analysen zum Status quo und Vorschläge zur Reform, Neuwied.
Kreyenfeld, M. (2004): Social structure and child care An analysis of the social and economic determinants of child care use, MPIDR Working Paper WP-2004-009, Rostock 2004
Kreyenfeld, Michaela (2007): Kinderbetreuung und soziale Ungleichheit, in: Becker, R., Lauterbach, W. (eds.) (2007): Bildung als Privileg? Erklärungen und Befunde zu den Ursachen der Bildungsungleichheit, 2nd edition, VS- Verlag für Sozialwissenschaften, Wiesbaden 2007
Lamb, M. E. (1998): Nonparental Child Care: Context Quality, Correlates and Consequences", in: Damon, W., Sigel, I.E., Renninger, K.A. (eds.), Handbook of Child Psychology (Vol. 4), Child Psychology in Practice, 5th edition, Wiley, New York 1998
Levin, H. M., Schwartz, H. L. (2007): Educational vouchers for universal pre-schools, in: Economics of Education Review, Vol. 26 (2007), pp. 3–16
Lynch, R. G. (2004): Exceptional Returns. Economic, Fiscal, and Social Benefits of Investment in Early Childhood Development, Economic Policy Institute, Washington, D. C. 2004
Merkle, L. E. (1994): Frauenerwerbstätigkeit und Kinderbetreuung, Physica-Verlag, Heidelberg 1994
OECD (2004): Early Childhood Education and Care Policy in The Federal Republic of Germany, OECD County Note, 26 November, Paris 2004
OECD (2005): Education at a Glance, Paris 2005
OECD (2006): Starting Strong II, Early Education and Care, Paris 2006
Parker, M. D. (1989): Vouchers for Day Care of Children: Evaluating a Model Program, in: Child Welfare, Vol. 68 (6) (1989), pp. 633–642
Perspektive Deutschland (2006): Projektbericht Perspektive-Deutschland 2005/06, Düsseldorf, http://www.perspektive-deutschland.de/files/presse_2006/pd5-Projektbericht.pdf (Download: July 10th 2007)
Rauschenbach, T., Schilling, M. (2007): Erwartbare ökonomische Effekte durch den Ausbau der Betreuungsangebote für unter Dreijährige auf 750.00 Plätze bis 2013, Deutsches Jugendinstitut, München 2007
Spiess, C. K. (1998): Staatliche Eingriffe in Märkte für Kinderbetreuung. Analysen im deutsch-amerikanischen Vergleich, Campus Verlag, Reihe Wirtschaftswissenschaften, Frankfurt a.M. and New York 1998
Spiess, C. K., Kreyenfeld, M., Wagner, G. G. (2000): Kindertageseinrichtungen in Deutschland. Ein neues Steuerungsmodell bei der Bereitstellung sozialer Dienstleistungen, in: DIW-Wochenbericht, Vol. 67 (18) (2000), pp. 269–275
Spiess, C. K., Schupp, J., Grabka, M.M., Haisken-De New, J. P., Jakobeit, H. and Wagner, G. G. (2002a): Abschätzung der Brutto-Einnahmeneffekte öffentlicher Haushalte und der Sozialversicherungsträger bei einem Ausbau von Kindertageseinrichtungen, Nomos Verlag, Baden-Baden 2002
Spiess, C. K., Büchel, F., Frick, J. R. (2002b): Kinderbetreuung in West- und Ostdeutschland: Sozioökonomischer Hintergrund entscheidend, in: DIW-Wochenbericht, Vol. 69 (31) (2002), pp. 518–524
Spiess, C. K., Tietze, W. (2002): Qualitätssicherung in Kindertageseinrichtungen – Gründe, Anforderungen und Umsetzungsüberlegungen für ein Gütesiegel, in: Zeitschrift für Erziehungswissenschaft, Vol. 5 (1) (2002), pp. 139–162
Spiess, C. K. (2002): Gutscheine – ein Ansatz zur Finanzierung und Steuerung im Kindertagesstättenbereich, in: Dohmen, D., Cleuvers, B. A. (eds.): Nachfrageorientierten Bildungsfinanzierung – Neue Trends für Kindertagesstätte, Schule und Hochschule, Bertelsmann Verlag, Gütersloh 2002 (Schriftenreihe zur Bildungs- und Sozialökonomie, Band 1), pp. 33–50
Spiess, C. K., Büchel F., Wagner, G. G. (2003): Children's School Placement in Germany: Does Kindergarten Attendance Matter?, in: Early Childhood Research Quarterly, Vol. 18 (2003), pp. 255–270

Spiess, C. K., Wrohlich, K. (2005): Wie viele Kinderbetreuungsplätze fehlen in Deutschland?, in: DIW-Wochenbericht, Vol. 72 (14) (2005), pp. 223–227

Statitisches Bundesamt (2007a): 89% der 3- bis 5-Jährigen in Kindertagesbetreuung, press report from March 8, 2007, Wiesbaden

Statitisches Bundesamt (2007b): Statistik der Jugendhilfe. Ausgaben und Einnahmen. Revidierte Ergebnisse 2005, Wiesbaden 2007

Stutzer, A., Dürsteler, R. (2005): Versagen in der staatlichen Krippenförderung – Betreuungsgutscheine als Alternative. Crema Working Paper Number 26, 2005

TAG – Gesetz zum qualitätsorientierten und bedarfsgerechten Ausbau der Tagesbetreuung für Kinder (Tagesbetreuungsausbaugesetz) (2004), in: Bundesgesetzblatt, Part 1, Number 76, pp. 3852–3854.

Tietze, W. (ed.) (1998): Wie gut sind unsere Kindergärten? Eine Untersuchung zur pädagogischen Qualität in deutschen Kindergärten. Beltz, Weinheim 1998

Tietze, W. (2007): Sozialisation in Krippe und Kindergarten, mimeo.

Viitanen, T. K. (2003): Experimental Evidence of a Private Childcare Voucher, mimeo, http://cemmap.ifs.org.uk/resources/files/docs/eea_viitanen.pdf (Download: August 5th 2007).

Wrohlich, K. (2005): The Excess Demand for Subsidized Child Care in Germany. DIW Diskussionspapier Number 470, Berlin, in: Applied Economics (forthcoming).

Wrohlich, K. (2007): Evaluating Family Policy Reforms Using Behavioral Microsimulation. The Example of Childcare and Income Tax Policy Reforms in Germany. Doctoral Thesis, Free University of Berlin; published online: http://www.diss.fu-berlin.de/2007/531 (Download: September 10th 2007).

Early Childhood Education and Care in Germany: The Status Quo and Reform Proposals

Summary

The high returns of early childhood education and care (ECEC) services, especially for disadvantaged children, are receiving more and more attention in the economic research. The viewpoint of educational economics may be expected to contribute particularly important findings on these services. The present paper offers an overview of the most important issues currently facing the German ECEC system. First, with regard to specific German governance and funding issues, it outlines public organizations and authorities responsible for this aspect of education and illustrates the supply and demand sides of the ECEC market using the most recent official statistics and comparing these findings with other European countries. Second, it discusses the specific issue of rationing and the problem that attendance rates only provide information on the group of parents who received one of the limited spots available in the German system. Furthermore, while quality issues are not a major focus of this paper, they are mentioned here as well. Third, the paper summarizes studies on the utilization of ECEC services in Germany based on representative national data sets, also referring to empirical studies that have focused on the correlation between school outcomes and ECEC attendance. Finally, some important issues at the top of the political agenda are highlighted, and the use of a federal voucher approach is discussed from an economic perspective.

Frühkindliche Bildungs- und Betreuungseinrichtungen: Der Status Quo und Ansätze für Reformen

Zusammenfassung

Der Bereich frühkindlicher Bildungs- und Betreuungseinrichtungen nimmt im deutschen Bildungswesen einen zunehmend bedeutenden Stellenwert ein. Ökonomische Analysen belegen die hohen Renditen von öffentlichen Investitionen in diesen Bereich, insbesondere wenn sie Kindern aus sozioökonomisch benachteiligten Familien zukommen. In diesem Überblicksbeitrag wird eine Einführung in das deutsche System frühkindlicher Bildungs- und Betreuungseinrichtungen gegeben, in dem zunächst die Finanzierungs- und Organisationsstrukturen dargestellt werden. Der Beitrag umfasst auf der Basis aktueller Daten eine Beschreibung der Angebots- und Nachfrageseite. Darüber hinaus werden die Ergebnisse empirischer Studien zusammengetragen, welche die Nutzung von Kindertageseinrichtungen beschreiben und auch deren Zusammenhang mit dem späteren Schulerfolg analysieren. Der Beitrag schließt mit einer Darstellung der aktuellen politischen Diskussion. Dabei wird insbesondere auf die Finanzierungsalternative von Bundesgutscheinen für die Betreuung in Kindertageseinrichtungen eingegangen und ökonomisch bewertet.

WWW.GABLER.DE

Clearly structured case studies of successful growth companies

Holger Ernst | Stefan Glänzer | Peter Witt (Eds.)
Success Factors of Fast Growing Companies
Selected Case Studies
2005. x, 276 pp., 80 Fig., 4 Tab. Softc.
EUR 29,90
ISBN 978-3-409-12706-6

This book presents a unique range of case studies of fast growing firms in different stages of their development. The companies covered in this volume mainly belong to modern high-tech industries like electronic commerce, biotechnology, software and others. From an investigation of their corporate histories, the authors derive the major success factors in the management of fast growing companies.

The Editors
Prof. Dr. Holger Ernst is a professor of technology and innovation management at the Otto Beisheim Graduate School of Management (WHU).
Dr. Stefan Glänzer is a serial entrepreneur and a lecturer at the WHU.
Prof. Dr. Peter Witt is the Otto Beisheim Professor of Entrepreneurship at the WHU.

Order your copy now: kerstin.kuchta@gwv-fachverlage.de
Telefon +49(0)611. 7878-626

KOMPETENZ IN SACHEN WIRTSCHAFT

The Economics of Tracking and Non-Tracking

Volker Meier, Gabriela Schütz

Abstract

- There exists substantial variation across OECD countries as to whether and how students are grouped in classes according to perceived ability.
- Economic analyses stress that there is joint production of human capital in schools, where output increases with rising mean ability in the class. Ability tracking may therefore be particularly helpful for talented students. At the same time, weak students may benefit from ability grouping via tailored and specialised courses.
- The vast majority of the econometric literature suggests that tracking promotes inequality in academic achievement. By contrast, the empirical literature on the impact of tracking on average test scores of students is inconclusive. Only few studies find a significant association, and they include both positive and negative estimates.

Keywords Tracking · ability grouping · peer group effects · school systems

JEL: I20

PD Dr. Volker Meier (✉)
is senior researcher at the Ifo Institute for Economic Research. His main fields of research are Labour Economics and Public Economics. Ifo Institute for Economic Research, Poschingerstr. 5, D-81679 Munich, Germany, E-mail: meier@ifo.de.

Dipl.-Vw. Gabriela Schütz (✉)
is junior researcher at the Ifo Institute for Economic Research. Her main field of research is Economics of Education. Ifo Institute for Economic Research, Poschingerstr. 5, D-81679 Munich, Germany, E-mail: schuetz@ifo.de.

A. Introduction

In the vast majority of OECD countries, some kind of ability grouping is employed within secondary schooling. In many cases this takes the form of explicit tracking where students somewhere between age 10 and age 16 are sorted into schools of different types. These schools offer a specific degree of academic orientation in their curriculum. The lower track schools often have some vocational orientation, while the higher track schools exhibit a more academic curriculum. In the last decades, several OECD countries moved towards detracking their school systems or decided to defer tracking to a later point in the schooling career. Movements in this direction were enacted in Sweden, the UK, Italy and Norway in the 1960s, in France and the US in the 1980s, and in Spain and Portugal in the 1990s. These measures were usually taken because of a perceived disadvantage of children with less favourable family background at the separation stages in education. Indeed, early tracking seems to induce a higher intergenerational correlation of school careers and wages. Thus, in tracked systems the final school degrees of parents and their rank in the wage distribution will to a higher extent be mirrored in the achievements of their children (Dustmann, 2004; Bauer and Riphahn, 2006; Pekkarinen et al., 2006).

Figure 1 shows the age at which students are first tracked in the different OECD countries. The age of first selection refers to a standard case and may show regional variations in countries in which the organisation of the school system is decentralised. Obviously, Germany and Austria have a boundary position in the comparison with other countries. Selection takes place after four years of schooling at age 10. Most of the OECD countries do not track their students before age 14. The upper boundary is set to age 16 and covers also education systems in which no tracking at all occurs over the course of compulsory schooling, like Sweden, Spain, New Zealand, Iceland, Finland, Denmark and Canada. Thus, among OECD countries there is no consensus on the best way to deal with heterogeneous ability among the student population.

Tracking of students into different types of schools is not the only possible way of grouping students according to ability. Countries with a comprehensive school system often employ streaming as a milder form of ability grouping. In this case, only some courses are taught at different levels of complexity. Streaming entails that students are placed into advanced classes for one subject and into standard classes for another subject. The existing literature largely ignores the distinction between tracking and streaming and treats the notions as synonymous. Since the main research questions on the impacts of ability grouping also apply to streaming, we also review the empirical evidence from countries in which students are all placed in the same type of school, like in the US. However, the distinction between tracking and streaming is of importance for empirical researchers trying to assess the relative merits of various forms of ability grouping.

Further, it should be noted that ability grouping often also occurs within a school system that officially does not employ any tracking or streaming measures. If the rich live apart from the poor and the children's ability levels are positively correlated with the income of their parents, schools located in rich areas will display a higher mean student ability than schools located in poor areas.

Two main questions are to be answered when considering the economics of ability grouping. The first question relates to a wider notion of *efficiency*. If the choice is between

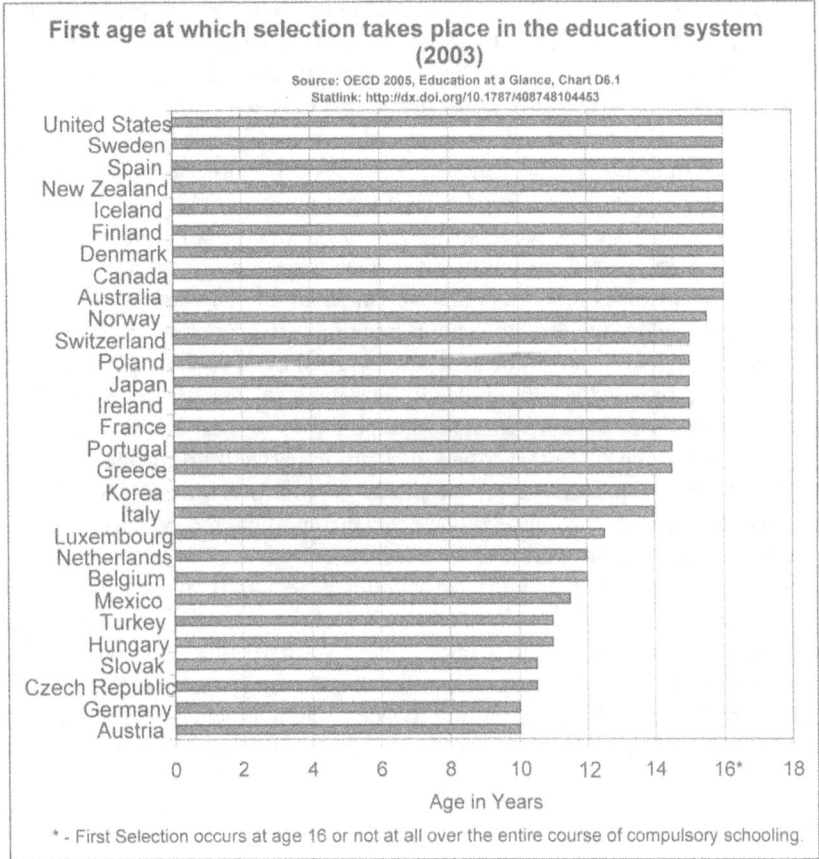

Fig. 1. Tracking in OECD countries

a school system with ability tracking at a given age and no tracking at all, which scheme will yield a higher aggregate sum of individual productivities net of costs of education? In an ex ante sense, a scheme would be called efficient if an individual who does not yet know his type in terms of innate ability would prefer the scheme under a veil of ignorance. In general, it cannot be expected that one scheme dominates the other, such that productivity is higher for any initial ability type. Employing the wider notion of efficiency makes it possible to rank the schemes if, for example, tracking increases productivities of high ability types and reduces productivities of low ability types. The second question deals with the *equality of opportunity* offered by the scheme in a narrower sense. Considering the same choice as before, which scheme leads to higher productivities for disadvantaged students?

Apart from the questions of efficiency and equality of opportunity in tracked or non-tracked systems, the more detailed structure of the tracking scheme is also to be considered. If ability grouping is beneficial, the next questions would be which form of ability grouping should be employed – different school types or streaming within schools –, and at which age tracking should be introduced.

There is clearly some intuitive expectation concerning the answers to the first two questions. The motive behind tracking is to increase output of the school system in terms of aggregate wages. By creating more homogenous classes, teaching becomes easier because the style of the course can be better adapted to the needs of the students. One main channel why this procedure may yield improved outcomes lies in faster accumulation of human capital of the more talented students. If this is indeed the case, a higher aggregate productivity measure may be achieved even if tracking reduces the future productivities of students sent to lower track schools. But it is not even clear whether tracking will reduce the productivity of students in the lower track. One would expect that teachers can help the less able students better when they no longer have to take care of students of high ability. In contrast, the main idea behind non-tracking is to guarantee equality of opportunity as long as possible. This will be achieved by a policy of equipping all students with the same level of knowledge. While ideally a tracking scheme also implies equality of opportunity ex ante, observations from several countries suggest that early tracking procedures are noisy in the sense that capabilities are imperfectly identified and predicted. Since the influence of parents on school choice is more pronounced when the child is younger, the intergenerational correlation of income and final school degrees is typically stronger the earlier tracking occurs.

The remainder of the paper is organised as follows. Section B reviews the contributions of economic theory to the analysis of tracking. As lots of predictions remain ambiguous, the empirical evidence surveyed in Section C deserves particular attention. We cover the US experience in effectively dealing with different streaming policies across high schools, analyses of regime changes in the UK and Sweden, and international comparisons building on international student achievement tests. Section D concludes and indicates directions for future research.

B. Theory

I. Peer group effects

When considering the question of which school system generates the highest output in terms of aggregate productivities of its students at a given total cost of education, the educational production function has to be taken into account. In an educational production function, an outcome variable describing human capital of a student at the end of school is related to input variables like initial ability of the student, number of schooling hours, class size, or teacher quality. With such a simplified approach, family background variables are often captured by measures of initial ability. If human capital is produced by the student, the teachers and some material resources, tracking would only matter if the material resources are spent in an unequal fashion afterwards or if the characteristics of the teachers would differ between the different school types. The interesting point is that we have joint production, where the abilities of all students in class enter as factors of production. This aspect is usually covered by incorporating mean ability in class in the production function. A higher mean ability increases the individual's output measure for given initial abilities and given resources spent on teaching. This positive impact of mean ability is called the *peer group effect*. It is usually interpreted as a consequence of joint learning where the students support each other.

Alternatively, the peer group effect may also express that the share of weak students who impose negative externalities on all pupils is reduced. Weak students tend to disrupt the learning process. This problem gives a rationale to sort out the weak students by tracking. The optimal class size in a higher track will exceed the optimal class size in a lower track because there are fewer disturbances. This theory can explain why empirical researchers typically fail to find the expected negative correlation between class size and educational outcomes (Lazear, 2001).

In the following, we consider an educational production function with only three inputs: initial ability of the student, mean ability in class, and resources spent on the student. Using such a simple approach is sufficient to highlight the main issues associated with the tracking decision.

The mere existence of peer group effects suggests that grouping classes according to ability at a given curriculum and given resources spent on each student has an effect on educational outcomes. If the sorting procedure works, individuals in higher tracks would benefit from tracking while individuals in lower tracks are harmed. However, the theoretical prediction on the consequences of peer group effects on the construction of output-maximising class structures is ambiguous. Arnott and Rowse (1987) maximise a welfare function in which welfare increases in each student's final human capital, but may fall with more inequality. They point out that the specific structure of the educational production function has to be considered when constructing an optimal class system. The educational production function they analyse is

(1) $\quad h = a^\alpha m^\beta e^\gamma$,

where h is human capital of the student as the output variable, a is his or her initial ability, m is mean ability in class, e is expenditure spent on the student, and $\alpha, \beta, \gamma \in [0,1)$ are production coefficients. Apart from boundary cases with zero marginal productivities, the production function exhibits positive and diminishing marginal productivities, and the factors of production are complements. Having mixed classes means that mean ability of the whole student population applies for every student. By contrast, tracking assigns students with a high initial ability a to classes with mean ability m above average. Accordingly, students with low initial ability are taught in classes with mean ability below average.

Increasing the marginal productivity of mean ability in class may both imply a tendency in favour of streamed classes and in favour of mixed classes. For example, starting at $\beta=0$, peer group effects are absent. Streaming may be used to exploit that educational resources e are more productive when being spent on more talented students. The predominant effect of introducing peer group effects by increasing β may then consist in the feature that gains from raising mean ability are particularly strong for low levels of mean ability in class. This implies a tendency in favour of mixed classes, as tracking would hurt weak students substantially while losses of able students from detracking are small. Increasing the strength of the peer group effect by further increasing β can then lead to a functional form in which gains from increasing mean ability are similar at all levels of mean ability and given ability of the student, and become very strong for talented individuals. Tracking will then yield the maximum aggregate human capital because the gains of the high ability students from tracking by far outweigh the losses of the low ability individuals.

One main effect of tracking is to make public schools more attractive relative to private schools. Epple et al. (2002) consider an environment with school competition, where private schools can set tuition fees and individuals are differentiated according to initial ability and household income. Private schools will always be stratified according to tuition, where the most expensive schools have the best peer quality among its students, and its student population exhibits the highest average household income. While private schools may in principle also employ ability tracking, a similar effect is achieved by prices that can be differentiated according to ability and parental income. Without tracking, mean ability in the student population in any public school will lie below mean ability in the weakest private school. This is a consequence of the fact that even the weakest private school charges a positive fee while all public schools are free. Introducing tracking in public schools with two tracks will attract students with intermediate ability from families with high income to public schools. Returning to the public system is attractive when these students are assigned to the higher track. The public lower track schools are still the weakest, but the public higher track schools will typically show a higher quality in terms of average ability in class than some private schools. Tracking then tends to harm students of low ability with low household income and particularly helps more able students with poor parents.

The use of tracking allows for a differentiation of the academic level across different types of schools. Employing a higher academic level in schools attended by stronger students may simply reinforce the ordinary peer group effect. Effinger and Polborn (1999) study a hierarchical school system with two school types in which raising the academic level yields a stronger increase in a higher school student's productivity if mean ability in class is higher. Households are free to choose to send children to the lower or the higher track school. The weakest students are always best served at the lower track school. Sending a child from a threshold household to the higher track school rather than to a lower track school is associated with negative externalities, because mean ability both in the higher track class and in the lower track class deteriorates. As these negative externalities are not taken into account by parents, too many students attend higher track schools under free school choice. This argument justifies binding recommendations. Further, schools choose the academic level to maximise the educational output of their students (Costrell, 1994). Higher track schools may not take into account that increasing the academic level deters weaker students from entering and imposing negative externalities. This provides an argument for centralised setting of academic standards, which yields higher standards than under a decentralised organisation.

A drawback of this argument is that higher academic levels also imply a risk of failure at school, In the US, the dropout rate in high school has been around 20 per cent in the nineties (Arum and Hout, 1998), and the loss of income arising from dropout rates has been substantial (Domazlicky et al., 1996; Thompson, 1998). If output losses are higher for more talented students, tracking procedures associated with adapting the academic standard implies a higher risk of human capital losses of talented students. In such a situation, a comprehensive system without tracking may well lead to a higher aggregate income (Meier, 2004).

II. Other arguments

Economic theory has also stressed the signalling value of education. According to this view, education is not necessarily productive per se. One main function of the school system is to provide prospective employers with some information about the productivity of the applicant. Given that ability screening in a tracking scheme works reasonably well, a selective system tends to be more informative than a comprehensive school system (Brunello and Giannini, 2004a). This is particularly true with respect to the assessment of students at the end of the ability distribution. If final grades are not comparable across students due to individualised courses and exams, the only reliable pieces of information are completion of school and school type, where only the selective scheme provides the latter signal. It can be argued, however, that this problem may be mitigated by introducing uniform examination procedures in order to make grades more informative.

Another key idea behind tracking is to exploit gains from specialisation. Rather than teaching similar curricula at different levels, tracking is often used to teach a more practical and vocational curriculum in the lower track and a theory-orientated and more academic curriculum in the higher track. A comprehensive system would incorporate elements of both tracks, which allows for more flexibility of the students. As expressed by Brunello and Giannini (2004b), human capital is kept more versatile. On the other hand, accumulation of human capital of a given type – academic or vocational – would be faster if the student specialises early. As the jobs ultimately require predominantly academic or predominantly vocational skills, a stratified school system with tracking producing the desired shares of skills is superior to a comprehensive scheme without tracking under perfect foresight. This argument is similar to the idea that segregated clubs are more efficient because the provision of public goods can be tailored to the preferences of the club members. The comprehensive scheme without tracking displays its strength in environments with a substantial amount of uncertainty.

If tracking is used for introducing specialised curricula, an interesting problem is to determine the optimum age at which students are separated. If separation starts too early, there is some risk of mismatch unemployment. As the separation of students determines the future shares of workers of different types, the resulting proportions may not fit well with the needs of the employers after completion of schooling. In addition, if there are frictions in matching in the job market, mismatches will occur where positions are filled with workers displaying specialisations that are not used in the job. Such mismatches are associated with higher output losses when specialisation at school starts earlier. Therefore, increasing frictions in the labour market imply that the optimal tracking age goes up (Ariga et al., 2006).

Moreover, the earlier tracking sets in, the noisier the test signal is when measuring true ability. Apart from the problem that ability is revealed only gradually, younger students show stronger differences in maturity. In fact, the younger students in class more often achieve an upgrading as a correction of a previous tracking decision (Puhani and Weber, 2007). Hence, losses from sending children to the wrong schools will be higher with earlier tracking. By contrast, if specialised curricula are introduced late, the gains from specialisation tend to be lower (Judson, 1998, Ariga et al., 2005).

Finally, Brunello et al. (2007) argue that technological progress in firms leads to a higher depreciation rate of vocational training. This reduces the gain from earlier specialisation as the acquired knowledge may already be obsolete when entering the job market. More academic tracks are not hurt by skill depreciation in a similar fashion. The appropriate policy in view of such a skill-biased technological change is to increase the share of students in the academic track and to separate the students later.

C. Empirical Analyses

I. Overview

For empirical researchers, the most obvious approach to analyse the consequences of tracking policies consists in monitoring major reforms or local reform experiments. However, because whether to employ tracking or not is a central structural element in education systems, reforms or experiments are rare. Therefore, empirical analyses of the effects of tracking often struggle with credible statistical methods to identify causal effects. The missing availability of policy experiments also explains why empirical research has taken different alternative approaches.

One main option is to exploit variation of ability grouping policies within and across schools. This route is pursued in many studies from the US. While tracking in the shape of sorting children into different types of secondary schools is uncommon, the US high schools display a substantial amount of heterogeneity with respect to their streaming policies for different subjects. As a consequence, the notion of tracking is not well-defined in many datasets. Additional problems arise if the measures of student performance are correlated to unobserved student characteristics that determine both school choice and track placement.

Another strand of the literature analyses institutional variations across countries using international achievement tests. This approach can avoid problems of explaining selection of students into tracking and non-tracking schools by omitting countries in which both types of schools exist. The major disadvantage lies in the fact that it is almost impossible to control for all relevant institutional differences between countries. For example, social policies may be crucial for achieving mixed classes in a comprehensive school system. Peer group effects are among the forces creating segregation of communities by internal migration, with schools in richer areas displaying a higher peer quality (see, for example, de Bartolome (1990)). In such a situation, moving toward more heterogeneous classes requires measures like augmenting the space for free school choice and subsidise transportation for pupils from poor areas to schools in rich areas. Other institutional features that affect the performance of schools in a country are the degree of school autonomy, centralised exams, and competition between schools (Woessmann, 2003).

II. Older literature on peer group effects

The effects of tracking have first been discussed in the United States in the context of peer group effects. Since it is a widely held belief that peer groups exert substantial influence on the educational production process, it is interesting to analyse the effect of a change in the composition in the peer group that may be caused by tracking.

Summers and Wolfe (1977) analyse the effect of peer group composition on students' achievements in the Philadelphia school district, using the change in the composite achievement score between the third and sixth grade as outcome variable. They find that a higher share of high achievers in a grade has a positive impact on low achievers, while the impact on high achievers is negligible. At the same time, a higher share of low achievers reduces the score of both low and high achievers. Hence, peer group effects are present for everybody and work strongest for weak students. However, the peer group measure used refers to school grades, but not classes. Yet, the presence of tracking implies that the composition of classes within the same grade differs with respect to their peer group quality.

Henderson et al. (1978) estimate peer group effects in elementary schools using achievement scores in French and mathematics between the first and the third grade of French speaking students in Montreal. The authors control for innate ability by including the first recorded IQ score of the student and at the same time also control for achievement in the previous grade. Peer group quality is measured by the mean IQ in the class or by the relative position of this mean IQ among all classes. In each case the coefficients of the peer group variables do not change with the student's ability, indicating similar peer group effects for all ability groups. Since the peer group effect is positive and concave, test score gains from increasing the class mean IQ by one point is diminishing with increasing mean ability. Henderson et al. (1978) therefore conclude that maximising the sum of scores would be achieved by mixed classes. Assuming that tracking separates students on the basis of IQ, and that peer group effects work similarly across grades and subjects, these results indicate a negative effect of tracking on overall achievement.

III. US studies

Since then, several contributions have aimed at determining the sizes of peer group effects in tracked and non-tracked US high schools. Hoffer (1992), Argys, Rees and Brewer (1996), Betts and Shkolnik (2000a), and Figlio and Page (2002) use rather similar datasets but slightly different approaches to address the effects of tracking. Hoffer (1992) and Betts and Shkolnik (2000a) both use the Longitudinal Study of American Youth (LSAY), while Argys et al. (1996) and Figlio and Page (2002) use the National Education Longitudinal Study of 1988 (NELS). Their results are similar in that tracking does not seem to be related to substantial efficiency gains. However, with respect to differential effects for students of different ability levels, the authors come to widely different conclusions.

Hoffer (1992) examines the effects of ability grouping between seventh and ninth grade and performs different analyses using mathematics and science scores. Information on the schools' use of ability grouping and on the level of the ability-grouped class that the students attended were gathered from teachers and school documents. The analysis starts with simple ordinary least squares regressions of later achievement on previous achievement, measures of social background and two sets of grouping indicators. First using a dummy indicating whether or not the school uses ability grouping, no evidence is found for a significant effect of ability grouping on average achievement. The second set

Tab. 1. Evidence from the US

Paper	Data	Country	Tracking /Streaming information	Outcome variable	Results
Hoffer (1992)	Longitudinal Study of American Youth (LSAY)	USA	a) Dummy variable if school uses ability grouping in math classes b) Teacher's evaluation of average ability level of class compared to other classes in same school	Test scores in mathematics and science in ninth grade	No effect of ability grouping on overall achievement. Placement in high group has positive effect, placement in low group has negative effect
Betts and Shkolnik (2000a)	Longitudinal Study of American Youth (LSAY)	USA	a) Dummy variable if school uses ability grouping in math classes. b) Teacher's evaluation of average ability level of class compared to other classes in same school.	Test scores in mathematics and science in ninth grade	No effect of ability grouping on overall achievement. Low ability children not affected by ability grouping, middle ability students harmed, high ability students gain
Argys et al. (1996)	National Education Longitudinal Study, 1988	USA	Teacher's evaluation: a) achievement level in mathematic class considered above average, average, below average, widely differing b) class is honours, academic, general or vocational track	Test scores in mathematics, tenth grade	Students in lower tracks gain from de-tracking, students in higher tracks lose. Detracking reduces average test scores by two percent
Figlio and Page (2002)	National Education Longitudinal Survey, 1988	USA	Tracking dummy a) from principals' reports: whether school uses ability grouping or tracking in math classes. b) combining answers from teachers' reports	Gain in math test scores between 8th and 10th grade	Overall, no effect of tracking. Using two-stage least squares: Tracking helps students in bottom third of test distribution

of grouping indicators consists of dummies indicating ability group level placement in high, middle and low group with non-grouped as the reference category. Thus, students in high, middle and low ability classes are compared to students in schools that supposedly do not use ability grouping. The results across different specifications indicate that placement in the high group has a weak positive effect, and that placement in the low group has a stronger negative effect. The results for the overall effects of grouping and the effects of group placement are not greatly changed by employing a propensity score method to encounter the criticism that grouped and non-grouped students are not comparable. This criticism relates to the fact that selection into grouped or ungrouped classes might be based on unobservable factors that are correlated with achievement, such as motivation, which would lead to biased estimates.

Betts and Shkolnik (2000a) prefer to use information on the ability level of the class provided by the teachers to compare grouped and non-grouped students at given class ability levels. Using this information might even better control for unobserved heterogeneity than a propensity score method. They control for average class ability both at grouping and at supposedly non-grouping schools using two different measures of class ability. Their first measure is based on teachers' reports on the average ability level of the class as compared to other classes in the same school. Their second measure is obtained by subtracting the mean achievement of the grade from the initial achievement and subsequently grouping the students into quartiles based on their normalized scores. Betts and Shkolnik regress student achievement on previous achievement, control variables and a set of dummy variables indicating membership in different ability groups and whether or not the school employs grouping according to the principal. The difference in the coefficients on class ability between grouped and non-grouped schools are used to identify the effect of being placed in a class of given ability in a school that officially groups. The overall effect of formal ability grouping on the average student is insignificant. This finding is in line with Hoffer (1992), but stands in contrast to Argys, Rees and Brewer (1996) who find a positive significant overall effect. Further, Betts and Shkolnik (2000a) find that children at the bottom of the ability distribution are not affected by ability grouping, that middle students are harmed, and that high ability students gain. The authors discuss and present several robustness checks which lead to insignificant estimates for the effects of grouping in the case of a propensity score method and to significant effects of grouping only for high ability children in the case of an instrumental variable approach. Their conclusion is that previous research by Hoffer (1992) and Argys et al. (1996) has overstated the differential effects of ability grouping across students of differing ability levels due to inadequate controls for class ability levels at supposedly ungrouped schools. On the other hand it can be argued that the approach used by Betts and Shkolnik (2000a) does not allow the correct identification of grouped and ungrouped classes and that the results should be reinterpreted as the effect of formal versus informal tracking (Rees et al., 2000).

Argys et al. (1996) infer from their analysis that abolishing tracking would lead to losses in efficiency. They consider the impact of tracking on test scores in mathematics at the end of the 10th grade. Two measures of grouping of students that were derived from survey questions to teachers are used separately in the analysis: the achievement level of the students in the class as compared to the average student in the same grade (above average, average, below average, heterogenous), and the track that the class could best be described as (honors, academic, general or vocational). For each track or ability group, achievement equations are estimated separately. Averaging predicted achievement in each track across all students in the sample gives an estimate of what the achievement of the average student would be if placed in a certain track or ability group. Comparing mean predicted achievement between tracks or ability groups, the authors find uneven effects of detracking schools. Students in below average classes or tracks would gain and students in above average classes or tracks would lose. The overall net effect of placing all students in heterogeneous classes would be a 2 percent drop in mathematics test scores.

Betts and Shkolnik (2000b) claim that the sizes of the effects reported by Argys et al. (1996) are overstated. They argue that group or track placement may be correlated with the error when students' initial achievement is only imperfectly measured, and that therefore the estimates will be systematically biased. Moreover, the selectivity correction used by Argys et al. (1996) appears not to correct for the correlation between track placement and initial achievement, but rather to increase the omitted ability bias. Betts and Shkolnik (2000b) also criticise that a 'heterogeneous' ability level of a class should not be used to compare grouped classes of differing ability levels to ungrouped classes, since it may mean different things to different teachers in different schools.

Using the same data as in Argys et al. (1996), Figlio and Page (2002) compare students' achievement growth between 8th and 10th grade only across schools, with some schools employing ability grouping measures while others do not. Figlio and Page divide the students according to their 8th grade math achievement into top, middle and bottom thirds of the test score distribution. Subsequently, they estimate separate regression equations for each of these subsets and include a dummy for whether the principal reports that the school tracks. The effect of tracking is statistically insignificant within each third of the student achievement distribution. Figlio and Page interpret this as evidence that lower test score gains observed among students in low ability tracks does not stem from tracking placement, but from unobserved factors that are correlated with track placement. Using alternative approaches to define the school as tracking or non-tracking, the authors again do not find evidence that tracking harms low-ability children. The authors also argue that a school's tracking status affects school choice. Therefore, a two-stage least squares analysis is performed to address the potential endogeneity of tracking status. The results from this exercise indicate that low-ability students may actually gain from being placed in schools that employ tracking.

The major problem of these US studies is the nonexistent definition of tracking and ability grouping in the survey questionnaires. Therefore, grouping measures may not be comparable across schools or even teachers. Moreover, two possible sources of endogeneity make it difficult to estimate causal effects of different tracking policies within any survey data. First, track placement may be correlated with unobserved factors such as motivation that both determine achievement and track placement. Second, the selection of students into schools is presumably endogenous. If parents tend to send talented children to schools employing tracking programmes, the results will be biased towards finding a positive effect of tracking on achievement.

IV. Impacts of reducing the variance in mean ability

In the last few years, some attempts have been undertaken to identify the pure peer group effect generated by tracking. By creating homogenous classes, tracking not only changes the mean ability in classes for students assigned to different tracks, but it also reduces the variance in ability. The impact of tracking on the level of the peer group effect is seen by measuring the effect of reducing the variance on the level of the student's test scores at given mean ability. In addition, tracking also affects the strength of the peer effect, which would be expressed by the change in test scores associated with varying mean ability. If individuals benefit from tailored courses in homogenous classes, the sum of these two effects is expected to be positive. As the results presented by Zimmer and Toma (2000) and Zimmer (2003) show, this is not necessarily the case.

Estimating peer group effects in a sample of students from five countries, Zimmer and Toma (2000) surprisingly find that a higher standard deviation of test scores within the class leads to higher individual student achievement. The strength of this effect, however, also depends on the mean ability of the class. Increasing the variance in ability within a class generates smaller effects when mean ability is higher, and higher effects when mean ability is lower. At the same time, low-ability students capture higher gains from a better peer set than high-ability students. Thus, low-ability students are the ones most affected by classroom composition. Zimmer (2003) uses only the US portion of the same dataset and shows that for low-ability and average-ability students tracking reduces the positive peer effect, whereas for high-ability students the peer effect is unaffected by the tracking procedure. His results also suggest that the institutional practice of tracking has a positive effect on low- and high ability students at low levels of peer quality; a situation which is more likely to occur in the presence of tracking. Thus, the positive effect of tracking may compensate weak students for losses associated with a reduction in peer group quality upon separation from stronger students. However, if both effects are combined, the loss of more able peers seems to outweigh the benefits of tracking for low- and average ability students.

V. Policy reforms

Other contributions to the empirical literature have tried to exploit institutional change or reforms over time. Since determining causal effects is very difficult in the context of student performance due to unobserved ability and family background and due to the difficulties in establishing the treatment effects on the non-treated, reforms in education systems offer a much more reliable basis for establishing causal effects. This approach is followed by Galindo-Rueda and Vignoles (2007) and Manning and Pischke (2006) for the United Kingdom and by Meghir and Palme (2005) for Sweden.

Galinda-Rueda and Vignoles (2007) use the National Child Development Study consisting of a cohort of individuals born in England and Wales in March 1958. The data contains the test scores of the individuals at age 7, 11, and 16, together with lots of individual and family characteristics. As the movement from the selective to the comprehensive school system was delayed or accelerated by local education authorities, both systems coexisted in the years under consideration. In their study, Galindo-Rueda and Vignoles take the test score in mathematics at age 16 as the dependent variable. Using a matching approach in which individuals with similar characteristics are compared to each other, their results indicate that a selective school system favours high ability students, whereas the impacts on middle and low ability students are insignificant. This implies that the selective school system had been more efficient in terms of average achievement. In contrast, Manning and Pischke (2006) argue that nothing can be learned from the education policy reform in England and Wales. They analyse the same data and perform similar analyses, but also test additional specifications. Using ability measures at age 11 as the outcome variable, that is before even entering secondary education, the authors are still able to show a negative effect of attending a comprehensive school. Since it is not possible that later attendance of comprehensive schools influences test scores during primary school years, these results indicate the presence of selection bias. Hence, results for specifications using age 16 ability measures are most likely biased as well and should not be interpreted casually. The selection into comprehensive and selective schools during the transition period seems to be based on unobservable characteristics that cannot be controlled for.

Tab. 2. Evidence from policy reforms

Paper	Data + Country	Reform information	Outcome variable	Results
Galinda-Rueda and Vignoles (2007)	National Child Development Study, England and Wales	Change from selective to comprehensive school system	Test scores in mathematics at age 16	Tracking helps high ability students, insignificant effects on others
Manning and Pischke (2006)	National Child Development Study, England and Wales	Change from selective to comprehensive school system	Test scores in mathematics at age 16 and 11	Selection bias cannot be ruled out. Applies also to Galinda-Rueda and Vignoles (2004)
Meghir and Palme (2005)	1948 and 1953 cohort survey, Sweden	Abolishment of tracking, extension of compulsory schooling, introduction of national curriculum.	Final educational attainment and annual earnings	Educational attainment and earnings increased for individuals with low-skilled fathers

The consequences of the Swedish education reform in the 1950s give strong evidence for an equalising effect of detracking, with gains arising for individuals of a less favourable educational background and losses for children of skilled parents. The reform not only abolished tracking after the sixth grade, but also entailed the extension of compulsory schooling and the introduction of a national curriculum. Meghir and Palme (2005) use the 1948 and 1953 cohort survey that collected information on individuals when they were in sixth grade. Data from these two cohort surveys was supplemented by information on final educational attainment from the 1990 Swedish education register and by information on annual earnings and employment status between 1985 and 1996 from the Swedish tax registers. Meghir and Palme find that the reform increased the educational attainment of individuals with unskilled fathers, with a particularly strong effect on the more able students. The increase in educational attainment beyond the new compulsory schooling level was stronger for women. Earnings of individuals with unskilled fathers increased significantly, with a more pronounced effect for women. The difference in the earnings increase between individuals of high or low ability was significant only for women. However, earnings of individuals with skilled fathers were negatively affected by the reform. One reason for this phenomenon can be traced to the fact that this group used to attend the academic track prior to the reform. The reform appears to have reduced both the quality of education for these individuals and their subsequent earnings. Since the Swedish reform included an increase in compulsory schooling and the establishment of a nationwide unified curriculum, it is not completely clear which part of the effects of the reform can be attributed to detracking.

VI. Interregional and international comparisons

Other papers have even more strongly focussed on family background, thereby not only considering the effects of tracking versus non-tracking, but more frequently also on the effects of the timing of tracking and of the number of distinct tracks available to secondary students. This applies both to studies exploiting regional variations across countries and to analyses of international student achievement tests.

Bauer and Riphahn (2006) estimate the effect of the timing of tracking on the educational mobility using within country variation in the timing of tracking between the 26 cantons in Switzerland. If tracking takes place at an early stage in the educational career, students' innate ability will be measured with a lot of noise. In this case, track placement will be dominated by the parental background of the students. Bauer and Riphahn analyse the difference in the predicted probabilities of attending the college-bound track for children of high and low educated parents and compare those differences between early and late tracking cantons. The results show that the impact of parental education on track placement varies depending on the timing of tracking. Early tracking greatly increases the relative advantage of children with highly educated parents. Applying a similar methodology to data referring to the German Federal States, Woessmann (2007) confirms these results.

Ammermüller (2005) employs data from two international student achievement studies PIRLS (Progress in International Reading Literacy Survey) and PISA (Programme for International Student Assessment) to analyse the effect of changes in the institutional structure of the education systems between primary and secondary schooling on the educational opportunities of children with differing family backgrounds. His dataset consists of student micro level, school and country level information for 12 of the 14 countries that participated both in PIRLS in 2001 and in PISA 2000. Using a difference-in-differences estimation approach, Ammermüller investigates how changes in institutional variables that occur between the primary and the secondary schooling level influence the strength of the influence of family background on the test score of students. One of the institutional changes that are considered in this analysis is the number of distinct school types or tracks that are available to students in secondary education. The results indicate that the number of school types is positively linked to the impact of parents' education and origin. Thus, the influence of parental background on student achievement is higher and – thus equality of educational opportunities is lower – in education systems that select their students into many different types of secondary schools.

Hanushek and Woessmann (2006) employ a differences-in-differences approach to analyse the question of whether the timing of educational tracking affects performance

Tab. 3. Evidence from international studies

Paper	Data	Country	Tracking information	Outcome variable	Results
Ammermüller (2005)	PIRLS 2001 and PISA 2000	12 countries	Number of distinct school types (tracks) in secondary education	Change in impact of family background on test achievement between primary and secondary schooling	Impact of family background higher with more school types (tracks) in secondary schooling
Hanushek and Woessmann (2006)	Several waves of PIRLS, PISA and TIMSS	18–26 countries	Dummy representing early tracking	Change in dispersion of student test scores between primary and secondary schooling	Early tracking increases inequality, tendency for tracking to reduce mean achievement
Schütz et al. (2005)	TIMSS 1995 and 1999	53 countries	Timing of tracking	Impact of family background on test achievement	Impact of family background higher when tracking occurs earlier
Brunello and Checchi (2006)	European Community Household Panel (ECHP), International Adult Literacy Survey (IALS), International Social Survey Programme (ISSP)	12–25 countries	Weighted indicator capturing share of population tracked into vocational stream and time spent in tracks	Educational attainment, literacy, employment, earnings	Effect of family background stronger with tracking, tracking reinforces dispersion of earnings
Waldinger (2006)	PIRLS 2001, PISA 2000 and 2003 and TIMSS 1995 and 1999	8–15 countries	Number of years spent in untracked system	Student test scores in reading and mathematics	Family background more important in countries that track early, inequality already present before tracking occurs

and inequality. Their dataset consists of different waves of the international student achievement tests PIRLS, PISA and TIMSS (Trends in International Mathematics and Science Study, formerly Third International Mathematics and Science Study). By matching tests measuring performance at the end of primary school (PIRLS 2000, TIMSS 1995 and 2003) with tests taken in secondary schools (PISA 2000 and 2003, TIMSS 1995, 1999 and 2003) they are able to compare inequality in student outcomes before selection takes place with inequality in outcomes after selection has taken place in some countries, but not in others. The matching of tests produces datasets containing between 18 and 26 countries depending on the subjects tested. The econometric analysis shows that early tracking increases inequality. With respect to the effects of tracking on average country performance, the picture is not consistent across countries and subjects but overall shows a tendency for early tracking to reduce average performance.

Evidence for the negative effects of streaming on the equality of educational opportunities is also provided by Schütz et al. (2005). Their analysis tries to provide an answer to the question of why the degree to which family background determines student achievement differs between countries. The authors use data from two international student achievement tests in mathematics (TIMSS 1995 and TIMSS 1999) to obtain a sample consisting of 54 countries. The degree of equality of educational opportunities that a country achieves is measured as the extent to which the number of books in the students' home influences test achievement. Several organisational features of the education systems are found to determine educational opportunity. The equality measure increases with a longer duration of the pre-primary educational cycle, a higher level of enrolment in pre-primary education and a higher age of first streaming. Later tracking is shown to reduce the strength of the influence of family background on student achievement. The authors also analyse whether the timing of streaming is connected to the overall level of educational achievement in the participating countries. Since country mean test achievement is independent of the age of first streaming, delaying the timing of tracking does not appear to have negative effects on average student performance.

Brunello and Checchi (2006) and Waldinger (2006) also investigate whether tracking contributes to increasing inequality of educational outcomes by strengthening the impact of family background variables. Brunello and Checchi use several datasets like the European Community Household Panel, the International Social Survey Programme, and the International Adult Literacy Survey, that all measure outcome variables of young adults in terms of wages, final educational attainment, or literacy. The stronger effect of family background with tracking is persistent when considering educational attainment, and tracking reinforces the dispersion of earnings. By contrast, the effect of family background on reading skills of young adults is weaker in countries that track earlier. This finding indicates that the opposite result that arises with the PISA 2003 literacy score data has to be taken with caution. Waldinger considers international student test scores of primary school students (PIRLS) and secondary school students (TIMSS and PISA). He confirms the findings that family background effects on student achievement are stronger in countries that track earlier. However, using a difference-in-differences approach, he shows that differences in the importance of family background between countries are already present before tracking takes place, and that actual tracking does not increase the importance of the family background characteristics. Hence, the differences across countries cannot directly be traced back to the tracking procedures. Yet, one drawback of this study is the relatively small sample of countries which is why it cannot be ruled out that some important variation is missing.

D. Conclusions

Although the literature on the consequences of ability grouping has spread out substantially during the last two decades, clear-cut messages have not emerged. Neither theory nor the empirical evidence gives a definitive answer to the question of which school system yields the maximum of total productivities, or the maximum aggregate test scores at some given grade in school. Theoretical considerations suggest that ability grouping is useful if either talented students can achieve a strong increase in performance or if substantial gains from specialisation can be expected. In contrast, keeping students of different ability levels in the same class makes sense when weak students benefit a lot from the presence of strong students. Delaying the age when tracking starts lowers the risk of mistakenly sending children to the wrong school type, but also reduces gains of appropriately placed students.

The empirical literature has until now failed to provide clear answers to the question of the impact of tracking on average achievements of students. While some studies have found negative effects of tracking, others have found evidence for positive effects. Since lots of studies fail to find a significant overall effect, it seems most likely that on average the tracking regime has no major effect on average achievement. However, the relative advantages of tracking or detracking may still depend on timing, the composition of the student population and institutional features. Further, insignificant or even negative effects of tracking on average test scores do not exclude positive impacts on productivities, because test results may not be perfect indicators of subsequent labour market performance. In particular, the tests may not capture possible gains from specialisation.

Empirical research has also investigated the impacts of tracking on the equality of educational opportunities and on the dispersion of achievements. There is a clear tendency that ability grouping increases the variance of school achievements in terms of test scores. Moreover, children of disadvantaged family background seem to benefit from delaying tracking and from a reduced availability of distinct types of secondary school tracks. Yet, speculations that ability grouping helps the talented individuals and harms the weak students are still hotly debated.

References

Argys, L. M., D. I. Rees and D. J. Brewer (1996). Detracking America's schools: equity at zero cost? Journal of Policy Analysis and Management 15, 623–645.

Ariga, K., G. Brunello, R. Iwahashi and L. Rocco (2005). Why is the timing of school tracking so heterogeneous? IZA Discussion Paper No. 1854, Bonn.

Ariga, K., G. Brunello, R. Iwahashi and L. Rocco (2006). On the efficiency costs of de-tracking secondary schools. IZA Discussion Paper No. 2534, Bonn.

Arnott, R., and J. Rowse (1987). Peer group effects and educational attainment. Journal of Public Economics 32, 287–305.

Arum, R., and M. Hout (1998). The early returns – the transition from school to work in the United States. In: W. Müller and Y. Shavit (eds.), From School to Work, Oxford, 471–510.

Bauer, P., and R. T. Riphahn (2006). Timing of school tracking as determinant of intergenerational transmission of education. Economics Letters 91, 90–97.

Betts, J. R., and J. L. Shkolnik (2000a). The effects of ability grouping on student achievement and resource allocation in secondary schools. Economics of Education Review 19, 1–15.

Betts, J. R., and J. L. Shkolnik (2000b). Key difficulties in identifying the effects of ability grouping on student achievement. Economics of Education Review 19, 21–26.

Brunello, G., and D. Checchi (2006). Does school tracking affect equality of opportunity? New international evidence. IZA Discussion Paper No. 2348, Bonn.

Brunello, G., and M. Giannini (2004a). Selective schools. Bulletin of Economic Research 56, 207–225.

Brunello, G., and M. Giannini (2004b). Stratified or comprehensive? The economic efficiency of school design. Scottish Journal of Political Economy 51, 173–193.

Brunello, G., M. Giannini and K. Ariga (2004). The optimal timing of school tracking: a general model with calibration for Germany. In: L. Woessmann and P. E. Peterson (eds.), Schools and the Equal Opportunity Problem, Cambridge, MA: MIT Press, 129–156.

Costrell, R. (1994). A simple model of educational standards. American Economic Review 84, 956–971.

de Bartolome, C. (1990). Equilibrium and inefficiency in a community model with peer group effects. Journal of Political Economy 98, 110–133.

Domazlicky, B. R. et al. (1996). Measuring the cost of high school noncompletion in Southeast Missouri. The Journal of Economics 22, 81–86.

Dustmann, C. (2004). Parental background, secondary school track choice, and wages, Oxford Economic Papers 56, 209–230.

Effinger, M. R., and M. K. Polborn (1999). A model of vertically differentiated education. Journal of Economics 69, 53–69.

Epple, D., E. Newlon and R. Romano (2002). Ability tracking, school competition, and the distribution of educational benefits. Journal of Public Economics 83, 1–48.

Figlio, D. N., and M. E. Page (2002). School choice and the distributional effects of ability tracking: does separation increase inequality? Journal of Urban Economics 51, 497–514.

Galinda-Rueda, F. and A. Vignoles (2007). The heterogeneous effect of selection in UK secondary schools. In: L. Woessmann and P. E. Peterson (eds.), Schools and the Equal Opportunity Problem, Cambridge, MA: MIT Press, 103–128.

Hanushek, E. A., and L. Woessmann (2006). Does educational tracking affect performance and inequality? Difference-in-differences evidence across countries. Economic Journal 116, C63–C76.

Henderson, V., P. Mieszkowski and Y. Sauvageau (1978). Peer group effects and educational production functions. Journal of Public Economics 10, 97–106.

Hoffer, T. B. (1992). Middle school ability grouping and student achievement in science and mathematics. Educational Evaluation and Policy Analysis 14, 205–227.

Judson, R. (1998). Economic growth and investment in education: how allocation matters. Journal of Economic Growth 3, 337–359.

Lazear, E. P. (2001). Educational production. Quarterly Journal of Economics 116, 777–803.

Manning, A., and J.-S. Pischke (2006). Comprehensive versus selective schooling in England and Wales: what do we know? IZA Discussion Paper No. 2072, Bonn.

Meghir, C., and M. Palme (2005). Educational reform, ability and family background. American Economic Review 95, 414–424.

Meier, V. (2004). Choosing between school systems: the risk of failure. Finanzarchiv 60, 83–93.

OECD (2005). Education at a glance, OECD: Paris.

Pekkarinen, T., R. Uusitalo and S. Pekkala (2006). Education policy and intergenerational income mobility: evidence from the Finnish comprehensive school reform. IZA Discussion Paper No. 2204, Bonn.

Puhani, P. A., and A. M. Weber (2007). How persistent is the age of school entry effect in a system of flexible tracking? Mimeo, University of Hannover.

Rees, D. I., D. J. Brewer and L. M. Argys (2000). How should we measure the effect of ability grouping on student performance? Economics of Education Review 19, 17–22.

Schütz, G., H. W. Ursprung and L. Woessmann (2005). Education policy and equality of opportunity. IZA Discussion Paper No. 1906, Bonn.

Summers, A. A., and B. L. Wolfe (1977). Do schools make a difference? American Economic Review 67, 639–652.

Thompson, M. A. (1998). Assessing the economic costs of high school noncompletion Journal of Economics and Finance 22, 109–117.

Waldinger, F. (2006). Does tracking affect the importance of family background on students' test scores? Mimeo, London School of Economics.

Woessmann, L. (2003). Schooling resources, educational institutions and student performance: the international evidence. Oxford Bulletin of Economics and Statistics 65, 117–170.

Woessmann, L. (2007). Fundamental determinants of school efficiency and equity: German states as a microcosm for OECD countries, CESifo Working Paper 1981, München.

Zimmer, R. (2003). A new twist in the educational tracking debate, Economics of Education Review 22, 307–315.

Zimmer, R. W., and E. F. Toma (2000). Peer effects in private and public schools across countries. Journal of Policy Analysis and Management 19(1), 75–92.

The Economics of Tracking and Non-Tracking

Summary

There exists substantial variation across OECD countries as to whether and how students are grouped in classes according to perceived ability. Economic analyses stress that there is joint production of human capital in schools, where output increases with rising mean ability in the class. Ability tracking may therefore be particularly helpful for talented students. At the same time, weak students may benefit from ability grouping via tailored and specialised courses. The vast majority of the econometric literature suggests that tracking promotes inequality in academic achievement. By contrast, the empirical literature on the impact of tracking on average test scores of students is inconclusive. Only few studies find a significant association, and they include both positive and negative estimates.

Die Ökonomik der Mehrgliedrigkeit von Schulsystemen

Zusammenfassung

Im internationalen Vergleich existieren sehr unterschiedliche Praktiken hinsichtlich der Aufteilung von Schülern auf Schulen unterschiedlicher Qualität oder Kurse mit unterschiedlichen Leistungsansprüchen. Die ökonomische Theorie betont die gemeinschaftliche Produktion des Humankapitals in der Klasse, wobei der Output durch eine höhere durchschnittliche Schülerqualität gesteigert werden kann. Die Trennung der Schüler nach einem Fähigkeitstest sollte vor allem auf talentierte Schüler positiv wirken. Schwächere Schüler könnten dabei durch auf sie zugeschnittene Kurse von der Trennung profitieren. Die empirische Literatur zeigt, dass ein längeres gemeinsames Lernen der Schüler die Chancengleichheit erhöht, indem es den Einfluss des familiären Hintergrunds auf den schulischen Erfolg reduziert. Im Hinblick auf die Frage nach der Wirkung von gegliederten Schulsystemen auf die durchschnittlichen Testleistungen besteht allerdings Uneinigkeit. Einige Studien finden positive Effekte und andere negative, was darauf hin deutet, dass es wahrscheinlich keinen signifikanten Zusammenhang gibt.

WWW.GABLER.DE

State-of-the-Art in European Management

Christian Scholz | Joachim Zentes (Eds.)
Strategic Management – New Rules for Old Europe
2006. viii, 314 pp., 32 Fig., 37 Tab. Hardc. EUR 64,00
ISBN 978-3-8349-0211-5

Lecturers and researchers at Saarland University's Europa-Institut present the latest findings and trends of their most important research topics. They discuss the present state of the art in European management, focussing on the areas of marketing & commerce, finance, human resource management & entrepreneurship, as well as European policy.

The Editors
Univ.-Professor Dr. Christian Scholz holds the chair of Business Administration, especially Organisation, Human Resource Management and Information Management at Saarland University, Germany. He is director of the Institute of Management Competence and director of the Europa-Institut at Saarland University, Germany.
Univ.-Professor Dr. Joachim Zentes holds the chair of Business Administration, especially Foreign Trade and International Management at Saarland University, Germany. He is director of the Institute of Commerce & International Marketing and director of the Europa-Institut at Saarland University

Order your copy now: kerstin.kuchta@gwv-fachverlage.de
Telefon +49(0)611. 7878-626

KOMPETENZ IN SACHEN WIRTSCHAFT

How Equal Are Educational Opportunities?
Family Background and Student Achievement in Europe and the United States

Ludger Wößmann*

Abstract

- This paper estimates the associations between family-background characteristics and student performance in the United States and 17 Western European school systems using student-level data from the TIMSS international student achievement test.
- The associations are strong both in Europe and the United States, remarkably similar in size on aggregate.
- On the preferred measure, France and Flemish Belgium achieve the most equitable performance for students from different family backgrounds, and Britain and Germany the least.
- Equality of opportunity is unrelated to countries' mean performance.
- Quantile regressions show little variation in the associations across the ability distribution in most countries.

Keywords Educational economics · equality of opportunity · student performance · family background · intergenerational mobility

JEL: I21, H52, J62

Prof. Dr. Ludger Wößmann (✉)
is Professor of Economics, esp. Economics of Education, at the Ludwig-Maximilians-University Munich and Head of Department Human Capital and Innovation at the Ifo Institute for Economic Research, Munich. Research fields: education economics, growth economics, innovation economics. Ifo Institute for Economic Research, Poschingerstr. 5, 81679 Munich, Germany, E-mail: woessmann@ifo.de,
Internet: www.cesifo.de/woessmann.

A. Introduction

Equality of opportunity for all citizens is a major concern in all open societies (cf., e.g., Roemer 1998). An important foundation for the future civil, social, and economic opportunities of citizens is laid in the education system. The importance of educational performance for future income and productivity of individuals and societies has been documented by a large literature (cf., e.g., Bishop 1992; Card 1999), and it is increasingly stressed that family background plays a crucial role in the formation of skills (cf., e.g., Cunha et al. 2006). However, no consistent evidence is available to what extent different countries achieve equal educational opportunities for children from different family backgrounds. Such evidence would be useful both because it could reveal an important feature of each country's equality of opportunity and because the comparison of equality of educational opportunity across countries may lead to a better understanding of how it may be achieved and why different countries achieve it to a different extent. This paper aims to present estimates of the extent of equality of opportunity in education in Western European countries and the United States that are directly comparable across countries.

The topic of equality of educational opportunity relates to the extensive economic literature on intergenerational earnings mobility, which looks at the relationship in earnings between parents and their children (cf. Solon 1999 for a survey). Because of the strong relationship between education and earnings, there should be a clear mapping between intergenerational mobility in education outcomes and intergenerational mobility in earnings. But while Solon (2002) shows how the literature on earnings mobility suffers from limitations in the comparability of data and concepts across countries, this paper uses internationally comparable data on students' educational performance to yield readily comparable estimates of educational mobility. Measures of intergenerational educational mobility have the additional advantage of providing contemporaneous evidence for children currently in school, while earnings mobility can only be measured with sufficient precision once the children have been in the labor market for a considerable period of time.

Evidence of substantial earnings returns to quantitative measures of education, like years of schooling, is abundant (cf. the surveys by Card 1999 and Ashenfelter et al. 1999). But the earnings returns to qualitative measures of education, like scores on cognitive achievement tests, seem to be even higher (in terms of standardized coefficient estimates; Boissiere et al. 1985; Bishop 1989, 1992) and increasing over time (Murnane et al. 1995). Furthermore, while returns to educational quantity decrease with an individual's time in the labor market, returns to educational quality increase (Altonji/Pierret 2001). Even among school dropouts, i.e. students with the lowest educational quantity, there are substantial earnings returns to basic cognitive skills (Tyler et al. 2000).[1] This suggests that qualitative measures of education such as cognitive achievement tests are better indicators for future economic opportunities than quantitative measures of education such as years of formal schooling.[2]

This paper therefore uses data from a large international comparative student achievement test – the Third International Mathematics and Science Study (TIMSS) – to estimate the associations between different measures of family background and children's test scores in middle school. For the purposes of this paper, the extent of equality of opportunity in education is thus measured by the size of the associations that several measures of students' family background have with the students' performance on standardized achievement tests of cognitive skills.

In effect, the estimates of equality of educational opportunity are derived by estimating the "home production" part of education production functions.[3] The TIMSS database contains both achievement data for representative samples of middle-school students in 17 Western European school systems (in 15 countries) and the United States, and abundant family-background data available from student background questionnaires. The fact that the same data-collection process was implemented in all countries allows for a direct comparison of estimated family-background effects across the European countries and the United States.[4]

The paper is structured as follows. Section B introduces the database and presents the empirical model. Section C presents the basic results on the associations between family background and student achievement in the 18 school systems. The discussion in this paper will focus on student performance in math, as this is generally viewed as being most readily comparable across countries. Math achievement has also been shown to be most strongly related to productivity (e.g., Bishop 1992).[5] Section D compares the general pattern of the evidence between Europe and the United States. Section E extends the analysis to quantile regressions to investigate whether there is heterogeneity in the associations across the conditional achievement distribution. Section F discusses whether the cross-country pattern of results suggests an equity-efficiency tradeoff in educational production. Section G summarizes the results and concludes on directions for future research.

B. Data and Method

This section discusses the TIMSS student performance database used in this paper, reports descriptive statistics for each country, and presents the empirical model to be estimated.

I. The TIMSS Student Performance Data

The Third International Mathematics and Science Study (TIMSS) is a large-scale cross-country comparative test of student achievement, conducted in 1995 by the International Association for the Evaluation of Educational Achievement (IEA), an independent international cooperative of national research institutions and government agencies which has been developing and conducting cross-national studies of student achievement since 1959.[6] From Western Europe, 17 separate school systems in 15 countries participated in TIMSS: Austria, Flemish and French Belgium, Denmark, England and Scotland, France, Germany, Greece, Iceland, Ireland, the Netherlands, Norway, Portugal, Spain, Sweden, and Switzerland.[7] The TIMSS database combines individual student-level performance data in math and science with extensive information from background questionnaires for nationally representative samples of students in each of the countries.

In TIMSS, the target population of middle school students to which each participating country administered the test was defined as those students enrolled in the two adjacent grades with the largest proportion of 13-year-olds at the time of testing.[8] TIMSS followed a curriculum-based test design, so that its questions are meant to reflect the students' current curriculum and are thus appropriate for them (cf. Martin/Kelly 1996; 1997). Thus, TIMSS covers the core material common to the curricula in the majority of participating countries, and every effort was made to help ensure that the items did not exhibit any bias towards or against particular countries. A matching analysis later performed between the test and the actual curriculum in each country showed that disregarding any items not covered in the country's intended curriculum barely affected the results.

Each participating country randomly sampled the schools to be tested in a stratified sampling design, and within each of these schools, generally one class was randomly chosen from each of the two grades and all of its students were tested in both math and science, yielding a representative sample of students within each country.[9] Schools in geographically remote regions, extremely small schools, and schools for students with special needs were excluded from the target population. Within sampled schools, disabled students who were unable to follow even the test instructions were excluded; students who merely exhibited poor academic performance or discipline problems were required to participate (Martin/Kelly 1996). The overall exclusion rate was not to exceed 10% of the total student population.[10]

As a general rule, each country was meant to sample at least 150 schools (Gonzalez/ Smith 1997). Response rates were not perfect (even after taking into account randomly selected replacement schools), though, while some countries sampled even more schools.[11] As reported in Table 1, Switzerland features the largest sample size of the countries considered in this paper with 11,722 students in 613 classrooms in 327 schools, while England has the smallest number of sampled students at 3,579 and the Netherlands has the smallest number of sampled classrooms (187) and schools (95).

TIMSS gave rigorous attention to quality control, using standardized procedures to ensure comparability in school and student sampling, to prevent bias, and to assure quality in test design and development, data collection, scoring procedures, and analysis. The TIMSS achievement tests were developed through an international consensus-building process involving inputs from international experts in math, science, and measurement, and were endorsed by all participating countries. Given the international standardization of the test results, the cooperative nature of the test development, its endorsement by all participating countries, and the substantial efforts to ensure high-quality sampling and testing in all countries, the TIMSS student performance and background data should be comparable across countries. This should also make the empirical estimates presented in this paper directly comparable across the different countries.

The performance data are merged with background data from TIMSS background questionnaires for each individual student.[12] The information on student- and family-background characteristics are mainly drawn from student background questionnaires, where students report the number of books in their home, the level of their parents' education, whether they live with both parents and were born in the country, and their sex and age. Additionally, school-principal background questionnaires provide information on the community location of the school. Except for student age, all background data are used as dummy variables in this paper.

Complete performance data are available for all the students participating in TIMSS. In terms of the background data, France did not administer the question students' country of birth. Furthermore, some students and school principals failed to answer some items in the background questionnaires. While in general, response rates are reasonable, in some countries data on parental education and community location are missing for more than 40 percent of the students (cf. Table A1 in the working-paper version of this paper (Wößmann 2004)). In cases of missing data, the values were imputed within each country for the analyses in this paper. This seems superior to dropping all students with missing data on some explanatory variables altogether, because the latter would disregard the information available for these students on other explanatory variables, would severely reduce the sample size in several countries, and would probably introduce bias because it seems likely that observations are not missing at random. Appendix 1 of the working-paper version of this paper (Wößmann 2004) presents the details of the method used to impute missing data, which uses both median imputation and imputation based on probit models relating the observations from students with original data to a set of "fundamental" explanatory variables available for all students.

Tab. 1. Descriptive Statistics
Student performance: Mean of international math test scores. Standard deviation in parentheses. Standard deviation in percent of country mean test score in brackets. Family-background measures: Country means. Standard deviations in parentheses for continuous variable (std. dev. for dummies equal roughly 2*mean*(1–mean), neglecting the weighting). Only non-imputed data for each variable. Weighted by sampling probabilities. Sample size: Absolute numbers.

	AUS	BFL	BFR	DEN	ENG	FRA	GER	GRE	ICE
Student performance	524.1	561.7	517.5	485.3	491.3	514.4	496.6	461.2	473.1
Standard deviation	*(89.9)*	*(85.3)*	*(83.1)*	*(83.1)*	*(92.7)*	*(78.3)*	*(88.2)*	*(89.6)*	*(73.3)*
Std. dev./score (in percent)	*[17.2]*	*[15.2]*	*[16.1]*	*[17.1]*	*[18.9]*	*[15.2]*	*[17.8]*	*[19.4]*	*[15.5]*
Books at home									
Less than one shelf (<=10)	0.11	0.09	0.06	0.03	0.06	0.05	0.08	0.05	0.01
One shelf (11-25)	0.16	0.16	0.10	0.09	0.13	0.19	0.14	0.23	0.05
One bookcase (26-100)	0.32	0.34	0.29	0.29	0.27	0.36	0.28	0.41	0.30
Two bookcases (101-200)	0.18	0.19	0.21	0.23	0.23	0.20	0.19	0.19	0.28
More than two bookcases (>200)	0.24	0.22	0.35	0.36	0.32	0.20	0.32	0.12	0.36
Living with both parents	0.85	0.90	0.85	0.86	0.83	0.86	0.83	0.84	0.84
Born in country	0.94	0.97	0.91	0.94	0.95	–	0.90	0.94	0.93
Sex (female)	0.52	0.50	0.52	0.51	0.47	0.50	0.51	0.48	0.49
Age	13.81	13.64	13.79	13.43	13.57	13.81	14.27	13.12	13.14
	(0.71)	*(0.76)*	*(0.91)*	*(0.64)*	*(0.58)*	*(0.91)*	*(0.82)*	*(0.74)*	*(0.58)*
Upper grade	0.49	0.54	0.54	0.55	0.51	0.49	0.49	0.48	0.50
Above upper grade	–	–	–	–	–	–	–	–	–
Community location									
Geographically isolated	0.00	0.00	0.00	0.07	0.04	0.00	0.02	0.03	0.07
Close to town center	0.43	0.39	0.56	0.23	0.33	0.39	0.48	0.52	0.42
Sample size									
Students	5,786	5,662	4,883	4,370	3,579	6,014	5,763	7,921	3,730
Classes	249	296	261	282	243	253	272	312	274
Schools	129	141	120	153	127	134	137	156	155

Tab. 1. (continued)

	IRE	NET	NOR	POR	SCO	SPA	SWE	SWI	USA
Student performance	513.5	529.0	481.8	438.3	481.1	467.6	517.1	544.6	487.8
Standard deviation	(90.8)	(85.2)	(82.8)	(63.7)	(86.5)	(74.2)	(90.2)	(91.2)	(90.9)
Std. dev./score (in percent)	[17.7]	[16.1]	[17.2]	[14.5]	[18.0]	[15.9]	[17.5]	[16.8]	[18.6]
Books at home									
Less than one shelf (<=10)	0.07	0.07	0.02	0.12	0.11	0.05	0.03	0.07	0.08
One shelf (11-25)	0.16	0.15	0.06	0.27	0.17	0.18	0.08	0.15	0.12
One bookcase (26-100)	0.34	0.34	0.25	0.31	0.29	0.33	0.24	0.31	0.28
Two bookcases (101-200)	0.21	0.20	0.23	0.13	0.19	0.19	0.24	0.21	0.21
More than two bookcases (>200)	0.22	0.24	0.44	0.17	0.25	0.25	0.41	0.27	0.31
Living with both parents	0.90	0.91	0.85	0.88	0.81	0.89	0.86	0.84	0.79
Born in country	0.97	0.95	0.95	0.92	0.92	0.97	0.92	0.88	0.93
Sex (female)	0.52	0.50	0.50	0.50	0.49	0.50	0.49	0.50	0.50
Age	13.93	13.82	13.37	13.97	13.22	13.76	13.94	14.07	13.74
	(0.70)	(0.80)	(0.60)	(1.11)	(0.60)	(0.86)	(0.88)	(1.01)	(0.72)
Upper grade	0.50	0.52	0.50	0.48	0.50	0.50	0.33	0.36	0.50
Above upper grade	–	–	–	–	–	–	0.34	0.29	–
Community location									
Geographically isolated	0.06	0.00	0.12	0.01	0.05	0.01	0.04	0.04	0.03
Close to town center	0.35	0.22	0.12	0.62	0.44	0.23	0.46	0.23	0.44
Sample size									
Students	6,203	4,084	5,736	6,753	5,776	7,596	8,855	11,722	10,973
Classes	261	187	287	283	257	309	535	613	529
Schools	132	95	249	142	128	154	270	327	183

II. Cross-Country Comparative Descriptive Statistics

TIMSS measured student performance separately in math and science, using an international achievement scale with scores having an international mean of 500 and an international standard deviation of 100. As shown in Table 1, the mean math performance in TIMSS of the Western European countries ranges from 438.3 in Portugal to 561.7 in Flemish Belgium. As a comparison, Singapore was the international top performer at 622.3, South Africa was the lowest performer at 351, and the United States scored an average of 487.8 test-score points in math. Portugal has the lowest variation in math performance among its students, both when measured by the absolute standard deviation in test scores (63.7) and relative to its mean performance (14.5). On the relative measure, Flemish Belgium and France also feature relatively low performance variations. At the other extreme, England has the highest standard deviation in absolute terms (92.7), while in relative terms it is Greece (19.4). The United States also shows a relatively large performance variation among its students.

Table 1 presents country means of the data on family background used in this paper. The number of books in the students' home is a general proxy for the educational background of the family that seems readily comparable across countries. The measure varies widely among the countries, with Portugal featuring relatively low and Norway relatively high values. The distribution across the five categories of books at home in countries such as England, Germany, and the United States is actually very similar.

Across Europe, the Netherlands had the lowest share of students not living with both parents at 9%, while Scotland had the highest share at 19%. The share was even higher in the United States at 21%. The share of immigrant students ranges from 3% in Flemish Belgium, Ireland, and Spain to 12% in Switzerland. The average age of the tested students ranges from 13.1 years in Greece and Iceland to 14.3 years in Germany.[13] In all countries, students are roughly equally divided into boys and girls, as well as between the two tested grades. Sweden and Switzerland tested students in a third grade above the other two, with roughly one third of their samples coming from each grade. In terms of the community in which the schools are located, Norway features a relatively high share of geographically isolated locations (12%) and a relatively low share of schools located close to the center of a town (also 12%). By contrast, several countries do not feature tested school in isolated areas, and 62% of Portuguese students visit a school close to a town center.

III. The Empirical Model

To quantify the extent of equality of educational opportunities for children from different backgrounds, the size of the associations between students' family background and their educational performance is estimated for each country in the following form:

(1) $\quad T_{ics} = F_{ics}\alpha_1 + D^F_{ics}\delta_1 + (D^F_{ics}F_{ics})\delta_2 + \varepsilon_{ics}$,

where T is the test score of student i in class c in school s and F is a vector of family-background variables. The coefficient vectors α_1, δ_1, and δ_2 are to be estimated. The inclusion of the imputation controls D^F and the structure of the error term ε are discussed below.

Usually being determined before children are in school, most family-background characteristics can be viewed as exogenous to student performance. Furthermore, there is no self-selection into the sample because 7th- and 8th-grade schooling is compulsory in Western Europe and the United States. The estimation intentionally does not control for school characteristics, such as schools' resource endowments or institutional features, as in standard education production functions, because the paper is interested in the total impact of family background on student performance, including any indirect effect that might work through families' differential access to schools or their influence on school policies.

It should be noted that the estimated family-background effects combine the joint impact of nature and nurture, the relative importance of which cannot be distinguished in this dataset. Thus, the estimates of equality of educational opportunities may to some extent reflect the effect of heritable ability.[14] However, the extent to which heritability can account for the cross-country variation in the findings should be limited.

It helps to clarify what the estimates of the coefficients α_1 on the family-background variables, and especially differences in the estimates across countries, mean and do not mean. Because the TIMSS data were generated by the same data-collection process in the different countries and are therefore directly comparable across countries, and given the technical constraints on the pedagogical process, the prior should be that the size of the *effect* of any family-background characteristic on students' educational performance should be the same everywhere. If this is not the case, this implies that there must be differences in how the school systems work. This does *not* reflect different *distributions* of family-background characteristics in the different populations, as evident in Table 1, which a priori do not necessarily constitute a reason that the performance gap between students with two different characteristics should differ.

As discussed in the previous section, some of the data are imputed rather than original. Generally, data imputation introduces measurement error in the explanatory variables, which should make it more difficult to observe statistically significant effects.[15] Still, to make sure that the results are not driven by imputed data, a vector of dummy variables D^F is included as controls in the estimation. The vector D^F contains one dummy for each variable in the family-background vector F that takes the value of 1 for observations with missing and thus imputed data and 0 for observations with original data. The inclusion of D^F as controls in the estimation allows the observations with missing data on each variable to have their own intercepts. The inclusion of the interaction term between imputation dummies and background data, $D^F F$, allows them to also have their own slopes for the respective variable. These imputation controls for every variable with missing values ensure that the results are robust against possible bias arising from data imputation.[16]

Further problems in the econometric estimation of equation (1) are that the explanatory variables in this study are measured at different levels, with some of them not varying within classes or schools; that the performance of students within the same school may not be independent from one another; and that the primary sampling unit (PSU) of the two-stage clustered sampling design in TIMSS was the school, not the individual student (see Section B.I). As shown by Moulton (1986), a hierarchical structure of the data requires the addition of higher-level error components to avoid spurious results. Therefore, the error term ε of equation (1) has a school-level and a class-level element in addition to the individual-student element:

(2) $\quad \varepsilon_{ics} = \eta_s + \nu_c + \upsilon_i,$

where η is a school-specific error component, ν is a class-specific error component, and υ is a student-specific error component. Clustering-robust linear regression (CRLR) is used to estimate standard errors that recognize this clustering of the survey design. The CRLR method relaxes the independence assumption and requires only that the observations be independent across the PSUs, i.e. across schools. By allowing any given amount of correlation within the PSUs, CRLR estimates appropriate standard errors when many observations share the same value on some but not all independent variables (cf. Deaton 1997).

Finally, TIMSS used a stratified sampling design within each country, producing varying sampling probabilities for different students (Martin/Kelly 1997). To obtain nationally representative coefficient estimates from the stratified survey data, weighted least squares (WLS) estimation using the sampling probabilities as weights is employed. The WLS estimation ensures that the proportional contribution to the parameter estimates of each stratum in the sample is the same as would have been obtained in a complete census enumeration (DuMouchel/Duncan 1983; Wooldridge 2001).

C. Results for Individual Countries

This section presents results on the effect of several family-background features on students' educational performance in the United States and 17 Western European education systems. The size of the family-background effects can be viewed as a measure of the equality of educational opportunities for children from different backgrounds. The results, reported in Table 2, start with several measures of the educational background of the family, followed by student characteristics and the community location.[17]

I. Families' Educational and Socio-Economic Background

The dataset includes two alternative general measures of the educational, social, and economic background of the students' families: the number of books in the students' home and the educational level of their parents. For several reasons, our preferred general measure is the number of books at home, a measure proposed and frequently used in sociological research (e.g., Esping-Andersen 2004). Students were asked to report in five given categories the total number of books that are in their home, not counting newspapers, magazines, or their school books. First, the number of books at home has repeatedly proved to be the single most important predictor of student performance in international tests. Second, the measure seems much more readily comparable across countries than parents' educational level, whose cross-country comparability may be limited because educational levels may not be easily comparable in the different countries. Third, Schütz et al. (2005) show that on a different international test that includes information on both books at home and family income, the correlation between the two does not differ in any significant way across countries, so that books at home can actually be viewed as a strong and internationally consistent proxy for general family background. And fourth, in TIMSS the books variable has the additional advantage over parental education of having substantially fewer missing observations in all countries.

Given these reasons for preferring the books measures, and given that books and parental education should not be entered jointly in the specification because they are alternative proxies for the same concept of general family background, our main specification includes only the books variable.[18] The specification does not make the assumption of a linear relationship, but rather uses all the information available in the background questionnaires and allows a more flexible functional form by including a dummy for each response category.

The number of books in the students' home is strongly and statistically significantly related to student performance in all European countries, as well as the United States. In the regressions reported in Table 2, England features the largest effect among all countries, with students from homes with more than two bookcases full of books performing 104.4 math test-score points better than students from homes with less than one shelf of books. Scotland (93.6) and Germany (84.9) also feature very large family-background effects on this account, followed by Austria, Ireland, Sweden, and the United States (76.1). At the other extreme, France features the lowest effect (20.9), and Flemish Belgium has the lowest effects when looked at relative to one shelf of books as the lowest category. A third country with relatively small effects is Portugal. This general pattern of results is

Tab. 2. Family Background and Student Performance

Least-squares regression within each country, weighted by students' sampling probabilities. Dependent variable: TIMSS math test score. Standard errors robust to clustering at the school level and heteroscedasticity in parentheses.

	AUS	BFL	BFR	DEN	ENG	FRA	GER	GRE	ICE
Books at home (residual category: less than one shelf (<=10))									
One shelf (11-25)	21.05*	19.71*	11.99°	16.16+	24.41*	-3.12	20.11*	14.17*	17.76
	(4.13)	(6.52)	(6.90)	(8.13)	(5.96)	(5.12)	(4.18)	(3.64)	(12.02)
One bookcase (26-100)	41.73*	33.91*	36.76*	36.39*	60.29*	12.86*	45.45*	40.97*	33.41*
	(4.70)	(7.78)	(5.01)	(7.65)	(6.45)	(4.78)	(5.05)	(4.61)	(10.63)
Two bookcases (101-200)	69.37*	45.36*	47.90*	51.13*	81.22*	24.17*	70.80*	57.70*	50.18*
	(5.88)	(8.40)	(5.31)	(8.02)	(6.62)	(5.11)	(6.25)	(5.99)	(10.48)
More than two bookcases (>200)	80.98*	40.32*	58.72*	61.88*	104.43*	20.85*	84.93*	63.10*	61.60*
	(5.39)	(7.70)	(5.49)	(7.58)	(7.77)	(5.50)	(6.04)	(6.21)	(11.50)
Living with both parents	-1.55	0.49	-5.80	3.69	4.51	8.40*	10.33*	14.44*	6.42°
	(3.16)	(4.25)	(4.67)	(3.78)	(4.27)	(2.53)	(3.05)	(2.57)	(3.86)
Born in country	25.73*	4.53	15.45+	20.64*	10.59	–	13.74*	5.55	7.19
	(6.68)	(8.38)	(6.18)	(6.28)	(7.42)		(4.96)	(4.46)	(5.66)
Female	-10.69*	-1.86	-13.84*	-12.61*	-9.13°	-12.06*	-8.70*	-9.89*	-2.32
	(2.93)	(7.71)	(3.54)	(2.71)	(4.87)	(2.04)	(3.34)	(2.03)	(2.97)
Age	-23.56*	-39.74*	-35.33*	-20.08*	7.03	-28.31*	-19.76*	-15.53*	-0.75
	(2.64)	(3.18)	(1.97)	(3.33)	(4.99)	(2.38)	(2.57)	(3.44)	(4.47)
Upper grade	54.36*	53.28*	60.98*	57.68*	23.00*	72.82*	45.03*	58.15*	27.13*
	(3.83)	(5.59)	(3.84)	(4.60)	(5.30)	(4.54)	(3.88)	(4.74)	(7.76)
Above upper grade	–	–	–	–	–	–	–	–	–
Community location (residual category: rural and outskirts)									
Geographically isolated	53.53*	–	–	-28.02+	-11.25	–	28.16	-10.23	-13.20+
	(9.58)			(10.93)	(11.42)		(32.43)	(6.83)	(6.14)
Close to town center	16.56+	-6.67	13.98°	-11.13°	-12.30	5.89	6.28	18.35*	3.48
	(7.33)	(10.06)	(7.43)	(6.33)	(8.51)	(5.45)	(10.46)	(4.98)	(5.27)
Imputation controls	yes	yes	yes	yes	yes	yes	yes	yes	yes
Students [unit of observation]	5,786	5,662	4,883	4,370	3,579	6,014	5,763	7,921	3,730
Schools [unit of clustering]	129	141	120	153	127	134	137	156	155
R^2	0.176	0.104	0.207	0.124	0.157	0.202	0.195	0.160	0.084
R^2 (without imputation controls)	0.167	0.100	0.196	0.115	0.148	0.193	0.174	0.145	0.076

Significance levels (based on standard errors robust to clustering at the school level): * 1%. – + 5%. – ° 10%

Tab. 2. (continued)

	IRE	NET	NOR	POR	SCO	SPA	SWE	SWI	USA
Books at home (residual category: < one shelf)									
One shelf (11-25)	16.40*	16.80+	11.88	9.74*	28.05*	16.09*	5.71	20.19*	11.69*
	(4.83)	(7.57)	(9.42)	(2.24)	(3.80)	(4.45)	(5.83)	(4.61)	(3.79)
One bookcase (26-100)	52.92*	40.90*	26.06*	21.60*	51.80*	34.58*	40.58*	42.77*	39.65*
	(5.17)	(6.85)	(8.40)	(2.54)	(3.92)	(4.31)	(5.19)	(4.78)	(3.68)
Two bookcases (101-200)	73.58*	56.86*	41.84*	35.44*	78.46*	48.02*	62.31*	62.78*	62.74*
	(5.59)	(6.93)	(9.00)	(3.03)	(5.05)	(4.84)	(5.22)	(5.40)	(4.65)
More than two bookcases (>200)	78.53*	68.40*	61.84*	39.19*	93.64*	58.45*	77.33*	74.13*	76.08*
	(5.83)	(7.78)	(8.64)	(3.61)	(5.10)	(4.64)	(5.26)	(5.59)	(5.33)
Living with both parents	14.90*	1.19	19.50*	1.31	9.00*	1.38	6.95+	9.84*	17.97*
	(3.68)	(4.94)	(5.55)	(2.27)	(2.86)	(2.59)	(3.10)	(2.58)	(2.98)
Born in country	-15.26*	9.84	21.81*	-6.73+	0.51	13.17*	28.04*	25.10*	0.31
	(5.87)	(6.65)	(4.90)	(3.04)	(4.50)	(5.06)	(4.12)	(4.15)	(4.76)
Female	-20.92*	-11.91*	-6.22*	-10.19*	-11.07*	-10.19*	-3.04	-14.15*	-9.80*
	(5.23)	(3.16)	(2.28)	(1.51)	(2.45)	(2.12)	(2.04)	(2.04)	(2.33)
Age	-29.18*	-32.66*	2.49	-14.54*	8.24°	-22.69*	-2.12	-18.51*	-23.37*
	(2.52)	(3.02)	(3.80)	(0.94)	(4.33)	(1.43)	(3.17)	(3.55)	(2.70)
Upper grade	58.09*	63.29*	40.28*	45.75*	27.97*	60.91*	41.39*	63.42*	47.14*
	(5.49)	(6.83)	(4.54)	(2.25)	(6.14)	(2.45)	(4.59)	(5.66)	(4.58)
Above upper grade	–	–	–	–	–	–	77.46*	124.22*	–
							(7.66)	(9.47)	
Community location (residual category: rural and outskirts)									
Geographically isolated	7.07	–	4.58	-21.73*	12.25	-47.38*	-20.27	2.30	-29.23*
	(13.38)		(7.68)	(5.75)	(8.43)	(2.36)	(13.93)	(14.86)	(7.73)
Close to town center	7.07	15.76	8.81	1.18	-3.03	4.67	12.27*	-4.67	-4.35
	(7.00)	(11.47)	(6.02)	(3.24)	(5.29)	(4.78)	(4.10)	(9.43)	(7.14)
Imputation controls	yes	yes	yes	yes	yes	yes	yes	yes	yes
Students [unit of observation]	6,203	4,084	5,736	6,753	5,776	7,596	8,855	11,722	10,973
Schools [unit of clustering]	132	95	249	142	128	154	270	327	183
R^2	0.159	0.171	0.136	0.175	0.180	0.191	0.215	0.255	0.158
R^2 (without imputation controls)	0.148	0.163	0.129	0.173	0.171	0.190	0.209	0.253	0.151

Significance levels (based on standard errors robust to clustering at the school level): * 1%. – + 5%. – ° 10%.

basically unaffected by which specific difference one looks at; e.g. it also holds for two bookcases relative to less than one shelf, more than two bookcases relative to one shelf, more than two bookcases relative to one bookcase, or two bookcases relative to one shelf. The effect sizes are very large indeed in almost all countries: In most countries, they are more than twice as large as the average performance difference between 7th and 8th graders, and equal nearly a whole standard deviation in TIMSS test scores (cf. Table 1).

The results suggest that the United States, which is often viewed as the country where everybody should have equal opportunities, features among the countries where children's educational performance is most strongly dependent on their family background. On the alternative family-background measure, parental education, the United States is even the country with the strongest association between family background and student performance among all countries, although the cross-country comparability of this measure may be hampered by differences in education systems. Still, the alternative family-background measure of parental education also features statistically significant associations with student performance in all Western European countries.

The relatively low intergenerational *educational* mobility in Britain mirrors previous findings of relatively low intergenerational *earnings* mobility in this country (cf. Dearden et al. 1997; Solon 2002). However, the Swedish results contrast with studies finding relatively high intergenerational earnings mobility in Sweden (cf. Björklund/Jäntti 1997; Solon 2002), suggesting that the latter is not predominantly driven by particularly strong equality in educational opportunities. This finding is in line with Björklund et al. (2004), who similarly show that the high intergenerational earnings mobility in Sweden in comparison to the United States does not seem to be related to the education system or to differences in the intergenerational transmission of quantities of education, but is almost exclusively driven by the lower earnings returns to education in Sweden.

Two neighboring countries of which one belongs to the group of countries with small family-background impacts on our preferred measure and the other to the group with large family-background impacts are France and Germany. In a French-German comparison of the impact of family background on educational attainment, Lauer (2003) hypothesizes that family background should have a larger impact on children's educational prospects in Germany than in France, mainly based on the observation that streaming takes place much earlier in the German school system than in the French one (cf. also Schnepf 2002; Dustmann 2004). However, her evidence suggests that the two countries prove surprisingly similar with regard to the impact of family background on educational attainment, i.e. on a measure of educational *quantity*. By contrast, my results show that when using a measure of educational *quality* instead, her hypothesis actually holds true. That is, the larger family-background effect in Germany materializes in terms of better educational performance of the children rather than higher educational attainment. One way to reconcile the two findings would be that certification regimes differ, so that the attainment certificates represent different ranges of actual skills in the two countries.

The extent to which the differing finding with regard to performance is due to the different streaming practices in the two systems is an open question, though, because the two systems also differ in several other important dimensions (see however Hanushek/ Wößmann 2006 and Schütz et al. 2005 for consistent evidence on the differentiating effects of early streaming). Most notably, France features a much more widespread prevalence of pre-primary education than Germany. Starting at the age of 3, more than 90% of children are enrolled in the French education system, while in Germany, this is not the case until the age of 7 (data for 1996 from OECD 1998). Of the children aged 2-4, 80% are enrolled in France but only 45% in Germany. This may be another impact factor lying behind the large French-German difference in family-background effects, and it could also account for the low family-background effect in Flemish Belgium where the 90% enrollment range also starts at the age of 3 and where 79% of children aged 2-4 are enrolled.

In interpreting the results, one has to bear in mind that family-background measures such as the number of books at home or parental education will be correlated with other, unobserved aspects of family background, such as parents' motivation or their willingness and capability to help with homework. Therefore, the estimated coefficients have to be interpreted as the effect of the respective variable and anything else that goes with it. In that sense, both the number of books at home and parental education serve as general proxies for the educational, social and economic background in the students' homes.

II. Single Parents, Immigrants, Other Student Characteristics, and Community Location

The regressions also take account of other, more specific measures of family background. In no country do students living with both parents perform statistically significantly worse than students not living with both parents, and they perform statistically significantly better in the United States and 8 Western European school systems. Only in Norway (18.7) is the effect larger than in the United States (15.5), and the next-largest effects are in Ireland, Greece, and Germany.[19]

The other considered student characteristics are also significantly related to student performance in many of the countries. Native students perform statistically significantly better than immigrated students in 10 European countries, but not in the United States (at least in math). The estimated effect is largest in Sweden (30.3), followed by Austria (25.9), Switzerland, Norway, and Denmark. By contrast, immigrated students actually perform statistically significantly (at least at the 5% level) better than native students in Ireland (13.2) and Portugal (6.1).[20]

With regard to students' gender, Flemish Belgium, Iceland, and Sweden are the only countries where girls do not perform statistically significantly worse in math than boys. The boys' lead is largest by far in Ireland (19.7), followed by Switzerland (13.3), French Belgium (13.1), and Denmark (12.6).

Controlling for grade differences, older students perform statistically significantly worse in most countries, which presumably reflects a grade repetition effect. In all countries, 8th-graders perform statistically significantly higher than 7th-graders. The performance difference ranges from 23.0 in England to 67.4 in France. In countries with small performance differences between grades (e.g., England, Iceland, Scotland, and to a lesser extent Norway and Sweden), the age effect tends to be low (in absolute terms), while it tends to be high in countries with strongly negative age effects (e.g., France, the Netherlands, and the two Belgian systems). This may reflect differences in the policies of how to deal with low-performing students. In the latter countries, the lowest-performing students regularly seem to be relegated into lower grades, so that the grade difference is relatively large, and at the same time the age effect is strongly negative since the relegated students are older but relatively low performing. By contrast, in the former countries, low-performing students generally seem not to be relegated to lower grades, so that the performance difference between grades is relatively low as the low-performers remain in upper grade, and age does not make much of a difference within grades and might even have a slightly positive effect on performance.

Finally, there is no clear pattern in the relative performance of schools by community location. In some countries, schools in geographically isolated locations perform much worse, while in others, they perform much better. Here, it should also be noted that most of the statistically significant estimates are based on very few observations, because only 2 schools in Austria and Portugal, and only 1 in Spain, are reported to be geographically isolated (cf. Table 1). There is also no clear pattern of results for schools located in communities close to the center of a town.

The explanatory power of the student and family background characteristics, when measured as the proportion of the test-score variation accounted for by the model (the R^2), is largest in Switzerland at 26.4% (disregarding the part "explained" by imputation controls), followed by French Belgium, Sweden, and France. At the lower end, 9.2% of the performance variation can be attributed to family background in Iceland, followed by Denmark, Norway, and Flemish Belgium. In the United States, it is 17.5%.

D. Equality of Educational Opportunity in Europe vs. the United States: The Aggregate Picture

The previous discussion already allowed a comparison of results for European countries with the United States at an individual-country level. To estimate more formally how the equality of educational opportunity compares between the United States and Europe as an aggregate, Table 3 reports the same model specification used above in Table 2 for the pooled sample of all students from the European countries and the United States. For each explanatory variable, the pooled regression includes an interaction term with a Europe dummy to test whether the family-background effect differs between Europe and the United States. The regression also controls for a whole set of country dummies to account for country fixed effects.

Comparing Europe as an aggregate to the United States, there is remarkably little difference in the direction, size, and significance of the family-background effects. Particularly when considering books at home as the main general measure of family background, the association with student performance actually barely differs between the "average" European country and the United States. At a low level of significance, there is a slight difference in the size of the performance difference between the lowest two categories, but as a general pattern, family background has a strong and comparable impact on student performance both in Europe and the United States.

The effect of students living with both parents is statistically significantly smaller in Europe than in the United States, but it is still statistically significantly positive. Europe differs from the United States in that immigrant students perform statistically significantly worse than native students, which is not the case in the United States. There is also

Tab. 3. Family-Background Effects in Europe vs. the United States
Least-squares regression pooling all countries, weighted by students' sampling probabilities. Dependent variable: TIMSS math test score. Standard errors robust to clustering at the school level and heteroscedasticity in parentheses.

	All countries	Interaction with Europe dummy
Books at home (residual category: < one shelf)		
One shelf (11-25)	11.54 *	6.73 °
	(3.73)	(3.97)
One bookcase (26-100)	40.41 *	1.15
	(3.66)	(3.93)
Two bookcases (101-200)	63.35 *	-3.59
	(4.62)	(4.88)
More than two bookcases (>200)	76.53 *	-5.41
	(5.28)	(5.51)
Living with both parents	18.07 *	-11.25 *
	(2.88)	(3.02)
Born in country	0.67	12.61 +
	(4.83)	(5.06)
Female	-9.87 *	0.37
	(2.31)	(2.49)
Age	-23.48 *	2.83
	(2.72)	(2.80)
Upper grade	47.24 *	6.21
	(4.55)	(4.69)
Above upper grade	–	117.29 *
		(3.40)
Community location (residual category: rural and outskirts)		
Geographically isolated	-29.30 *	24.69 *
	(7.60)	(8.58)
Close to town center	-6.75	10.94
	(6.75)	(6.96)
Imputation controls	yes	
Country dummies	yes	
Students [unit of observation]	115,406	
Schools [unit of clustering]	2,932	
R^2	0.245	
R^2 (without imputation controls)	0.241	

Significance levels (based on standard errors robust to clustering at the school level): * 1%. – + 5%. – ° 10%.

a difference in that students from schools located in geographically isolated areas perform statistically significantly worse in the United States, but not in Europe. However, the effects of students' age, gender, grade, and town-center location of schools do not differ significantly between Europe and the United States. All in all, when taking Western Europe as a whole, there is remarkably little difference in family-background effects to the United States, not even in their size.

E. Heterogeneity of Family-Background Effects by Ability

Given that 75-90% of the test-score variation in the different countries remains unexplained, a large part of the performance variation across students has to be attributed to omitted variables (in addition to measurement errors and random variation). This is not unexpected, because the basic learning ability of students – e.g., their innate ability or their learning motivation – remains unobserved and thus enters the error term ε of equation (1) (or, more precisely, the student-specific error component υ in equation (2)). However, it begs the question whether the family-background effects vary across the ability distribution of students. E.g., it may be of different importance to low-ability students compared to high-ability students whether they come from a disadvantaged family background. Such heterogeneity in the family-background effects can be detected by quantile regressions (cf. Koenker/Bassett 1978).

Student ability itself remains unmeasured, virtually by definition. However, once family-background effects are controlled for, the conditional performance distribution should be strongly correlated with ability (or, more precisely, with that part of ability that is not correlated with family background). For simplicity, this conditional performance distribution is termed "ability" in what follows. Quantile regressions estimate the effect of family background on student performance for students at different points on this ability distribution. While Eide/Showalter (1998) and Levin (2001) have applied the quantile regression method to the estimation of resource effects in education, Fertig (2003) seems to be the only country study that uses quantile regressions to estimate family-background effects. However, the distinction between family background and underlying ability seems to offer a particularly appealing analytical background for the estimation and interpretation of quantile estimates. The family-background proxy used in this section is again our preferred measure of the number of books at home.

The horizontal lines of Figure 1 replicate the least-squares coefficients on the four books-at-home dummies from Table 2 for each country. The relatively large effects in England and the relatively small effects in France are immediately apparent. The curved lines with dots report quantile-regression coefficients of the same model for 19 quantiles ranging from 0.05 to 0.95.[21] As a general pattern, these quantile-regression estimates are relatively constant across quantiles in almost all countries. This remarkable uniformity suggests that the family-background effects do *not* vary strongly with the underlying ability of students.

To the extent that they do, they tend to *increase* with quantiles in the vast majority of countries. This pattern of family-background effects slightly increasing with ability is particularly notable in Austria, England, Ireland, Norway, Spain, Sweden, and the United States. To a lesser extent, it may also be observed in French Belgium, France, Germany, Greece, Iceland, Portugal, Scotland, and Switzerland. However, England is the only country where a strong pattern of effect heterogeneity exists. In all these countries – albeit to varying degrees – a good family background is most important for high-ability children. Thus, for instance, while the performance lead of students from homes with more than two bookcases over students from homes with less than one shelf of books is 69.4 for students at the 10th percentile of the conditional performance distribution in England, it is 146.5 for students at the 90th percentile. This effect difference of 77.1 between the 10th and the 90th percentile in England compares, e.g., to a difference of only 5.3 in Switzerland (59.1 at the 90th percentile versus 53.7 at the 10th percentile). In the countries where no increasing pattern can be observed, the family-background effect seems to slightly shrink with ability in the Netherlands, be roughly U-shaped in Flemish Belgium, and inverted-U-shaped in Denmark.

The median regression can also be viewed as a test of the least-squares result for robustness against outliers. The conditional median function estimated by median regression minimizes the sum of the absolute residuals and is thus less prone to outliers than the conditional mean function estimated by least-squares regressions. In this sense, median regressions may better describe the central tendency of the data. As is evident from Figure 1, in most countries the least-squares and the median estimates do roughly coincide. In these countries, the initial least-squares results do not seem to be substantially biased by outlying observations. A difference between the two estimates in some countries suggests that the least-squares estimates may be affected to an extent by outliers. In Flemish Belgium, the median estimates are somewhat smaller than the least-squares estimates, suggesting that outliers seem to affect the least-squares coefficients in an upward direction. By contrast, in Austria, Denmark, and Norway, the median estimates are slightly larger than the least-squares estimates, suggesting that outliers seem to affect the least-squares coefficients in a downward direction.

F. Is There a Tradeoff Between Equality and Aggregate Performance?

Viewing the size of the family-background effects as a measure of the equality of educational opportunities for children from different backgrounds, the French school system seems to achieve the highest extent of equal opportunity, and the British systems the lowest. From a policy viewpoint, this begs the question whether equalizing educational opportunities must be bought by having to accept a lower overall level of performance, i.e. whether a tradeoff exists between educational equity and efficiency (as measured by mean performance per student).

To give a cross-country view on this question, Figure 2 plots the mean of the math achievement in each country against a measure of the family-background effect in the country, namely the performance difference between students with more than two bookcases at home and students with less than one shelf of books at home. From this scatter plot, it is evident that there is no direct relationship between average performance and the measure of equality of opportunity across countries. The cross-country correlation coefficient between the two measures is 0.002.

When using other proxies for family-background effects, the correlation with mean performance is similarly low, and often negative. For example, the correlation coefficient is –0.03 for the performance difference between students with more than two bookcases relative to students with one shelf as the proxy for family-background effects, –0.15 for more than two bookcases relative to one bookcase, and 0.11 for two bookcases relative to less than one shelf as well as one shelf. Likewise, using parental education as the family-background proxy, the correlation coefficient with mean math performance is –0.11 when considering the performance difference between students whose parents finished university relative to students whose parents had no secondary education, and –0.10 when considering finished university relative to finished secondary.

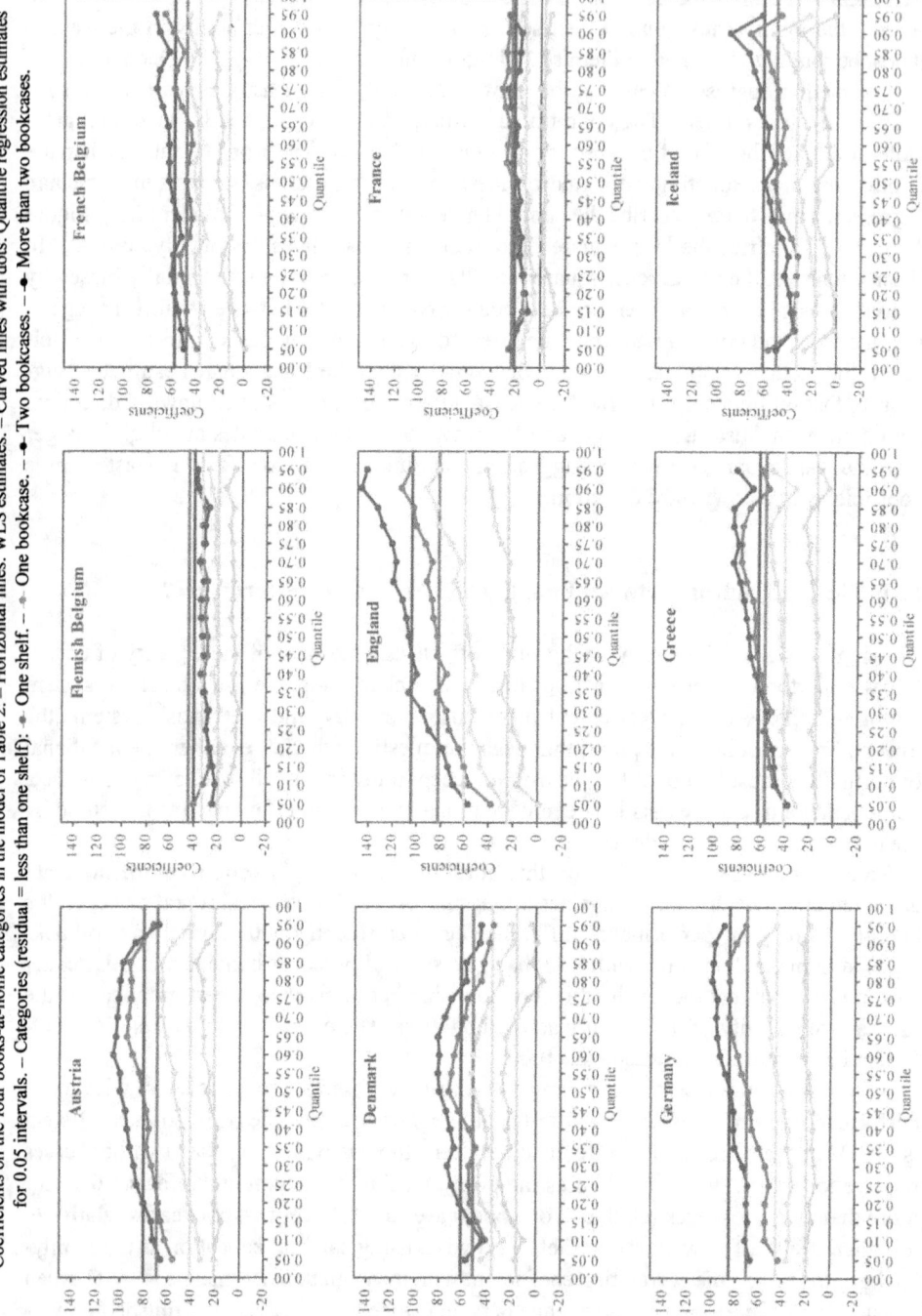

Fig. 1. Quantile Regression Estimates of Family-Background Effects

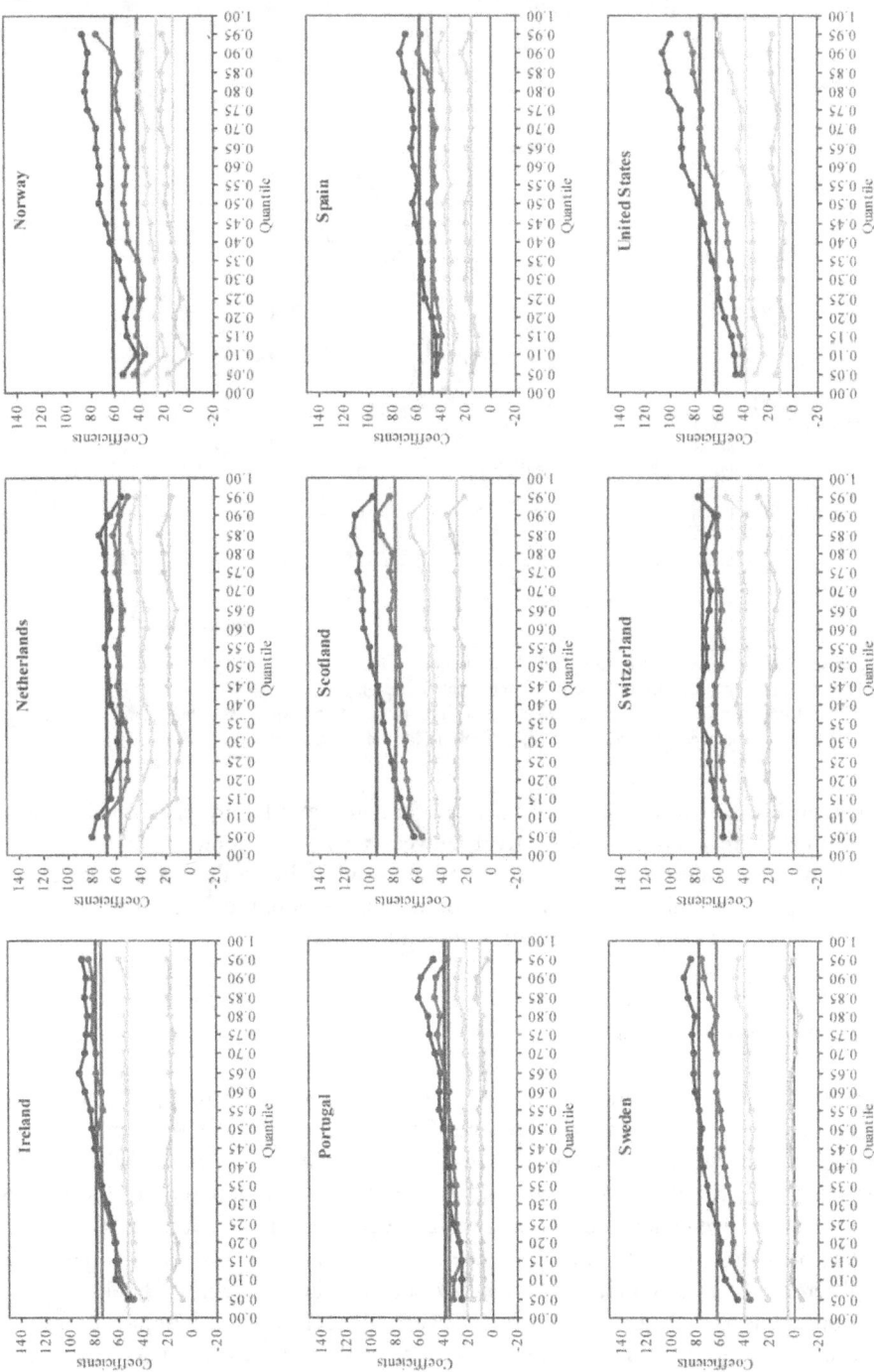

Fig. 1. (continued)

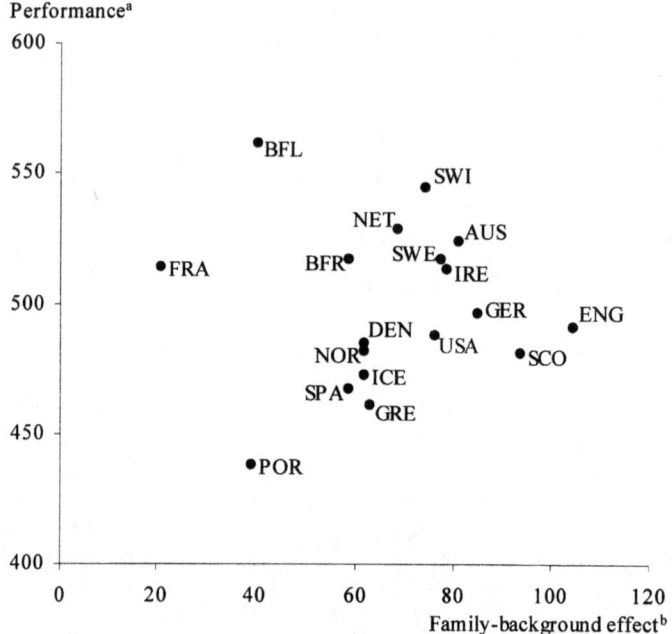

Fig. 2. Family-Background Effects and Mean Performance
Notes: [a] Mean performance on the TIMSS math test (cf. Table 1).
  [b] Performance difference between students with more than two bookcases at home and students with less than one shelf of books at home, controlling for the variables reported in Table 2.

Thus, the cross-country pattern of mean performance and family-background effects suggests that there is no obvious tradeoff between achieving efficiency in educational production and equality of educational opportunity. While being illustrative, this cross-country snapshot can give only a first descriptive impression, requiring much more in-depth analysis before any definite conclusion seems warranted.

G. Summary and Conclusions

This paper has presented consistent and comparable evidence on how equal educational opportunities are for children from different family backgrounds in Western European countries and the United States. The evidence is based on the estimated size of the impact that several measures of family background have on students' performance on the TIMSS international achievement test in lower secondary education. In all countries, the impact of family background on students' cognitive skills is strong. For example, the performance difference between children with the lowest and highest category of books at home easily surmounts a whole grade equivalent in nearly all countries. Furthermore, the model analyzed in this paper is able to account for at least 8.4% of the total test-score variation (in Iceland), and up to 25.5% (in Switzerland). Both the size of the individual effects and the explained proportion of the test-score variation dwarf the effects that have been found for school inputs such as class sizes, teacher characteristics, and resource endowments for the same countries and performance data (Wößmann 2005).

With regard to the general pattern of strong family-background effects, and even with regard to the particular size of most family-background effects, equality of educational opportunities in Western Europe (as an aggregate) seems remarkably similar to the United States. Still, there are also noteworthy variations across European countries. Using the number of books in the students' home as a proxy for the educational and socio-economic background of the family, France and Flemish Belgium achieve the most equitable performance for students from different backgrounds, and Britain and Germany the least. In most countries, family-background effects do not vary strongly for students of different underlying ability. If anything, the effects tend to be stronger for higher-ability children in some countries, most notably in England. Across countries, the size of the family-background effects is basically unrelated to mean performance, suggesting that there is no inevitable equity-efficiency tradeoff in educational production. More equal opportunities for students from different family backgrounds thus do not necessarily have to be bought with lower average performance.

The findings in this paper open the door for much more in-depth future research. For example, the paper has not looked into how family-background effects work through different channels – through peer formation, differential access to resources, or other impacts on school policies. Likewise, there might be important interactions between the family-background effects themselves, for example between parental education and immigration status. Other international datasets such as the TIMSS-Repeat and PISA studies may offer additional evidence, despite their drawbacks for the particular question analyzed in this paper (focusing on Western European countries in addition to the United States and looking at an age where the whole cohort is still in school). Furthermore, the international primary-school study PIRLS may yield evidence to better understand at which stage equality of opportunities are gained or lost in the different countries. Also, while this paper has focused mainly on basic cognitive skills in math as an educational output, there are many other outcomes of the educational process that should be considered in the future, such as social capabilities and motivation.

The results of this paper are generally in line with the broad pattern of the existing cross-country evidence on intergenerational earnings mobility, which found that the United States and the United Kingdom appear to be relatively immobile societies (Solon 2002). The evidence on intergenerational educational mobility presented here extends this pattern to a much wider range of countries. The understanding of how educational and earnings mobility relate and how the one transforms into the other might be greatly advanced if family-background and student-achievement data could be directly linked to data on labor-market outcomes in different generations.

The most auspicious and proximate road for future research, however, seems to be to look at what might lie behind the cross-country differences in the extent of equality of educational opportunities estimated in this paper. The results can feed future work trying to explain why some countries achieve more educational equality than others, by relating the estimated family-background effects to characteristic features of the school systems and societal institutions across countries. Such research might advance our understanding of how more equal educational opportunities might be achieved.

Endnotes

* *Acknowledgements:* I benefited from the hospitality of PEPG at Harvard University, the NBER in Cambridge, MA, and the European Commission (DG ECFIN) in Brussels. I would like to thank Sascha Becker, Anders Björklund, Francesca Fabbri, Torberg Falch, Thomas Fuchs, Charlotte Lauer, George Psacharopoulos, Emiliana Vegas, anonymous referees, and participants at conferences of the Royal Economic Society in Swansea, the European Association of Labour Economists in Lisbon, the International Institute of Public Finance in Milan, the CESifo area conference on Employment and Social Protection, the Universities of Konstanz, Linz, Mainz, and Munich (CES), Cornell University, RWI (Essen), DIPF (Frankfurt), the Tinbergen Institute (Amsterdam), and the European Commission for valuable comments and discussion, and Andreas Ammermüller for research assistance in the construction of the country-specific databases.

1 For an overview of additional evidence on positive effects of cognitive test scores on individual labor-market performance and macroeconomic growth, see Hanushek/Wößmann (2007).

2 While recent research stresses the relevance of both cognitive and non-cognitive skills for economic outcomes, the data analyzed in this paper are only on cognitive skills.

3 Cf. Wößmann (2005) and Wößmann/West (2006) for comparable European and US estimates of the "school production" part of education production functions, i.e. the effects of schools' resource endowments on students' educational performance.

4 Most existing studies on education production functions are restricted to individual countries. While most US studies include some control for family background, they tend to focus on resource effects with little direct focus on family-background effects (cf. Hanushek 2002, p. 2082). Of the few studies on educational production from European countries, exceptions discussing family-background effects include Ammermüller et al. (2005), Björklund et al. (2003), Brunello/Checchi (2005), Feinstein/Symons (1999), Fertig (2003), Häkkinen et al. (2003), Lindahl (2001), and Wolter/Vellacott (2003).

5 Results on science performance are available from the author upon request.

6 Comparable large-scale international student achievement tests are the repeat study of TIMSS in 1999, which included only five Western European countries, and the Programme for International Student Assessment (PISA), conducted in 2000 by the Organisation for Economic Co-operation and Development (OECD). The PISA target population of 15-year-old students might suffer from self-selection into the sample of students in some countries, while schooling is compulsory for the TIMSS target population of 13-year-olds in all countries considered in this paper. Also, the PISA test is not curriculum-based.

7 Thus, among the bigger Western European countries, only Finland and Italy are missing in TIMSS.

8 In most countries, this corresponded to 7th and 8th grade of formal education (excluding pre-primary education). Exceptions are Denmark, Norway, Sweden, and the German-speaking cantons of Switzerland, where tested students had 6/7 years of formal education, as well as England and Scotland with 8/9 years (Martin/Kelly 1997).

9 In Germany, one Bundesland (Baden-Württemberg) did not participate in TIMSS, and in Switzerland, four cantons did not participate. Denmark and Greece had unapproved sampling procedures at the classroom level (Beaton et al. 1996).

10 England was the only country not to meet this general rule with an overall exclusion rate of 11.3% because it excluded schools that were selected for specific national evaluation samples.

11 As a general guideline, TIMSS required participation rates of 85% or higher. This was not met by Austria, French Belgium, the Netherlands, and Scotland. Flemish Belgium, England, and Germany met the participation rates only after replacement schools were included, as did the United States (Beaton et al. 1996).

12 The background questionnaires are available at http://timss.bc.edu/timss1995i/database/ UG1_Sup2.pdf.

13 Germany actually chose to test its 7th and 8th grade level to provide a decent curricular match, although that meant not testing the two grades with the most 13-year-olds. This breach of the official TIMSS age/grade specification led to German students being substantially older than those in most other countries.

14 More able parents, who obtained more education, may have more able children, who then perform better on the performance tests. Behrman/Rosenzweig (2002) show for Minnesota twins that heritable ability is a likely source of the correlation between the quantitative educational attainment of mothers and their children. This is not found for fathers, though, and Behrman et al. (1999) find a causal impact of mothers' schooling on their children's schooling, working through home teaching, in rural India during the green revolution. Similarly, Sacerdote (2002) and Plug/Vijverberg (2003) find somewhat contrary evidence on the relative importance of the nature and nurture components in the effect of parental background on children's educa-

tional outcomes. Given that abilities are both inherited and acquired, Cunha et al. (2006) conclude that the traditional distinction between nature and nurture is scientifically obsolete.
15 Fuchs and Wößmann (2007) employ an adjustment mechanism for standard errors suggested by Schafer and Schenker (2000) that accounts for the degree of variability and uncertainty in the imputation process as well as for the share of missing data and find that all qualitative results are highly robust to the alternatively computed standard errors.
16 Testing for robustness of results to the imputations by dropping missing observations showed that none of the central results are sensitive to the data imputation. Detailed results are available upon request.
17 The presentation of this paper focuses on results for math performance; results for science performance are quite similar and available from the author upon request.
18 Results for the alternative measure of parental education are available from the author upon request.
19 Cf. Piketty (2003) for French evidence suggesting that it is not parental separation per se, but rather parental conflicts which have a negative impact on children's school performance.
20 Because the strong correlation between the immigration status of parents and children regularly causes problems of multicollinearity, only the latter was included in the regressions and the former left out, with the evident ensuing consequences for the interpretation of results.
21 Confidence intervals are not shown for expositional reasons. For the least-squares estimates, standard errors are reported in Table 2. The precision of the quantile-regression coefficients is roughly comparable in size.

References

Altonji, J.G./Pierret, C.R. (2001): Employer Learning and Statistical Discrimination, in: Quarterly Journal of Economics, Vol. 116, No. 1, pp. 313–350.
Ammermüller, A./Heijke, H./Wößmann, L. (2005): Schooling Quality in Eastern Europe: Educational Production During Transition, in: Economics of Education Review, Vol. 24, No. 5, pp. 579–599.
Ashenfelter, O./Harmon, C./Oosterbeek, H. (1999): A Review of Estimates of the Schooling/Earnings Relationship, with Tests for Publication Bias, in: Labour Economics, Vol. 6, No. 4, pp. 453–470.
Beaton, A.E./Mullis, I.V.S./Martin, M.O./Gonzalez, E.J./Kelly, D.L./Smith, T.A. (1996): Mathematics Achievement in the Middle School Years: IEA's Third International Mathematics and Science Study (TIMSS), Chestnut Hill, MA: Boston College.
Behrman, J.R./Foster, A.D./Rosenzweig, M.R./Vashishtha, P. (1999): Women's Schooling, Home Teaching, and Economic Growth, in: Journal of Political Economy, Vol. 107, No. 4, pp. 682–714.
Behrman, J.R./Rosenzweig, M.R. (2002): Does Increasing Women's Schooling Raise the Schooling of the Next Generation?, in: American Economic Review, Vol. 92, No. 1, pp. 323–334.
Bishop, J.H. (1989): Is the Test Score Decline Responsible for the Productivity Growth Decline?, in: American Economic Review, Vol. 79, No. 1, pp. 178–197.
Bishop, J.H. (1992): The Impact of Academic Competencies on Wages, Unemployment, and Job Performance, in: Carnegie-Rochester Conference Series on Public Policy, Vol. 37, pp. 127–194.
Björklund, A./Edin, P.-A./Freriksson, P./Krueger, A. (2004): Education, Equality and Efficiency: An Analysis of Swedish School Reforms during the 1990s. IFAU Report 2004:1, Uppsala: Institute for Labour Market Policy Evaluation.
Björklund, A./Jäntti, M. (1997): Intergenerational Income Mobility in Sweden Compared to the United States, in: American Economic Review, Vol. 87, No. 5, pp. 1009–1018.
Björklund, A./Lindahl, M./Sund, K. (2003): Family Background and School Performance During a Turbulent Era of School Reforms, in: Swedish Economic Policy Review, Vol. 10, No. 2, pp. 111–136.
Boissiere, M./Knight, J.B./Sabot, R.H. (1985): Earnings, Schooling, Ability, and Cognitive Skills, in: American Economic Review, Vol. 73, No. 5, pp. 1016–1030.
Brunello, G./Checchi, D. (2005): School Quality and Family Background in Italy, in: Economics of Education Review, Vol. 24, No. 5, pp. 563–577.
Card, D. (1999): The Causal Effect of Education on Earnings, in: Ashenfelter, O./Card, D. (eds.): Handbook of Labor Economics, Volume 3A, pp. 1801-1863, Amsterdam: North-Holland.
Cunha, F./Heckman, J.J./Lochner, L./Masterov, D.V. (2006): Interpreting the Evidence on Life Cycle Skill Formation, in: Hanushek, E.A./Welch, F. (eds.): Handbook of the Economics of Education, Volume 1, pp. 697–812, Amsterdam: North-Holland.

Deaton, A. (1997): The Analysis of Household Surveys: A Microeconometric Approach to Development Policy, Baltimore: The Johns Hopkins University Press.
Dearden, L./Machin, S./Reed, H. (1997): Intergenerational Mobility in Britain, in: Economic Journal, Vol. 107, No. 1, pp. 47–66.
DuMouchel, W.H./Duncan, G.J. (1983): Using Sample Survey Weights in Multiple Regression Analyses of Stratified Samples, in: Journal of the American Statistical Association, Vol. 78, No. 383, pp. 535–543.
Dustmann, C. (2004): Parental Background, Secondary School Track Choice, and Wages, in: Oxford Economic Papers, Vol. 56, No. 2, pp. 209–230.
Eide, E./Showalter, M.H. (1998): The Effect of School Quality on Student Performance: A Quantile Regression Approach, in: Economics Letters, Vol. 58, No. 3, pp. 345–350.
Esping-Andersen, G. (2004): Untying the Gordian Knot of Social Inheritance, in: Research in Social Stratification and Mobility, Vol. 21, pp. 115–138.
Feinstein, L./Symons, J. (1999): Attainment in Secondary School, in: Oxford Economic Papers, Vol. 51, No. 2, pp. 300–321.
Fertig, M. (2003): Who's to Blame? The Determinants of German Students' Achievement in the PISA 2000 Study. IZA Discussion Paper 739, Bonn: Institute for the Study of Labor.
Fuchs, T./Wößmann, L. (2007): What Accounts for International Differences in Student Performance? A Reexamination using PISA Data, in: Empirical Economics, Vol. 32, No. 2-3, pp. 433–464.
Gonzalez, E.J./Smith, T.A. (eds.) (1997): User Guide for the TIMSS International Database: Primary and Middle School Years, Chestnut Hill, MA: Boston College.
Häkkinen, I./Kirjavainen, T./Uusitalo, R. (2003): School Resources and Student Achievement Revisited: New Evidence from Panel Data, in: Economics of Education Review, Vol. 22, No. 3, pp. 329–335.
Hanushek, E.A. (2002): Publicly Provided Education, in: Auerbach, A.J./Feldstein, M. (eds.): Handbook of Public Economics, Volume 4, pp. 2045–2141, Amsterdam: North-Holland.
Hanushek, E.A./Wößmann, L. (2006): Does Early Tracking Affect Educational Inequality and Performance? Differences-in-Differences Evidence across Countries, in: Economic Journal, Vol. 116, No. 510, pp. C63–C76.
Hanushek, E.A./Wößmann, L. (2007): The Role of School Improvement in Economic Development. NBER Working Paper 12832, Cambridge, MA: National Bureau of Economic Research.
Koenker, R./Bassett, G.Jr. (1978): Regression Quantiles, in: Econometrica, Vol. 46, No. 1, pp. 33–50.
Lauer, C. (2003): Family Background, Cohort and Education: A French-German Comparison Based on a Multivariate Ordered Probit Model of Educational Attainment, in: Labour Economics, Vol. 10, No. 2, pp. 231–251.
Levin, J. (2001): For Whom the Reductions Count: A Quantile Regression Analysis of Class Size and Peer Effects on Scholastic Achievement, in: Empirical Economics, Vol. 26, No. 1, pp. 221–246.
Lindahl, M. (2001): Summer Learning and the Effect of Schooling: Evidence from Sweden. IZA Discussion Paper 262, Bonn: Institute for the Study of Labor.
Martin, M.O./Kelly, D.L. (eds.) (1996): Third International Mathematics and Science Study Technical Report, Volume I: Design and Development, Chestnut Hill, MA: Boston College.
Martin, M.O./Kelly, D.L. (eds.) (1997): Third International Mathematics and Science Study Technical Report, Volume II: Implementation and Analysis – Primary and Middle School Years, Chestnut Hill, MA: Boston College.
Moulton, B.R. (1986): Random Group Effects and the Precision of Regression Estimates, in: Journal of Econometrics, Vol. 32, No. 3, pp. 385–397.
Murnane, R.J./Willett, J.B./Levy, F. (1995): The Growing Importance of Cognitive Skills in Wage Determination, in: Review of Economics and Statistics, Vol. 77, No. 2, pp. 251–266.
Organisation for Economic Co-operation and Development (OECD) (1998): Education at a Glance: OECD Indicators, Paris: OECD.
Piketty, T. (2003): The Impact of Divorce on School Performance: Evidence from France, 1968-2002. CEPR Discussion Paper 4146, London: Centre for Economic Policy Research.
Plug, E./Vijverberg, W. (2003): Schooling, Family Background, and Adoption: Is It Nature or Is It Nurture?, in: Journal of Political Economy, Vol. 111, No. 3, pp. 611–641.
Roemer, J.E. (1998): Equality of Opportunity, Cambridge, MA: Harvard University Press.
Sacerdote, B. (2002): The Nature and Nurture of Economic Outcomes, in: American Economic Review, Papers and Proceedings, Vol. 92, No. 2, pp. 344–348.
Schafer, J.L./Schenker, N. (2000): Inference With Imputed Conditional Means, in: Journal of the American Statistical Association, Vol. 95, No. 449, pp. 144–154.

Schnepf, S.V. (2002): A Sorting Hat That Fails? The Transition from Primary to Secondary School in Germany. Innocenti Working Papers 92, Florence: UNICEF Innocenti Research Centre.

Schütz, G./Ursprung, H.W./Wößmann, L. (2005): Education Policy and Equality of Opportunity. CESifo Working Paper 1518, Munich: CESifo.

Solon, G. (1999): Intergenerational Mobility in the Labor Market, in: Ashenfelter, O./Card, D. (eds.): Handbook of Labor Economics, Volume 3A, pp. 1761–1800, Amsterdam: North-Holland.

Solon, G. (2002): Cross-Country Differences in Intergenerational Earnings Mobility, in: Journal of Economic Perspectives, Vol. 16, No. 3, pp. 59–66.

Tyler, J.H./Murnane, R.J./Willett, J.B. (2000): Do the Cognitive Skills of School Dropouts Matter in the Labor Market?, in: Journal of Human Resources, Vol. 35, No. 4, pp. 748–754.

Wolter, S.C./Coradi Vellacott, M. (2003): Sibling Rivalry for Parental Resources: A Problem for Equity in Education? A Six-Country Comparison with PISA Data, in: Swiss Journal of Sociology, Vol. 29, No. 3, pp. 377–398.

Wooldridge, J.M. (2001): Asymptotic Properties of Weighted M-Estimators for Standard Stratified Samples, in: Econometric Theory, Vol. 17, No. 2, pp. 451–470.

Wößmann, L. (2004): How Equal Are Educational Opportunities? Family Background and Student Achievement in Europe and the United States. CESifo Working Paper 1162, Munich: CESifo.

Wößmann, L. (2005): Educational Production in Europe, in: Economic Policy, Vol. 20, No. 43, pp. 445–504.

Wößmann, L./West, M.R. (2006): Class-Size Effects in School Systems Around the World: Evidence from Between-Grade Variation in TIMSS, in: European Economic Review, Vol. 50, No. 3, pp. 695–736.

How Equal Are Educational Opportunities?
Family Background and Student Achievement in Europe and the United States

Summary

This paper estimates the associations between family-background characteristics and student performance in the United States and 17 Western European school systems using student-level data from the TIMSS international student achievement test. The associations are strong both in Europe and the United States, remarkably similar in size on aggregate. On the preferred measure, France and Flemish Belgium achieve the most equitable performance for students from different family backgrounds, and Britain and Germany the least. Equality of opportunity is unrelated to countries' mean performance. Quantile regressions show little variation in the associations across the ability distribution in most countries.

Wie gleich sind die Bildungschancen?
Familiärer Hintergrund und Schülerleistungen in Europa und den USA

Zusammenfassung

Dieser Beitrag liefert eine mikroökonometrische Schätzung des Zusammenhangs zwischen Eigenschaften des familiären Hintergrundes und Schülerleistungen in den USA und 17 westeuropäischen Schulsystemen anhand der Schülermikrodaten des internationalen TIMSS-Schülervergleichstests. Der Zusammenhang ist sowohl in Europa als auch in den USA sehr stark, und er unterscheidet sich bei aggregierter Betrachtung Europas kaum zwischen Europa und den USA. Bei dem bevorzugten Maß erreichen Frankreich und das flämische System in Belgien die ausgeglichensten Leistungen für Schüler mit unterschiedlichem familiärem Hintergrund, und Großbritannien und Deutschland die ungleichsten. Die Chancengleichheit weist keinen signifikanten Zusammenhang mit den Durchschnittsleistungen der Länder auf. Quantilregressionen zeigen in den meisten Ländern kaum Variation zwischen Kindern mit unterschiedlichem Leistungsniveau in dem Zusammenhang zwischen familiärem Hintergrund und Schülerleistungen.

Public Universities, Tuition and Competition – A Tiebout Model

Robert Schwager*

Abstract

- A simple model is presented where states decide on, and finance, universities which are attended by local but also by non-resident, mobile students.
- The efficient allocation is characterised. By means of an example, it is shown that efficiency may require to concentrate mobile students in a small number of "elite" universities.
- Un-coordinated decisions by the states are shown to satisfy the same first order conditions as the efficient allocation provided that the states have the right to charge a tuition fee reflecting the costs induced by an additional student.
- If tuition is banned or capped by the federal government, inefficient quality choices and insufficient admission numbers are likely to emerge.
- The analysis supports the assignment of responsibility for higher education to the *Länder* in the German federation. The right of the *Länder* to run universities should, however, be complemented by an unconstrained right to decide on tuition fees.

Keywords Higher education · migration · fiscal externality · club good · tuition

JEL: H75, I28, H77

Prof. Dr. Robert Schwager (✉)
is Professor of Economics at Georg-August-Universität Göttingen and a research professor at Centre for European Economic Research (ZEW), Mannheim. His field of research is public economics, with special emphasis on fiscal competition and federalism, tax policy, and publicly provided education. Georg-August-Universität Göttingen, Wirtschaftswissenschaftliche Fakultät, Platz der Göttinger Sieben 3, 37073 Göttingen, Germany, E-mail: rschwag@uni-goettingen.de

A. Introduction

In recent years, the assignment of responsibilities for higher education between the German states (*Länder*) and the federation (*Bund*) has undergone several changes. This development started when the constitutional court voided, in two rulings issued in 2004 and 2005,[1] two provisions amending the federal directive on universities (*Hochschulrahmengesetz*). The first of these provisions regulated the structure of personnel at state universities, and the second one stipulated that tuition fees are illegal. In both cases, the court ruled that the federation had no jurisdiction over the matter concerned, and hence strengthened the role of the states in higher education. In 2006, both chambers of parliament voted in favour of a set of changes to the vertical assignment of functions in the German federation.[2] Included in this package was a decision to abolish the 50% matching grant so far provided by the federation to state investment in university buildings.[3] In the same time, the states were granted more autonomy in running universities, a movement which meanwhile has culminated in a plan by the federal government to abolish the *Hochschulrahmengesetz* altogether.[4]

These developments have not been greeted with unequivocal welcome. Specifically, it is feared that un-coordinated competition in higher education leads to insufficient funding of universities. This opinion is based on a fiscal externality arising from the mobility of students across states. When a state government designs its universities, it will weigh the cost of education, paid out of the state budget, against the benefit procured by the university to the population of that state. This trade-off, however, does not include the benefits accruing to students who enter the state's universities but originate from other states. A state government which is responsible to the local electorate will disregard these benefits and hence, from a social point of view, will spend too little on universities. Similarly, the incentives to invest in higher education are reduced if part of the native high school graduates attend universities in other states. Büttner and Schwager (2004) provide empirical evidence showing that this fiscal externality is operating in the German federation. Using data on state expenditures for higher education, they find that a state spends less on universities if the neighboring states spend a lot. Thus, it seems that states whose high-school graduates can easily move or even commute to universities in other states drive down their own expenditures for higher education.

The objective of the present contribution is to put this empirical evidence, and the underlying fiscal externality argument, into a theoretical perspective. For this purpose, a standard fiscal competition model is presented. In this model, universities are run and paid for by sub-national governments out of tax revenues raised locally. There are both immobile and mobile students. Since state governments take only the interests of native students and taxpayers into account, neglecting the benefit of immigrant students, one might expect that the above mentioned under-provision of university education results. This is not the case, however, if the states have the right to raise tuition fees at a level which is at their discretion. It is shown that when this instrument is available, the willingness to pay for education by non-resident students is completely internalised in the state budget, and that by consequence, the Tiebout equilibrium is efficient.

A fiscal externality re-emerges, however, if the states do not have the right to choose the tuition level. If the federal government bans tuition, as was the case in the former

Hochschulrahmengesetz, or more generally, fixes tuition fees at any arbitrary level, the states' decisions on the quality of higher education are distorted. If tuition is capped at a low level, it is likely that the quality of universities deteriorates, and that an insufficient number of students is admitted. The upshot of this analysis is that un-coordinated subnational policies in higher education are not, by their nature, inefficient. Rather, any inefficiencies arise from an insufficient set of instruments in the hands of the states. In particular, the right to set tuition levels should complement the right to run universities.

The model presented here is rooted in the traditional theory of local public economics, pioneered by Tiebout (1956), and its non-spatial counterpart, the theory of clubs initiated by Buchanan (1965). Most previous applications of this approach in the field of education focus on primary or secondary education, rather than on universities like the present work. Correspondingly, in such models it is typically assumed that parents either move together with their children so as to enjoy a good public school financed out of local property taxes (for example, Miceli, 1993, and Nechyba, 1999), or that they pay tuition to a private profit maximising institution (for example, Epple and Romano, 1998). While this kind of work is motivated by US or British institutions, Büttner and Schwager (2004) and Kemnitz (2007) present models which are more closely tailored to the German system of financing higher education through state budgets. In Büttner and Schwager (2004), two states choose the qualities of their universities in the presence of student mobility, creating the fiscal externality described above. In this setup, the introduction of exogenous, small tuition fees is shown to locally improve the allocation. Since no decentralised tuition choice is modelled, however, it remains open in that paper to what extent tuition fees can restore efficiency.

Similar to the result presented here, Kemnitz (2007) shows that tuition fees improve educational quality when states are responsible for universities. Beyond several modelling details, the work by Kemnitz (2007) and the present paper mainly differ in the way the interest of native students is taken into account in the objective function of state governments. In Kemnitz's model, the earnings of these students are valued by state policy makers only insofar as they raise the state's tax revenues. Contrary to that, in the present model, native students' utilities enter the local objective function with the same weight as those of the taxpayers. Thus, the present paper pursues a more traditional welfare-economic approach, where the benefit of everyone in society counts, whereas the objective function in Kemnitz (2007) is rather motivated by public choice considerations, valuing only the interests of the majority of voters. It is remarkable, and strengthens the case for tuition fees in the context of decentralised education policies, that these two approaches reach a similar conclusion.

The present paper, and the work cited so far, deals with mobile incoming students. Another strand of literature considers students who attend university in their home region but move after graduation. Such mobility prevents states from recovering, through taxation of education-enhanced earnings, the public expenditures invested in their native students. In such a setting, as shown by Wildasin (2000), decentralised public provision of higher education is inefficient. Moreover, the structure of higher education is biased in favour of skills, such as legal studies, which are not internationally applicable (see Poutvaara, 2004, 2005). While this is clearly an interesting and relevant fiscal interaction, it is chiefly brought about by the fiscal competition for mobile (here, human) capital. In order to focus on the fiscal externality created by providing costly education to non-residents, this kind of fiscal competition is not considered in the present paper.

The rest of the paper is organised as follows. In section B, the model set-up is described. In section C, efficient allocations are characterised and illustrated by a numerical example. Decentralised policies are analysed in section D. There, the central result identifying Tiebout equilibria and efficient allocations is presented. Moreover, the impact of federally mandated tuition levels is examined and possible alternatives to tuition fees are discussed. The concluding section E discusses the implications of the results for higher education policy and the federal structure in Germany.

B. The model

The model describes a federation consisting of J jurisdictions, called states, which are labelled $j = 1,2,\ldots, J$. Each state provides tertiary education in a system of public universities. Individual universities are not modelled as separate actors. This is motivated by the fact that, in spite of a certain autonomy granted to public universities, these institutions are still largely under the control of state governments. In the following, the university system is consequently described, and referred to, as consisting of one university in each state. The university in state j provides education at a quality $q_j \geq 0$. This variable captures all aspects of the university which are relevant for educational success, measured by the job prospects of graduates. For example, major determinants of quality may be the qualification of the faculty as researchers and teachers, the availability of books and computing facilities, the office hour time a teacher accords to each student, etc.

In state j, there are $l_j > 0$ immobile, "local", students. They study in their home state and receive a wage $w_l(q_j)$ which depends on the quality of the education received. In addition, there are $M > 0$ mobile students in the federation who can choose where to study. A mobile student who obtains his education in state j will earn a wage of $w_m(q_j)$. Both functions w_l and w_m are increasing in quality, $w'_m > 0$, $w'_m > 0$, and concave, $w''_l \leq 0$, $w''_m \leq 0$.[5]

The fact that the wage function w_l and w_m may differ means that the two groups of students are not only differentiated by their readiness to leave home, but also by characteristics relating to the educational success, such as academic ability or motivation. For example, mobile students may be more able academically than immobile students, so that they benefit more from whatever education is given to them. This may correspond to a society where it is the brightest or most energetic students who migrate, possibly because being confined to their home state would limit their intellectual and professional opportunities. In the converse case, where mobile students obtain a lower wage than local ones, mobility is related to a relatively inferior ability to take advantage of education. This might describe a student population who move away from home for lifestyle rather than academic reasons, such as to get away from the surveillance of parents, or to enjoy the attractions of big cities.

The cost of providing higher education in state j depends on the quality q_j which is supplied, and the number of students enrolled at the state's university. Total enrolment consists of the l_j local students together with m_j mobile students who study in state j. The cost function in state j is given by $c^j(q_j, l_j + m_j)$. It is assumed to be convex, with first derivatives $c_q^j > 0$, $c_m^j > 0$ and second derivatives $c_{qq}^j > 0$, $c_{mm}^j > 0$, and $c_{qm}^j \geq 0$. This cost function describes how much money has to be spent in state j if an education of quality q_j is to be provided to $l_j + m_j$ students.

Naturally, costs increase in the quality of education. Moreover, costs also rise when more students are to be educated. Thus, the cost function displays crowding costs, as is common in Tiebout or club good models. In the context of a university, crowding costs arise when an increase in enrolment either directly induces a rise in public expenditures for the university, or indirectly makes additional costs necessary so as to maintain the quality. An example for the first case might be the costs for additional copies of teaching material which have to be provided to each student. An example for the second case is provided by the common experience of a classroom which becomes so crowded that it is difficult to follow the presentation of the instructor. The formulation used here implies that once quality is chosen, the government compensates any quality decline triggered in this way by an increase in the number of students. Thus, when classrooms are about to become overcrowded, the government will provide for new space and/or hire additional instructors so as to maintain the desired quality.

Mobile students obtain a utility u_o if they do not study at all. Since in a decentralised setting, states may choose not to admit any mobile students, this is a relevant case, as will be seen in subsection D.II. In contrast, a no-study-option is not explicitly considered for the immobile students. Rather, its is assumed that in each state $j = 1, 2, ..., J$, there is some (potentially small) quality level q_j such that the aggregate net value of providing higher education to the local students, $l_j w_1(q_j) - c_j(q_j, l_j)$, is larger than their aggregate utility if they do not study. This essentially says that everywhere, at least some young people are able enough so that providing higher education to them is the best choice for society.[6]

The model is closed by introducing a third group of individuals who are immobile, do not study, and have to pay, through their taxes, for the higher education provided in their home state. To use a convenient label, these agents are called the "parents". This group represents all agents in society who are not currently potential students. This includes both former students who now have reached working age[7] and individuals who never study. Essentially, the role of the parents in the model is to provide the resources necessary to finance universities. The endowment of the parents in any state, although not explicitly modelled, is thus assumed to be, in each of the various scenarios analysed in sections C and D, sufficiently large to pay for the costs of higher education provided in this state.[8]

C. Efficient policies

I. First-order conditions

Aggregate welfare is expressed, in monetary units, by the sum of the payoffs accruing to the three types of agents in all states. That is, welfare W is given by the difference between the wages earned by immobile students and the wages or reservation utilities enjoyed by mobile students, and the provision costs incurred in all states. A Pareto efficient allocation is then characterised by the solution of the following optimisation problem:[9]

(1) $$\max_{(q_j,m_j)_{j=1,...,J}} W(q_1,...,q_J,m_1,...,m_J) = \sum_j l_j w_l(q_j) + \sum_j m_j w_m(q_j)$$
$$+ \left(M - \sum_j m_j\right) u_o - \sum_j c^j(q_j, l_j + m_j)$$

(2) s.t. $M - \sum_j m_j \geq 0$

(3) $m_j \geq 0$ for all $j = 1, 2, ..., J$.

The constraints (2) and (3) require that in aggregate, at most the total number of mobile students can be enrolled somewhere, and that the number of mobile students in each state is non-negative.

Associating the Lagrange variables λ to the constraint (2), and α_j to the non non-negativity constraint (3) applying to state j, the necessary conditions[10] for an efficient allocation are, for $j = 1, ..., J$,

(4) $\frac{\partial L}{\partial q_j} = l_j w'_l(q_j) + m_j w'_m(q_j) - c^j_q(q_j, l_j + m_j) = 0,$

(5) $\frac{\partial L}{\partial m_j} = w_m(q_j) - u_o - c^j_m(q_j, l_j + m_j) - \lambda + \alpha_j = 0,$

together with the appropriate complementary slackness conditions. From equality (4) one derives the condition

(6) $l_j w'_l(q_j) + m_j w'_m(q_j) = c^j_q(q_j, l_j + m_j)$

for an efficient quality q_j. At an efficient allocation the aggregate marginal willingness to pay for quality by all students enrolled in state j, local and mobile ones, is equated to the marginal cost of quality. This condition, which is reminiscent of the Samuelson condition for the efficient provision of a public good, illustrates the club good nature of higher education. Students can be excluded from using the university, so that only the willingness to pay of those who are admitted to state j's university is taken into account. Once admitted, however, all students benefit from the same quality, and hence their willingness to pay has to be added.

For a state j which, in an efficient allocation, should admit a positive number m_j of mobile students, one has $\alpha_j = 0$. Thus, from (5), it follows

(7) $w_m(q_j) - u_o - c^j_m(q_j, l_j + m_j) = \lambda.$

Similarly, if the efficient allocation requires that some state does not admit any mobile students, from $\alpha_j \geq 0$, one has

(8) $\quad w_m(q_j) - u_o - c_m^j(q_j, l_j) \leq \lambda$,

with a strict inequality except for the borderline case where the non-negativity constraint (3) is just not binding. The left-hand sides in (7) and (8) give the net social benefit from educating an additional mobile student in state j. This benefit consists of the gain in wage procured to the student by studying in state j rather than foregoing higher education, net of the marginal crowding cost inflicted by this student on the taxpayer in state j. Thus, according to (7), in an efficient allocation mobile students are allocated across space such that the net marginal benefit of educating them is equalised across all universities which do admit mobiles students. There may, however, be some universities which would provide a net benefit which is below this amount; according to (8), these universities should not admit any mobile students.

The level of the common net benefit $\lambda = w_m (q_j) - u_o - c_m^j (q_j, l_j + m_j)$ of educating mobile students is determined by their scarcity, measured by the shadow price λ. If $\lambda > 0$, then $\sum_j m_j = M$. Thus, if it pays socially to educate mobile students at some university, then all students end up attending a university. Conversely, if some students do not attend university, $\sum_j m_j < M$, then for all students, the net benefit of higher education drops to zero.

The efficient inter-regional distribution of higher education institutions can display two qualitatively quite different patterns. On the one hand, mobile students might be distributed more or less evenly across states, with the quality of education in all states being similar, taking into account the interests of, and crowding costs induced by, the mobile students. Alternatively, the efficient university system in the federation may be very heterogeneous, with a few universities taking in all mobile students, whereas the remaining institutions cater to a purely local audience. In order to shed some light on the economic effects which cause one of these two scenarios to prevail, in the following subsection a simple example is presented which displays, for different parameter values, both kinds of solutions.

II. An example

In the example, there are two states, J = 2, which are symmetric. In both states j = 1,2 there is an equal number of local students $l_j = L/2$, and the cost function is the same and given by

(9) $\quad c^j(q_j, l_j + m_j) = c(q_j, \frac{L}{2} + m_j) = \frac{1}{2}q_j^2 + \frac{k^2}{2}(\frac{L}{2} + m_j)^2$.

In this cost function, the parameter $k \geq 0$ measures the importance of enrolment-related crowding costs. As seen from the cross derivative $c_{qm} = 0$, an increase in the number of students has no impact on the marginal cost of quality. While clearly special, this case has an interesting interpretation. As mentioned in section B, quality of education is, among other things, also related to the scientific reputation of the faculty teaching at the university. Now it seems plausible that the marginal cost of enhancing reputation, say by hiring a star professor, is more or less the same in large and in small universities. Thus, the separable cost function (9) fits rather well the case where quality of education is mainly driven by the scientific qualification of the faculty.

For immobile students, the marginal wage impact of a better education is normalised to unity, so that $w_1(q_j) = q_j$. Mobile students obtain a wage given by $w_m(q_j) = wq_j$, where $w > 0$ is a constant. Relating to the two types of mobile students discussed in section B, $w > 1$ ($w<1$) corresponds to a mobile student population which is more able (less able) than the immobile students.

In the following, two allocations are compared, an integrated allocation (I) where in each state, half of the mobile students are enrolled, and a segregated (S) one, where all mobile students gather in one jurisdiction, say state 1.[11] In the integrated allocation, the condition (6) for the optimal quality q^I in each state reads $(L/2) w_1'(q^I) + (M/2)w_m'(q^I) = c_q(q^I, (L+M)/2)$. With $w_1' = 1$, $w_m' = w$ and $c_q(q) = q$, this yields $q^I = (L+Mw)/2$. Inserting $q_1 = q_2 = q^I$, $l_1 = l_2 = L/2$, and $m_1 = m_2 = M/2$ in (1), one finds

$$(10) \quad \begin{aligned} W^I &= L \cdot w_1(q^I) + M \cdot w_m(q^I) - 2c(q^I, \frac{L+M}{2}) \\ &= \frac{1}{4}[(L+Mw)^2 - k^2(L+M)^2] \end{aligned}$$

for the welfare reached in an integrated allocation.

In the segregated allocation, the quality in state 1, where all M mobile students are enrolled, can be derived from the first order condition $(L/2)w_1'(q_1^s) + Mw_m'(q_1^s) = c_q(q_1^s, (L/2) + M)$, yielding $q_1^s = (L/2) + Mw$. The quality in state 2, where only local students are educated, follows from $(L/2)w_1'(q_2^s) = c_q(q_2^s, L/2)$, and hence is $q_2^s = L/2$. Using (1) again, the welfare

$$(11) \quad \begin{aligned} W^S &= \frac{L}{2} \cdot w_1(q_1^s) + M \cdot w_m(q_1^s) - c(q_1^s, \frac{L}{2} + M) + \frac{L}{2} \cdot w_1(q_2^s) - c(q_2^s, \frac{L}{2}) \\ &= \frac{1}{8}[(L+2Mw)^2 - k^2(L+2M)^2 + (1-k^2)L^2] \end{aligned}$$

in the segregated allocation can be derived.

Comparing both welfare levels from (10) and (11), one finds that

(12) $W^I \geq W^S$ if and only if $k \geq w$.

Thus, in the example, both kinds of university landscape discussed in the end of subsection I can emerge as the efficient allocation, depending on the parameters k and w. The integrated university system, where throughout the federation, universities cater to some mobile students and provide the same quality, is superior if (and only if) crowding costs in teaching are important, i.e., k is high, and the mobile students are not very able compared to the immobile students, i.e., w is low. Relating this result to the motivation for mobility discussed in section B, the integrated university system seems to be specifically appropriate if student mobility is induced by lifestyle rather than by academic considerations, and if increasing numbers of such students strongly disrupt the education process. Conversely, if crowding costs are moderate and the wage premium for mobile graduates is high, a segregated university system appears to be best. If mobile students are motivated by academic ambition, and can expect a high return to a good education, then it may well be worthwhile, from a federation-wide point of view, to establish a very small number of high-quality ("excellent") universities in just a few states. All mobile students (the "elite"), will attend these universities, whereas the rest receive an education at their local university which is tailored to their moderate abilities.

This result obtains from the trade-off between crowding costs on the one hand, and the benefit from concentrating students on the other hand. High crowding costs suggest that one should avoid packing too many students in one university, and hence call for an even distribution of students across states. The benefit from concentrating students arises from a scale effect and from a specialisation effect. The larger the number of students enrolled in one university, the larger is the aggregate benefit derived from a given quality. Moreover, segregating all mobile students in one university allows to tailor the quality of education more closely to the specific demand of the two different groups of students. In the example, the higher the wage for mobile students, the more important it is to take advantage from scale and specialisation benefits. Thus, the benefit from concentration rises in the wage premium for mobile graduates.

D. Decentralised decisions

I. Tiebout equilibrium

In this section, decentralised choices of higher education policies are examined and compared to the efficient allocation described in subsection C.I. Each state $j = 1, ..., J$ chooses the quality q_j of its universities, the number m_j of mobile students to be admitted, and a tuition fee t_j charged to each student.

All mobile students are alike, and they can move without costs. Therefore, in an equilibrium, all of them must obtain the same utility level. Denoting this utility level by u_m, the fact that pursuing higher education is voluntary implies $u_m \geq u_o$. Moreover, universities in state j will only attract mobile students if the wage obtained after graduating from j's university, net of tuition, is at least as large as the utility obtainable otherwise. Thus, in order to be able to enrol a positive number $m_j > 0$ of mobile students, state j's quality and tuition policies have to satisfy $w_m(q_j) - t_j \geq u_m$.

State governments pursue the interest of their native population. This encompasses the wages of immobile students, $l_j w_i(q_j)$, net of tuition expenses paid by them, $l_j t_j$. Moreover, the state government represents the interests of immobile parents who bear the net fiscal burden induced by the university. This burden consists of the difference between tuition revenues from immobile and mobile students $(l_j + m_j)t_j$ and the operating costs of the university, $c^j(q_j, l_j + m_j)$. In the present analysis, states are considered to behave competitively, in the sense that a single state does not feel itself to be large enough to affect, by its decisions, the equilibrium utility u_m of mobile students. This implies that the government of any state j, although it might be caring also for the mobile students originating from j, cannot affect, and hence does not have to take into account, the well-being of those students.

Aggregating the payoffs of the immobile students and the parents of state j, and observing that the tuition paid by immobile students cancels out, one obtains the maximization problem of state j

(13) $\max_{q_j, t_j, m_j} W_j(q_j, t_j, m_j) = l_j w_1(q_j) + m_j t_j - c^j(q_j, l_j + m_j)$

(14) s.t. $\left[w_m(q_j) - t_j - u_m\right] m_j \geq 0$,

(15) $m_j \geq 0$.

Here, condition (15) rules out negative numbers of mobile students, and constraint (14) ensures that mobile students are willing to apply to the university in j if a positive number $m_j > 0$ is to be admitted.

An equilibrium consists of a vector of qualities, tuition fees, and admission policies for all states, $(q_j, t_j, m_j)_{j=1}^J$, and a utility level $u_m \geq u_o$ for mobile students such that (q_j, t_j, m_j) solves state j's maximization problem (13) to (15), and such that in aggregate, states do not admit more than the total number of students, $M - \sum_{j=1}^J m_j \geq 0$. In addition, optimality of the mobile students' decision requires $\sum_{j=1}^J m_j = M$ if $u_m > u_o$ and $u_m = u_o$ if $\sum_{j=1}^J m_j < M$. Thus, if higher education is worthwhile for a student, every student is admitted at some university. Conversely, if there are students who choose not to pursue university education, the utility of mobile graduates is driven down to the utility level of non-graduates.

In order to solve the maximisation problem (13) to (15), the Lagrange multipliers μ_j and α_j are associated to the constraints (14) and (15) respectively. Then, the necessary conditions for an optimum are

(16) $\dfrac{\partial L}{\partial q_j} = l_j w_1'(q_j) - c_q^j(q_j, l_j + m_j) + \mu_j m_j w_m'(q_j) = 0$,

(17) $\dfrac{\partial L}{\partial t_j} = m_j - \mu_j m_j = 0$,

(18) $\dfrac{\partial L}{\partial m_j} = t_j - c_m^j(q_j, l_j + m_j) + \mu_j \left[w_m(q_j) - t_j - u_m\right] + \alpha_j = 0$,

together with the complementary slackness conditions corresponding to the constraints (14) and (15).

Considering first the case where the state wants to admit mobile students, $m_j > 0$, one observes from (17) that $\mu_j = 1$. Inserting in (16) leads to the efficiency condition (6). Thus, conditional on the number of mobile students, a state chooses the efficient quality. Moreover, from complementary slackness and $m_j > 0$, $\mu_j > 0$, it follows that

(19) $\quad w_m(q_j) - t_j = u_m.$

Thus, a state which admits mobile students to its universities will raise tuition so high that the package composed of quality and tuition is just attractive enough to get applications. Moreover, with $m_j > 0$, one must also have $\alpha_j = 0$. Using this together with (19) in (18), one obtains

(20) $\quad t_j = c_m^j(q_j, l_j + m_j).$

An additional student is thus charged the marginal crowding cost he inflicts on the provider. Combining (20) with (19), one finally arrives at

(21) $\quad w_m(q_j) - c_m^j(q_j, l_j) = u_m.$

Thus, in an equilibrium, the net social benefit of educating an additional student in state j is equal to the utility this student obtains elsewhere.

In the case $m_j = 0$, condition (16) again reduces to the efficiency condition (6), with only local students determining the quality in this case. Moreover, since anyway, no mobile student is admitted, the choice of the tuition level is not determined in an optimum. Consequently, also in this case, the tuition level can be set equal to marginal crowding costs, $t_j = c_m^j(q_j, l_j)$, without reducing the value of the objective function. Moreover, as seen from (17), also the value of the Lagrange variable μ_j is not determined if $m_j = 0$. Choosing a positive value $\mu_j > 0$, (18) then reduces to

(22) $\quad w_m(q_j) - c_m^j(q_j, l_j) - u_m = -\dfrac{\alpha_j}{\mu_j} \leq 0$

with a strict inequality except for the limiting case where the non-negativity constraint (15) is just not binding. Therefore, if $m_j = 0$ is optimal, the net social benefit of admitting a student to the university in state j must be less than the utility achievable for mobile students at other places or without university education.

To show that an efficient allocation can be supported as a Tiebout equilibrium, it remains to show that there is a utility level u_m obtained by mobile students in the equilibrium such that the conditions (21) and (22) determining decentrally optimal enrolment coincide with the corresponding conditions for the welfare maximising assignment of students to universities, (7) and (8). This is achieved with $u_m = \lambda + u_o$. That is, the equilibrium utility level u_m is chosen to be equal to the sum of the value of education in the efficient allocation, λ, plus the utility u_o obtained by a mobile student if she foregoes higher education. With this equilibrium utility level, the efficient choices are also optimal for the states. Finally, the solution to the welfare maximisation problem implies that all mobile students are enrolled at some university if $\lambda = u_m - u_o > 0$. Conversely, if it is efficient to leave some mobile students without higher education, then $\lambda = u_m - u_o = 0$.

To summarise, the analysis in this subsection has shown that there is no market failure intrinsic to a decentralised provision of higher education. This is true in spite of the fact that state governments do not care about the utility of immigrating students who take advantage of the quality of education provided by local taxpayers. The main institutional requirement for this result to obtain is that states are free to choose a tuition level which adequately reflects the cost of providing university education. In the following, it is examined how the equilibrium is affected if this requirement is not met.

II. Federal regulation

In order to account for this kind of institutional restriction, in the present subsection, the central government fixes tuition levels at some arbitrary values $\bar{t}_j$ for all states $j = 1, 2, ..., J$, which the states are not allowed to exceed nor undercut. The federally mandated tuition levels need not be uniform across states. For example, it is conceivable that federal policy makers, for equity reasons, wish to impose lower tuition fees in East Germany. Moreover, no specific level of the values $\bar{t}_j$ is assumed, although the politically relevant case clearly is given by a tuition cap which, for social policy reasons, is rather low.

With predetermined tuition level $\bar{t}_j$, state j only decides on quality and enrolment. Thus, its decision problem (13) to (15) changes to

(23) $\quad \max\limits_{q_j, m_j} W_j(q_j, \bar{t}_j, m_j) = l_j w_l(q_j) + m_j \bar{t}_j - c^j(q_j, l_j + m_j)$

(24) $\quad \text{s.t.} \ [w_m(q_j) - \bar{t}_j - u_m] m_j \geq 0,$

(25) $\quad m_j \geq 0.$

The necessary conditions for an optimum are

(26) $\quad \dfrac{\partial L}{\partial q_j} = l_j w'_l(q_j) - c^j_q(q_j, l_j + m_j) + \mu_j m_j w'_m(q_j) = 0,$

(27) $\quad \dfrac{\partial L}{\partial m_j} = \bar{t}_j - c^j_m(q_j, l_j + m_j) + \mu_j [w_m(q_j) - \bar{t}_j - u_m] + \alpha_j = 0,$

with the complementary slackness conditions on both restrictions.

Also with fixed tuition level, state j may optimally choose to admit mobile students ($m_j > 0$) or not ($m_j = 0$). In a solution with $m_j > 0$, one has $\alpha_j = 0$ and $\mu_j [w_m(q_j) - \bar{t}_j - u_m] = 0$. This implies with (27) that (20) holds for $t_j = \bar{t}_j$. That is, admission is chosen so that the predetermined tuition just covers marginal crowding costs. Regarding the quality of the university in state j, two scenarios can emerge. Firstly, like in the case with unconstrained tuition, it is possible that the migration constraint (24) is binding so that (19) holds with $t_j = \bar{t}_j$. In the case of a fixed tuition, this equation alone determines the quality q_j. That is, if the state cannot adjust the tuition level so as to extract the rent from mobile students, it will achieve the same result by reducing the quality of the education. Consequently, the efficiency condition (6) does not govern the quality choice anymore. Instead, equation (26) gives the value of the Lagrange multiplier

(28) $\quad \mu_j = \dfrac{c_q^j(q_j, l_j + m_j) - l_j w_1'(q_j)}{m_j w_m'(q_j)},$

where q_j is determined by (19) with $t_j = \bar{t}_j$, and m_j is then determined, using q_j, by (20). Since μ_j must not be negative, this solution arises if

(29) $\quad c_q^j(q_j, l_j + m_j) - l_j w_1'(q_j) \geq 0.$

If the values q_j, m_j determined from (19) and (20) fail to satisfy (29), then the second scenario applies, where a positive rent is left to the mobile students, $w_m(q_j) - \bar{t}_j > u_m$. This requires $\mu_j = 0$, and hence in this case, from (26), one derives

(30) $\quad l_j w_1'(q_j) = c_q^j(q_j, l_j + m_j)$

for the quality q_j. Just as in the efficiency condition (6), the state government takes into account the impact of mobile students on the marginal cost of providing quality. It disregards, however, the willingness to pay for quality by the mobile students.

Which one of these solutions arises depends on the level of the tuition $\bar{t}_j$. If tuition is very low, a low quality q_j will be sufficient to attract applications by mobile students. Such a low quality, however, will be too low from the point of view of the local students, i.e., (29) fails. Then, it is preferable for the state j to increase quality, even if this leaves some rent to the mobile students. Conversely, if the tuition is very high, a high quality will be needed to make mobile students ready to study in state j. Then, (29) will hold, and the state, in order to attract lucrative immigrant students, pays for a quality which exceeds the one which would be best for the local students.

In both cases, with fixed tuition, the quality choice is distorted. Except for the coincidental case where $\mu_j = 1$, the condition (6) is violated. It should be noted that this result is independent of the level of the federally imposed tuition $\bar{t}_j$. Even if $\bar{t}_j$ is rather high, the benefit of an increase in quality accruing to mobile students is not valued correctly by the state government, since it is not allowed to adjust tuition accordingly. Thus, in contrast to a common complaint issued by representatives of universities, the distortion of quality is not exclusively due to insufficient funding. Rather, it is the consequence of a mismatch in the assignment of decisions and revenues across layers of the public sector.

Turning now to the case where it is optimal for state j not to admit any mobile students, $m_j = 0$, then from (26), the locally optimal quality q_j will be chosen according to the efficiency condition (6) with $m_j = 0$. Such a solution can arise if, with this quality q_j, either $w_m(q_j) - \bar{t}_j - u_m \leq 0$, or $\bar{t}_j - c_m^j(q_j, l_j) \leq 0$, or both. If both of these inequalities hold, it follows $w_m(q_j) - c_m^j(q_j, l_j) - u_m \leq 0$. Thus, in this case, educating a mobile student in state j would provide a net social benefit which falls short of the utility which this student can expect elsewhere, and would therefore be socially wasteful. With an arbitrary tuition $\bar{t}_j$, it may also be that no mobile students are enrolled at the university in state j although it would be efficient to do so. This may occur if one has $w_m(q_j) - \bar{t}_j - u_m < 0$ and $\bar{t}_j - c_m^j(q_j, l_j)$

≥ 0 or $w_m(q_j) - \bar{t}_j - u_m \geq 0$ and $\bar{t}_j - c_m^j(q_j, l_j) < 0$. The first case corresponds to a tuition level which is set too high. The state is willing to admit some mobile students, but these do not apply because the education provided is not worth the tuition. In the second case, which corresponds to a tuition cap which is set fairly low, mobile students are happy to apply to the university in state j but admitting them does not pay off for the state.

Collecting the arguments from the previous discussion, and focussing on the realistic case of a low tuition level, it appears likely that in the nationwide equilibrium, some mobile students are not admitted to any university, while others are. At the same time, in order to satisfy the needs of the local students, states will provide a quality which is better than the one necessary to attract mobile students. Thus, some mobile students will have to part without education, and some will obtain an education which provides them with a rent, making them strictly better off than those who are rejected by all universities.

A federally mandated tuition level thus creates a fiscal externality which is not present when states are allowed to choose tuition levels freely. This externality works in two dimensions. With a fixed tuition, there is no flexible price signal relating the benefit of mobile students to quality improvements performed by state governments, and so quality is distorted. Moreover, if tuition is capped at a low level, states are reluctant to admit mobile students because they are not compensated for the crowding costs induced by increasing numbers of students. As a consequence, a university landscape emerges which, at a certain level of abstraction, is reminiscent of the German experience throughout the last three decades: The quality of education is chosen rather low, without taking into account the benefit of mobile students; there is a permanent shortage of university places; and student applications have to be rationed.

III. Alternative fiscal instruments

For the sake of analytical clarity, the formal model presented so far considers only a restricted set of fiscal instruments, i.e., tuition fees and a lump sum tax on immobile residents. In order to interpret the results in a policy-oriented discussion, the present subsection enlarges the focus by taking other fiscal instruments into account. Specifically, it will be discussed how taxes paid by graduates and inter-governmental transfers might interfere with the efficiency result obtained in subsection I.

For the discussion of income taxes paid by graduates, it is worthwhile to distinguish between taxation by the federation and by the states. A federal tax reduces the net income of graduates. If tuition is not deductible from the tax base, such a tax makes it less attractive to take up university education. In the same time, the revenue collected at most partially[12] accrues to the state government, and thus only part of it can be used to improve the university provided by the state. As a result, a federal income tax is likely to reduce the overall quality of higher education. While this vertical fiscal externality is a matter of concern, it is somewhat peripheral to the issue of inter-state migration which is at the heart of the present paper. The reason is that a uniform federal tax will reduce incentives to study in all states in a similar way.[13] Thus, the federal tax will reduce human capital accumulation, but will not strongly distort its inter-regional allocation.

Contrary to a federal tax, the revenues of a state income tax paid by graduates will fully accrue to the states and thus can be used to finance universities. Moreover, when the state has autonomy over the tax schedule, it can choose the tax rate so as to reflect the marginal crowding costs of educating an additional student. Mobile students will then choose the university which provides the highest income net of taxes, rather than net of tuition fees. This shows that, in the structure described by the model, a state income tax paid by graduates is equivalent to the tuition fee. Implementing this tax in practice, however, could be difficult for at least two reasons. Firstly, in order to provide the right incentives for students, the tax cannot be designed as a general income tax, where only the level, but not the source of income matters for the tax liability. Rather, the tax bill of a graduate would have to exceed the one of a non-graduate with the same income by the marginal cost of education. It is reasonable to expect that Germany's constitutional court would rule such a differentiation to be unconstitutional on the grounds that it violates horizontal equity. Secondly, and more fundamentally, students would simply evade the graduate tax by moving to a low-tax state after graduation.[14] To overcome this, states where graduates work would have to collect graduate taxes on behalf of the states which have provided the education. Since no state has an incentive to administer a tax whose revenues accrue to others, a federal clearing and enforcement mechanism would be needed – a rather cumbersome and dispute-prone institution. The upshot of this discussion is that, although equivalent in a narrow theoretical setting, a graduate tax which is levied ex post is much more difficult to implement than a tuition fee which is paid ex ante.

Instead of the individual student paying tuition, the government of her home state could pay an equivalent amount to the state where the student takes up higher education. Such a system has been suggested for Germany under the name of "*GefoS*",[15] and is used in Switzerland.[16] It creates the right incentives for state governments as long as they take into account the benefit accruing to emigrating students. Students, however, would not care about the transfer paid by their home state and thus would choose the best universities, regardless of the cost of education. In order to avoid this, students themselves would have to bear differences in tuition levels at the margin. A way to achieve this is offered by vouchers. According to this idea, each high school graduate obtains a voucher representing a certain amount of tuition fees, and is free to choose whether and where to study. Once a student takes up higher education in another state than her home state, the home state transfers the amount guaranteed by the voucher to the university where the student is enrolled. If this is a high quality institution charging more than the voucher, the student would have to top up the voucher. Conversely, a student who is satisfied to attend a low quality university, or none at all, should be allowed to cash in the difference between the voucher and the tuition charged. In essence, a voucher-based intergovernmental transfer system is thus a lump sum subsidy paid to mobile students by the taxpayers of the home state.

E. Conclusion

In this paper, a standard Tiebout model has been applied to higher education. It was shown that an efficient allocation can be decentralised to states competing for mobile students, provided that the states have the right to choose tuition fees according to crowding costs. When such fees are ruled out by federal legislation, states are likely to run down the quality of universities and to provide too few places for students.

From this result, one concludes that the abolition of the ban on tuition fees forced by the constitutional court in its 2005 ruling is a step in the right direction. Specifically, tuition fees are an essential part of a decentralised system of providing higher education, as we have it in Germany. In order to get an idea about the likely level of the tuition fee required, a look at actual expenditures per student is worthwhile. A first benchmark for such a figure is obtained by simply dividing total expenditures for higher education by the number of students enrolled. For example, relating the amount spent in 2005 by German higher education institutions in the fields of law, business/economics, and the social sciences, to the number of students enrolled in these fields during the winter term 2005/06, one arrives at expenditures per student of € 2547.[17] A much more sophisticated approach has been followed by Lüdeke and Beckmann (1998) who, in addition to current outlays, assess imputed rents for university buildings and implicit pension liabilities for professors. These authors estimate the annual cost of educating a student in the social sciences to be € 5581 in prices of 1994; for some other fields like theology and medical studies, they find substantially higher costs.[18] Their approach does not distinguish, however, between average and marginal crowding costs. This is attempted in Kraus (2004). Using data on current expenditures for the years 1996-1999 from all business/economics departments in Germany, Kraus estimates the marginal cost of an additional student in these fields, evaluated at the enrolment size which minimises cost per student, at € 1799 p.a. Although the wide variation of these numbers obviously leaves a lot of room for interpretation, it seems plausible that the maximal tuition fee of € 1000 currently levied falls short of the true marginal cost of educating an additional student. Thus, an increase seems warranted. Moreover, one would expect, and welcome from a welfare-theoretic point of view, a stronger differentiation of fees across universities and across fields of study, so as to reflect differences in quality and production costs.

As a more fundamental conclusion, the analysis presented here suggests that there is nothing inherently wrong with decentralised policy in higher education. Following Tiebout's insight, an excludable good, which higher education certainly is, can be provided by competing jurisdictions in an efficient way if users can be charged accordingly. For a long time the German system, until recently characterised by federal regulation of state universities and a ban on tuition fees, did not nearly conform to this ideal. Rather, the current state of German universities may serve as an example for the consequences of the general structural deficit of German federalism: States are quite autonomous in their spending decisions, but do not have the right to decide on their own revenues – be it tuition, in the case of universities, or taxes, for all kinds of public goods provided by states. Since revenue-raising and spending authority is out of line, states do not face the correct incentives, and hardly take efficient decisions. Germany will have a long way to go so as to bridge this gap, but, with recent reforms in higher education, at least has started on this journey.

Endnotes

* *Acknowledgements:* Part of this research was done while the author was visiting the Institute for Federalism and Intergovernmental Relations (IFIR) at the University of Kentucky. I am grateful for the hospitality I experienced there. I thank the participants of the Symposium 'Economics and Management of Education' at the University of Konstanz, two anonymous referees, and the editors of the special issue, Dominque Demougin and Oliver Fabel, for helpful comments and suggestions. Financial support by IFIR and the DFG (in the priority programme 1142 'Institutional Design of Federal Systems') is gratefully acknowledged.

1. BVerfG, 2 BvF 2/02 vom 27.7.2004 and 2 BvF 1/03 vom 26.1.2005.
2. This motion has become known as *Föderalismusreform I*. The laws enacting the reform are Gesetz zur Änderung des Grundgesetzes vom 28. August 2006, BGBl 2006, Teil I, Nr. 41, S. 2034, and Föderalismusreform-Begleitgesetz vom 5. September 2006, BGBl 2006, Teil I, Nr. 42, S. 2098.
3. *Gemeinschaftsaufgabe Hochschulbau*, Art. 91a Abs. 1 Nr.1 GG a.F.; see BMF (2006), p. 87.
4. See BMBF (2007).
5. This formulation ignores any consumption utility derived from studying at specific locations. While clearly, such considerations are relevant for many students (see Fabel et al., 2002), at least some mobile students seem to care about the academic quality of the university they attend (see Büttner et al., 2003). One could integrate such location specific attractions without altering the basic logic of the argument, for example by adding a state-specific leisure term to the wage function $w_m(q_j)$.
6. By this assumption, one avoids having to deal with the case where it is efficient for some state to close down its universities altogether – an outcome which is neither realistic nor interesting.
7. With this interpretation, the present set-up can be considered to be a shortcut for an overlapping generation model where young agents study and old agents pay taxes.
8. The presence of immobile agents with "deep pockets" distinguishes the public university featuring in the present model from a private institution. A private university, even if it is not for profit, would have to break even, whereas any losses incurred by the public university can be covered by taxing immobile resources.
9. Here and in the following, summations are taken over all states $j = 1, 2, ..., J$.
10. It is well known that in club good, or Tiebout, economies where the number of users of a public good is endogenous, standard convexity assumptions on preferences and technologies alone do not guarantee that first-order conditions are sufficient for a maximum (see, for example, Starrett, 1988, p. 77-83 and Schweizer, 1996). Since the present contribution is focussed upon the interpretation of Tiebout economies in the field of higher education, it is not attempted here to deal with this issue mathematically. Thus, only first order conditions are considered.
11. For simplicity, in the example, the utility u_o obtained by a mobile non-graduate is assumed to be so low that in an efficient allocation, all mobile students attend a university.
12. In Germany, states obtain 42.5% of income tax revenues (Art. 106 Abs. 3 S. 2, Abs. 5 GG).
13. Some second order effects may arise from a progressive tax schedule since students are disproportionately discouraged from attending high quality universities.
14. This effect is at the heart of Wildasin's (2000) inefficiency result. The analysis presented here suggests that autonomy to set tuition fees at the university level will restore efficiency even in Wildasin's context of mobile graduates. The proof of this claim is left for future work, or to the reader.
15. *"Geld folgt Studierenden"* (Money follows students), see CHE and Stifterverband (1998, 1999).
16. See *Interkantonale Universitätsvereinbarung (IUV) vom 20. Februar 1997*.
17. Sources: Statistisches Bundesamt (2007a, Table 1.4; 2007b, Table ZUS-06), own calculations.
18. Lüdeke and Beckmann (1998, Table 1, p. 10).

References

Buchanan, J., 1965. An economic theory of clubs. Economica 32, 1–14.
Bundesministerium der Finanzen, 2006. Monatsbericht des BMF, August 2006. Downloadable from http://www.bundesfinanzministerium.de/lang de/DE/Aktuelles/Monatsbericht des BMF/2006/08/060816agmb003.html
Bundesministerium für Bildung und Forschung, 2007. Schavan: Mehr Autonomie für die Hochschulen in Deutschland: Kabinett beschließt Aufhebung des Hochschulrahmengesetzes. Pressemitteilung 098/2007, 9. Mai 2007. Downloadable from http://www.bmbf.de/press/2044.php
Büttner, T., M. Kraus, and J. Rincke, 2003. Hochschulranglisten als Qualitätsindikatoren im Wettbewerb der Hochschulen. Vierteljahreshefte zur Wirtschaftsforschung 72, 252–270.
Büttner, T. and R. Schwager, 2004. Regionale Verteilungseffekte der Hochschulfinanzierung und ihre Konsequenzen. In: W. Franz, H.J. Ramser, and M. Stadler (eds.), Bildung. Tübingen: Mohr-Siebeck, 251–278.
CHE and Stifterverband (ed.), 1998. Modell für einen Beitrag der Studierenden zur Finanzierung der Hochschulen (Studienbeitragsmodell). Gütersloh and Essen.
CHE and Stifterverband (ed.), 1999. InvestiF und GefoS – Modelle der individuellen und institutionellen Bildungsfinanzierung im Hochschulbereich. Gütersloh and Essen.
Epple, D. and R. Romano, 1998. Competition between private and public schools, vouchers, and peer group effects. American Economic Review 88, 33–62.
Fabel, O., E. Lehmann, and S. Warning, 2002. Der relative Vorteil deutscher wirtschaftswissenschaftlicher Fachbereiche im Wettbewerb um studentischen Zuspruch: Qualität des Studiengangs oder des Studienortes? Zfbf – Schmalenbachs Zeitschrift für betriebswirtschaftliche Forschung 54, 509–526.
Kemnitz, A., 2007. Educational federalism and the quality effects of tuition fees. Dresden Discussion Paper in Economics No. 08/07, Dresden.
Kraus, M., 2004. Schätzung von Kostenfunktionen für die bundesdeutsche Hochschulausbildung: Ein konzeptioneller Ansatz im empirischen Test. ZEW Discussion Paper 04-36, Mannheim.
Lüdeke, R. and K. Beckmann, 1998. Social costs of higher education: Production and financing – The case of Germany (1994). Mimeo, Universität Passau.
Miceli, T., 1993. The decision to regionalize in the provision of education: An application of the Tiebout model. Journal of Urban Economics 33, 344–360.
Nechyba, T., 1999. School finance induced migration and stratification patterns: The impact of private school vouchers. Journal of Public Economic Theory 1, 5–50.
Poutvaara, P., 2004. Educating Europe: Should public education be financed with graduate taxes or income-contingent loans? CESifo Economic Studies 50, 663–684.
Poutvaara, P., 2005. Public education in an integrated Europe: Studying to migrate and teaching to stay? ZEI Working Paper B 03, 2005, Universität Bonn.
Schweizer, U., 1996. Endogenous fertility and the Henry George Theorem. Journal of Public Economics 61, 209–228.
Starrett, D., 1988. Foundations of public economics. Cambridge: Cambridge University Press.
Statistisches Bundesamt, 2007a. Bildung und Kultur: Finanzen der Hochschulen. Fachserie 11, Reihe 4.5, 2005. Wiesbaden.
Statistisches Bundesamt, 2007b. Bildung und Kultur: Studierende an Hochschulen. Fachserie 11, Reihe 4.1, Wintersemester 2005/2006. Wiesbaden.
Tiebout, C., 1956. A pure theory of local expenditures. Journal of Political Economy 64, 416–424.
Wildasin, D., 2000. Labor market integration, investment in risky human capital, and fiscal competition. American Economic Review 90, 73–95.

Public Universities, Tuition and Competition – A Tiebout model

Summary

A simple Tiebout model is presented where states provide university education to both immobile and mobile students. State governments choose the quality of public universities by trading off the value of education for the local immobile student population and the costs, net of tuition revenues, of running the university. The quality of education and the assignment of students to universities in an efficient allocation are characterised. It is shown that decentralised decisions result in efficient choices if states are allowed to choose tuition levels freely. If tuition is capped, inefficiently low qualities are likely to arise.

Staatliche Hochschulen, Studienbeiträge und Wettbewerb – Ein Tiebout-Modell

Zusammenfassung

Es wird ein einfaches Tiebout-Modell vorgestellt, in dem Länder Universitäten bereit stellen, die sowohl von einheimischen als auch von auswärtigen Studenten besucht werden. Bei der Bestimmung der Qualität der Ausbildung berücksichtigen die Länder den Nutzen der Ausbildung für die einheimischen Studenten und die Kosten der Hochschule abzüglich der eingenommenen Studiengebühren. Die effiziente Allokation wird charakterisiert. Es wird gezeigt, dass dezentrale Entscheidungen zur effizienten Wahl der Hochschulqualität führen, wenn das Niveau der Studiengebühren von den Ländern frei gewählt werden kann. Wenn die Studiengebühren durch Bundesgesetz begrenzt werden, kommt es typischerweise zu ineffizient niedriger Qualität.

WWW.GABLER.DE

Consulting – quo vadis? Critical perspectives on the consulting sector

Jean-Paul Thommen | Ansgar Richter (Eds.)
Management Consulting Today
Strategies for a Challenging Environment
2004. 180 pp., 38 Fig., 1 Tab. Softc. EUR 36,90
ISBN 978-3-409-12584-0

Leading management consultants and academics discuss the development of the consulting industry and of the firms that have decisively shaped the sector. The authors provide in-depth insights into the leadership of top management consultancies, the strategy and structure of consulting firms, the changing dynamics of client-consultant relationships, and the development of new consulting approaches..

The Editors
Prof. Dr. Jean-Paul Thommen is Professor of Business Administration, in particular Organisational Behaviour and Human Resource Management, at the European Business School in Oestrich-Winkel, Germany. He is also Adjunct Professor at the University of Zurich and a Visiting Lecturer at the University of St Gallen.
Ansgar Richter, PhD, is Assistant Professor of Organisation and Human Resources Management at the European Business School in Oestrich-Winkel, Germany.

Order your copy now: kerstin.kuchta@gwv-fachverlage.de
Telefon +49(0)611. 7878-626

KOMPETENZ IN SACHEN WIRTSCHAFT

Young Researchers in the Field of Management: Assessing the Relation between the Work Environment for Creativity and Job Satisfaction, Self-Confidence, and Publication Productivity

Marina Fiedler, Isabell M. Welpe, Arnold Picot*

Abstract

- This study assesses different dimensions of the work environment (i.e. organizational encouragement, supervisory encouragement, organizational impediments and workload pressure) with its relation to job satisfaction, self-confidence, and publication productivity of junior faculty in the field of management. We use pre-tested scales from creativity research that have acceptable factor structures, internal consistencies, and test-retest reliabilities to test our hypotheses with logistic (satisfaction and confidence) and linear regression analyses (publication productivity). The results indicate that organizational encouragement has a strong positive influence and workload pressure a strong negative influence on job satisfaction, self-confidence, and publication productivity. We believe that the paper can provide two important contributions: First, it offers a first account of the working conditions of junior faculty in the field of management in German-speaking Europe. Second, it introduces creativity-enhancing work environment as unit of analysis to the field of research on job satisfaction, self-confidence, and academic productivity. By simultaneously measuring both positive and negative dimensions of the work environment in respect of creativity, our research aims at separately assessing these working conditions' influence on job satisfaction, self-confidence, and professional productivity – three variables that are considered highly relevant for a successful research career.

Keywords Junior faculty · creativity · research · publication productivity · job satisfaction · self-confidence · working conditions · work environment

JEL: A29, M20, M53, O31

Dr. Marina Fiedler (✉)
Assistant Professor, Munich School of Management (Ludwig-Maximilians-University). Institut für Information, Organisation und Management, LMU München, Ludwigstr. 28, 80539 München, Germany;
E-mail: fiedler@lmu.de

Dr. Isabell M. Welpe (✉)
Assistant Professor, Munich School of Management (Ludwig-Maximilians-University). Institut für Information, Organisation und Management, Ludwig-Maximilians-Universität München, Ludwigstr. 28, 80539 München, Germany; E-mail: welpe@lmu.de

Prof. Dr. Dres. h.c. Arnold Picot (✉)
Full Professor, Munich School of Management (Ludwig-Maximilians-University). Institut für Information, Organisation und Management, Ludwig-Maximilians-Universität München, Ludwigstr. 28, 80539 München, Germany; E-mail: picot@lmu.de

A. Introduction

Previous research has demonstrated that the institutional environment functions as a mechanism for stabilizing expectations, thus influencing behavior (Downey et al., 1975; North, 1990). We want to add to this body of literature by examining the institutional environment of junior faculty (i.e. habilitation candidates – "Habilitanden", postdoctoral researchers, and junior professors), specifically the work environment in respect of creativity, as all research is rooted in creative and innovative ideas. We examine the work environment's influence on the job satisfaction, self-confidence, and publication productivity[1] of junior faculty in the field of management in Germany, Austria, and Switzerland. We concentrate on these three dependent variables since they are of central importance for developing a successful research program and career as a junior researcher.

Job satisfaction is one of the best-researched concepts in work psychology (e.g., Locke, 1976; Staw, 1984; Locke and Latham, 1990; Price, 1997; Saari and Judge, 2004; Judge, Bono, Erez, and Locke, 2005). *"Research on job satisfaction per se probably peaked in the 1960s and then declined when the presumed link between satisfaction and productivity was called into question"* (Staw, 1984, p. 631). However, actual studies show that job satisfaction is associated with absenteeism, fluctuation, and organizational inefficiency (Dormann and Zapf, 2001), as well as the working life's quality, the work's impact on the employee's mental health, and the relationship between work and family life (Staw, 1984). Job satisfaction is important in the young researcher context, as the time span for being appointed to a tenured position is rather short and the opportunity costs of pursuing this career are rather high. Hence, if junior faculty researchers are dissatisfied with their chosen career path, we can assume that they won't be motivated to become successful researchers and professors, but will instead leave academia.

Self-confidence is associated with creating and seizing opportunities, with motivating others, and with performance improvement efforts (Barnard, 1938; Keegan, 1987; Bass, 1990; Fedor et al., 2001). For example, Aycan (2004) identifies self-confidence as a key success factor for female managers. With meta-analytic data, Hiller and Hambrick (2005) demonstrate that self-esteem – a concept closely related to self-confidence – correlates 0.85 with generalized self-efficacy and 0.64 with emotional stability. At the very least, self-confidence may just make a person happier (Tirole, 2002), which is important to succeed in a field characterized by strong competition for appointments, as well as low acceptance rates in respect of prestigious journal publications.

Finally, the importance of publication productivity for evaluating a researcher's performance is comparatively undisputed. As part of the ongoing and rapidly progressing "Americanization" and internationalization of academic institutions in German-speaking Europe (Kieser, 2004), there is constantly increasing pressure on management faculty to publish in top-tier international journals (Müller-Camen and Salzgeber, 2005). However, in comparison with their Anglo-American colleagues, junior faculty in German-speaking Europe not only lack first and even second-hand experience with prestigious international publications (Backes-Gellner and Schlinghoff, 2004), but also face a number of institutional and organizational hurdles, such as a higher teaching and administration load. All of these factors influence their opportunities to build knowledge or gain experience in the area of international publications. Hence, this study aims at assessing the relation between the work environment for creativity and job satisfaction, self-confidence, and publication productivity.

B. Conceptual Model and Hypotheses

Antecedents of job satisfaction, self-confidence, and publication productivity can be clustered into three areas: institutional, personality, and interaction factors. In their meta-analysis, Dormann and Zapf (2001) conclude that the maximum effect of personality variables as determinants of job satisfaction is expected to be 30 per cent. Similarly, creativity research showed that novel and useful ideas do not only depend on personality traits such as intrinsic motivation and openness (Barron and Harrington, 1981; Eysenck, 1983; Eysenck 1993; Baer, 1998; Ai, 1999), but are also influenced by the work environment (Tushman, 1977; Kohn and Schooler, 1978; Basadur et al., 1982; Amabile et. al, 1996; Amabile, 1997; Ekvall and Ryhammer, 1998). Prior research has demonstrated that the institutional and situational setting influences behavior substantively.

Thus, we propose to examine the current work environment of junior researchers who aim to be professors in the management field. We focus our analysis on the work environment's influence on job satisfaction, self-confidence, and publication productivity. Studies show that institutional factors such as facet tasks, incentive systems, qualification possibilities, and work ecology have a significant influence on job satisfaction (Baumgartner and Udris, 2005; Cohrs and Abele, 2005; Fischer and Fischer, 2005). However, a junior faculty's weekly working day is dominated by teaching and research (Fiedler, Welpe and Picot, 2006) – tasks that are often perceived as rather challenging, highly ambiguous, and uncertain regarding the output. Consequently, there is a demand for a great deal of creativity and self-organization. Furthermore, traditional incentive systems and institutionalized qualification possibilities, such as those that are common in a firm environment, do not apply in the field of junior faculty.

We therefore focus our analysis of the impact of institutional antecedents on job satisfaction, self-confidence, and publication productivity on the work environment for creativity. This is in accordance with Staw (1984), who asks that an examination be undertaken of how individual and organizational factors interact to make an organization creative. By analyzing the literature as well as studying high- and low creativity projects Amabile et al. (1996) have developed scales to analyze the organizational and contextual foundations of creativity. Four of these scales seem to be especially appropriate for the academic field, since they take account of the specific conditions (e.g., a high degree of work autonomy and task ambiguity) in research and education. These scales are organizational encouragement, supervisory encouragement, organizational impediments, and workload pressure. The first two are considered beneficial, while the last two are considered to be obstructive in respect of creativity (Amabile et al. 1996; Amabile, 1997; Amabile, 1998; Amabile and Conti, 1999; Amabile et al. 2002; Amabile et al., 2005). We will next look at these four factors' relation to job satisfaction, self-confidence, and publication productivity.

The Relation between Organizational und Supervisory Encouragement and Job Satisfaction, Self-Confidence, and Publication Productivity

"*Job satisfaction is the extent to which a person reports satisfaction with both, intrinsic and extrinsic features of the job*" (Warr et al., 1979, p. 133). In a recent longitudinal study, Amabile et al. (2005) find that creative thought events have a positive influence on positive affect. An encouraging research organization is characterized by the valuing of risk-taking when approaching research questions; a collaborative idea flow; a fair, supportive evaluation; as well as the reward and recognition of new ideas (Amabile et al., 1996). Such a research organization should thus have a positive influence on the job satisfaction of junior researchers. It is furthermore characterized by a challenging yet reaffirming climate that contributes positively to junior researchers' self-confidence or to their belief in themselves and in their abilities. Moreover, we believe that an environment with the above attributes will stimulate junior researchers to aim at prestigious publications, which ought to enhance their publication productivity.

Whereas the organizational encouragement comprises the whole chair climate, supervisory encouragement deals with the specific relation between the habilitation candidate and the advisor. Supervisory encouragement is characterized by trustful interactions between the habilitation advisor and the habilitation candidate, and supervisory support of the candidate's work and ideas. The conclusion that Amabile (1998, p. 83) offers regarding managers could also apply to habilitation advisors: "*Most managers are extremely busy. (...) It is therefore easy for them to let praise for creative efforts – not just creative successes but unsuccessful efforts, too – fall by the wayside. One very simple step managers can take to foster creativity is to not let that happen.*" In their study, Pomaki, Maes and ter Doest (2004) find that autonomy in setting goals, supervisory encouragement, work group encouragement, and a low work load predict 30% of the variance in employees' job satisfaction. Supervisory encouragement should thus have a positive impact on a junior researchers' job satisfaction and self-confidence i.e., their belief that they will manage to publish enough journal articles to be appointed to a professorship, that they will be nationally as well as internationally acknowledged by the scientific community, and their belief that they will eventually be a tenured full professor.

Furthermore, supervisory encouragement should also be positively related to publication productivity. Studies of professionals' careers suggest that an important predictor of early career productivity is supervisors' and advisors' influence on their students (Polanyi, 1966; Williamson and Cable, 2003). Advisors could encourage junior researchers by providing direct training, feedback on manuscript drafts, counseling in respect of their research agenda's development, and advice regarding appropriate research outlets for their work (Müller-Carmen and Salzgeber, 2005). Although, advisors are mostly unable to function as a role model for learning how to publish in international journals, we hypothesize that their encouragement of this activity is an important factor in motivating junior faculty members to seriously consider the question of prestigious international publishing. Hence, we propose the following hypotheses:

H1a: Organizational encouragement is positively related to job satisfaction.
H1b: Organizational encouragement is positively related to self-confidence.

H1c: Organizational encouragement is positively related to publication productivity.
H2a: Supervisory encouragement is positively related to job satisfaction.
H2b: Supervisory encouragement is positively related to self-confidence.
H2c: Supervisory encouragement is positively related to publication productivity.

The Relation between Organizational Impediments and Workload Pressure and Job Satisfaction, Self-Confidence, and Publication Productivity

Research shows that goal success produces satisfaction (Locke, 1965; Graaf-Zijl, 2005). The dilemma is, of course, that easy goals produce more satisfaction than difficult ones, but difficult goals produce higher performance than easy ones (Locke and Latham, 1990). Locke and Latham (1990) therefore propose that goals should be set in a two-tier system. Each individual would have a challenging but fully achievable minimum goal (e.g., a publication worth a C-rating in the VHB-JOURQUAL in the case of a junior researcher) and a stretch goal (e.g., an A+ publication according to the VHB-JOURQUAL rating). They conclude that this would ensure some basic level of job satisfaction and yet motivate high work performance (Locke and Latham, 1990). Consequently, we can assume that if an institutional environment is predominantly characterized by unrealistic goals regarding research output, researchers will most probably display low levels of satisfaction, both because these goals are attained less frequently and because they yield a lower degree of satisfaction for any given performance outcome (Locke, 1965).

Therefore, an organizational environment that is characterized by political problems and destructive critique of new ideas in research and teaching, as well as unrealistic expectations of what junior researchers can achieve with regard to research productivity will have a hindering influence on self-confidence and publication productivity. The last relation can be illustrated with the following example from Amabile et al. (2002, p. 52): *"Darwin spent decades reading scientific literature, making voyages on the HMS Beagle to the Galapagos and other exotic destinations, carrying out painstakingly detailed observations, and producing thousands of pages of notes on those observations and his ideas for explaining them. It's inconceivable that his breakthrough would have occurred if he'd tried to rush it."* They conclude from an analysis of more than 9000 diary entries in a study of 177 employees in seven U.S. companies that workload pressure often leads to overworked, fragmented, and burned out employees (Amabile et al., 2002).

Hence,

H3a: Organizational impediments are negatively related to job satisfaction.
H3b: Organizational impediments are negatively related to self-confidence.
H3c: Organizational impediments are negatively related to publication productivity.
H4a: Workload pressure is negatively related to job satisfaction.
H4b: Workload pressure is negatively related to self-confidence.
H4c: Workload pressure is negatively related to publication productivity.

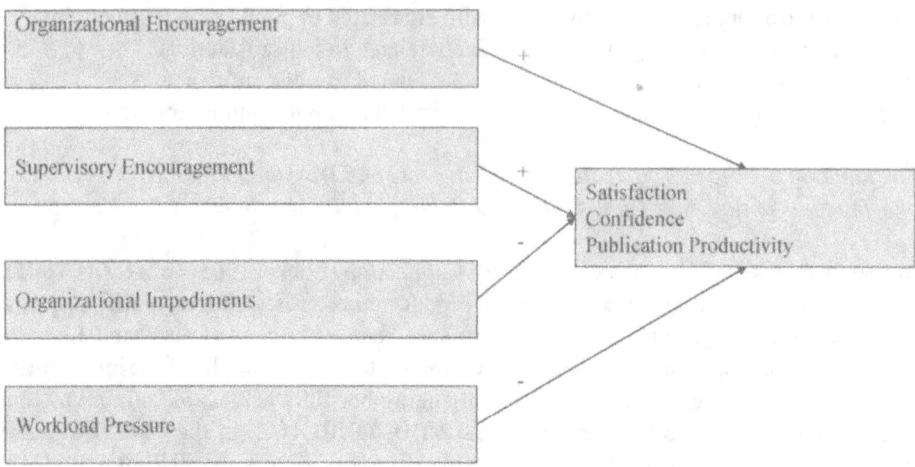

Fig. 1. Hypothesized model

C. Data and Method

I. Sample, survey design, and data collection

We combined primary and secondary data to examine the relation between the work environment for creativity and job satisfaction, self-confidence and publication productivity. We collected primary data on the several dimensions of the working environment related to creativity and junior faculty's self-confidence and job satisfaction through a pre-tested survey of junior management faculty in German-speaking Europe, using adapted validated scales by Amabile et al. (1996) during the period 6 April 2005 and 6 May 2005. The total design method as suggested by Dillman (1978) was used for the survey process. We collected secondary data on the publication productivity of all junior faculty in Austria, Germany, and Switzerland via website and database research in 2006.

The survey approach was necessary as publicly available information does not provide the level of detail that was needed for this study in respect of all variables. Nor does publicly available information include fine-grained information concerning junior faculty members' subjective attitudes and the characteristics of their work environment. Previous research, however, supports the reliability and validity of self-reported measures in the university context (Rogelberg et al., 2001; Fiedler et al., 2007; Fiedler and Welpe, forthcoming), especially if other sources are unavailable (Dess and Robinson, 1984), as was also the case in this study. A detailed pre-test was undertaken before the actual survey was carried out. In the context of the pre-test, several versions of the questionnaire were sent to and completed by members of the population, which led to the revision and more precise specification of the survey instrument.

In the context of the pre-test, the reliability, as well as the constructs' convergent and discriminant validity were also investigated. To ensure that a high proportion of the answers was valid, the questionnaires were sent directly to junior faculty members, using a key informant approach (Huber and Power, 1985).

Since there is no comprehensive database for this population, the empirical investigation was based on a hand-collected database, which aimed at identifying *all* junior faculty members in German-speaking Europe (Germany, Switzerland, and Austria). The German Academic Association for Business Research (VHB) provided us with a database of management junior faculty in these countries, which we reviewed, revised and updated. To ensure validity, the sample was restricted in the following way: The junior management faculty members had to be associated with a university based in German-speaking Europe; either aiming at the degree "Venia Legendi", or being employed as Junior Professor or Assistant Professor and they had to be in the process of pursuing a tenured academic position as professor. Criteria that led to exclusion from the sample were a tenured position at a university without the aim to get appointed as professor, termination of the goal to pursue a career in academia, non-completion of a PhD thesis, and affiliation with a university in a non-German-speaking country at the time of the survey. In cases of doubt, we contacted the individual junior faculty member personally to verify the aforementioned criteria. Furthermore, we also asked the divisional heads to forward the names of all junior faculty members in their respective division. In addition to the pre-selection of respondents and in order to guarantee the answers' validity, a series of control questions within the questionnaire checked whether the respondents were indeed junior faculty members and affiliated with universities in German-speaking Europe.

In total, we identified 574 junior faculty members, of which 74.56% came from Germany (n=428), 13.07% from Austria (n=75), 9.58% from Switzerland (n=55), and 2.70% from other countries (n=16). The authors estimate that the database is "sufficiently representative" as it does not contain any systematic omission errors (Bortz and Döring, 1995, p. 452). The final sample of completed surveys consists of 431 junior faculty members, which constitutes a highly satisfactory response rate of 75.1%. 70% of those who completed the survey were internal Habilitanden, 7% were external Habilitanden, 3% were junior professors and 20% had another position, such as "Akademischer Rat," "Lehrstuhlvertretung," "Privatdozent," and "Assistenzprofessor." Our sample contains 74.2% men and 25.8% women. The average age is 36.4 years for both Habilitanden and Junior Professors.

We collected secondary data on publication productivity a year after our junior faculty survey in order to account for the time it takes for the work environment to have an effect on publication output. The secondary data collection was done through databases and website searches from April 2006 until September 2006. We systematically searched for personal websites, WISO and EBSCO (Business Source Premier) databases, and cross-compared the results obtained in order to ensure exact and accurate data collection. Of the original 574 persons, only 449 were available for the database analysis due to their being offered an appointment as tenured full professor in the meantime or having abandoned an academic career. Figure 2 gives an overview of the timeline of the data collection period.

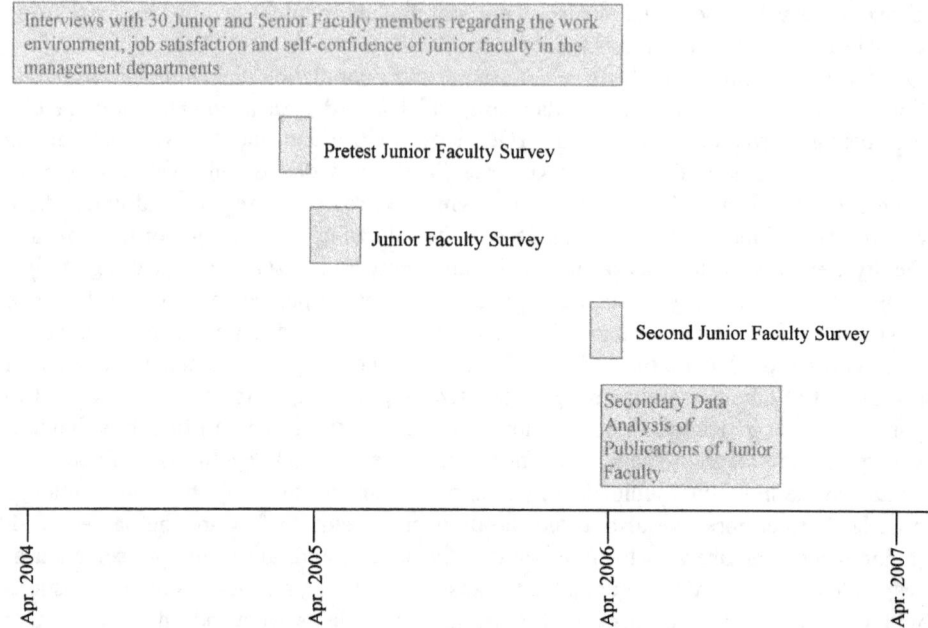

Fig. 2. Timeline of Data Collection Periods

II. Measures

In order to test the hypotheses, this study uses both established and newly developed scales. The known variables were mostly taken from original works and adapted to the university context. The construction of new measurement instruments in this study followed the suggestions of the American Psychological Association (2001). Based on an in-depth literature research on the different dimensions of job satisfaction, and self-confidence, definitions were developed of job satisfaction and self-confidence in the university context. In order to ensure the validity of the concepts, a number of items were generated. These item lists were discussed and supplemented by 16 expert interviews. After a pilot study (n = 30), the reliability of the individual constructs was checked, which exceeded the threshold value of 0.70 of Cronbach's Alpha. An exploratory factor analysis confirmed that all items loaded on to their respective constructs. After the data collection, the measurement instruments were again checked to ensure sufficient reliability and validity. In order to ensure the dimensionality of the constructs, principal component analyses were conducted followed by reliability analyses (Hair et al., 1998).

The next section provides an overview of the operationalisation of the variables in the university context. With the exception of the control variables, all items were measured on 1-7-point Likert scales. The respective constructs were each measured with four to twelve items.

1. Dependent variables

Job satisfaction. On a seven-point Likert scale, the respondents indicated whether they would again decide to become academics; whether, with the benefit of hindsight, they would again aim to be a professor; whether they would advise their PhD students to aim for a professorship in Germany/Austria/Switzerland; how satisfied the were with their academic careers to date; and whether they would again take up an academic career. Cronbach's Alpha for this variable is 0.78. Job Satisfaction was dichotomized by a median split in order to be included as a dependent variable in the logistic regression analysis.

Self-confidence. The "self-confidence" construct pertains to the extent to which the junior faculty members believe in a positive career development for themselves. The respondents indicated whether they believe that they will obtain the publications required for their first appointment as full professor, whether they believe that they will be able to apply for positions abroad, will receive recognition as scholars within Germany, and will be appointed as full and tenured professors within the next five years. Cronbach's Alpha for this variable is 0.77. Self-confidence was dichotomized by a median split in order to be included as a dependent variable in the logistic regression analysis.

Publication productivity. The publication productivity was determined through a secondary data collection during which journal publications were weighted as follows: In line with the rating value as indicated in the VHB-JOURQUAL, we weighted journal publications with the following mean values: A+-publications with 9,5; A-publications with 8,5; B-publications with 7,5; C-publications with 6,5; D-publications with 5,5; and E-publications with 3,5 points. Only journal articles of at least six pages were included in the collection, as book reviews, comments, and other short contribution, even if they do appear in prestigious journals, often do not have to undergo a peer-assessment procedure.

2. Independent variables

In order to analyze the work environment in respect of creativity in a university context, we adapt the validated scales by Amabile et al. (1996). As the KEYS Questionnaire developed by Amabile et al. (1996) was designed for traditional organizations, we had to adapt the scales and items to the university context. We focus on the following scales: organizational encouragement, supervisory encouragement, organizational impediments, and workload pressure. Table 1 indicates how we measured the four dimensions and specifies the median, minimum and maximum, and reliability values for the different creativity constructs used in the study. All constructs exceed the required reliability threshold value (Hair, Tatham, Anderson, and Black, 1998) of 0.70 (Cronbach's Alpha).

Since data collection by means of a survey always runs the risk of common method bias (Podsakoff, MacKenzie, Lee, and Podsakoff, 2003), we felt the need to validate the subjective measures by contacting those junior faculty members who had answered our survey in 2005 again in April 2006 and asking them again about the their job satisfaction and self-confidence. The reliability and validity of both constructs are supported by the significant correlations between the 2005 and 2006 measures (i.e., .0.5; $p < 0.001$ for organizational encouragement, .0.52; $p < 0.001$ for organizational impediments, and 0.59;

$p < 0.001$ for workload pressure). Thus, the items used in our study, do provide a valid measure for assessing different dimensions of the work environment.

3. Control variables

Career age. In keeping with Crane (1965), career age was calculated by subtracting the year of the dissertation from the year 2006.

Gender. The literature on publication productivity consistently indicates differences between male and female faculty members and suggests that men produce greater quantities of publications than women (e.g., Cole and Zuckerman, 1991; Stephan, 1998). To control for possible gender effects in our model, we include gender in the regression analyses.

Academic division. Junior faculty members belong to different academic divisions and fields of specialization. In the regressions, we controlled for the following divisions: Banking/Finance, Business Taxation, University Management, International Management, Logistics, Marketing, Public Management, Operations Research, Organization, Human Resources, Production Management, Accountancy, Technology and Innovation management, Environmental Economics, Computer Studies in Economics and Scientific Theory.

III. Test for systematic distortion of the data

In order to detect any systematic distortions in the collected data, several controls were employed following the procedures suggested by Podsakoff, et al. (2003). The authors tested whether the data were distorted by using of a single measurement instrument (Podsakoff et al., 2003). To do so, Harman's single-factor test (Podskaoff and Organ, 1986) was employed and the results indicate that no factor explains more than 25% of the variance, which is a commonly accepted threshold value (Hair et al., 1998). In addition, the authors conducted a follow-up survey in order to test the validity of the perceptual measures (see section C II. 2.).

Since the respondents gave their answers at different points of time, it is also possible that time could influence the given answers. Consistent with Armstrong and Overton (1977), the respondents' answers were divided into two groups: early and late respondents. Their answers were then compared with regard to the items included in this study. Armstrong and Overton (1977) verified that in respect of a survey, late answers are similar to non-answers. If there are no differences between early and late answers in a survey, it is assumed that non-answers do not distort the data. A t-test on both groups revealed no significant (5% level) differences and it is therefore fair to assume that no distortion of the data has occurred due to time.

Before detailing the results of the regression analyses, a brief discussion of other issues observed in the data is warranted. An examination of the correlations indicated that the correlations between the independent variables are below the required 0.50 threshold value (Hair et al., 1998). Both the variance inflation and the condition index were calculated as part of the regression computations to check whether multi-collinearity occurred. The variance inflation values of all variables are below the recommended 1.3 and, consequently, far below the valid threshold value of 10. The condition index values (Hair et al., 1998) lie between 1 and 11.3. A condition index is a summary of the collinearity diag-

Tab. 1. Scales for measuring the work environment in respect of the creativity of junior researchers (adapted from Amabile et al. (1996)

Scale Name	Number of Items/ Cronbach's Alpha/ Median/ Min Max	Description	Items
Organizational Encouragement	12/ 0.960/ 58/ 13-84	An organizational culture that encourages creativity through the fair, constructive judgment of ideas, reward and recognition of creative work, mechanisms for developing new ideas, an active flow of ideas, and a shared vision of what the organization is trying to do.	The organizational environment in which I'm doing research and teaching ... ... encourages people to approach research questions and problems creatively. ... encourages fair and constructive judgment of research ideas. ... encourages fun at the work place. ... has methods for identifying new research questions and problem solutions. ... encourages a lively and collaborative flow of ideas ... encourages people to take research risks. ... is characterized by an professional yet relaxed atmosphere. ... has a dynamic and inspiring work climate. ... is creative and innovative. ... encourages exercising new ideas. ... is characterized by an constructive and positive atmosphere ... encourages one to admit mistakes.
Supervisory Encouragement	7/ 0.909/ 37/ 7-49	A supervisor who serves as a good work model, sets goals appropriately, supports the work group, values individual contributions, and shows confidence in the work group.	My Habilitation advisor ... ... keeps his promises ... does not exploit me ... acts with my best interests in mind ... gives professional support. ... gives emotional support. In professional demanding situations ... ... I trust the advice of my Habilitation advisor. ... I trust the scientific judgment of my Habilitation advisor.
Organizational impediments	4/ 0.839/ 9/ 4-28	An organizational culture that impedes creativity through internal political problems, harsh criticism of new ideas, destructive internal competition, an avoidance of risk, and an overemphasis on the status quo	The organizational environment in which I'm doing research and teaching is characterized by ... ... many political problems. ... destructive critique of new ideas in research and teaching. ... destructive internal competition. ... personal conflicts.
Workload pressure	4/ 0.746/ 16/ 5-28	Extreme time pressures, unrealistic expectations regarding productivity, and distractions from creative work	My work environment is characterized by ... strong time pressure/stress. ... unrealistic expectations regarding what junior researchers can achieve in research productivity. ... too many distractions from research. ... no time to develop my ideas.

noses. A generally accepted rule for the interpretation of the condition index is that values above 15 signify a possible collinearity and that values above 30 denote a definite collinearity. The results of our analyses suggest that in this study, multi-collinearity is not a problem. Table 2 presents the descriptive results of junior faculty's work environment:

D. Results

As can be seen in table 2, organizational encouragement is highest for junior faculty members in the operations research and logistics academic divisions. Supervisory encouragement is highest in operations research and business taxation academic divisions. Organizational impediments as well as workload pressure are highest in the public and university management divisions.

Regarding the publication productivity of junior faculty researchers we find the following distribution (figure 3):

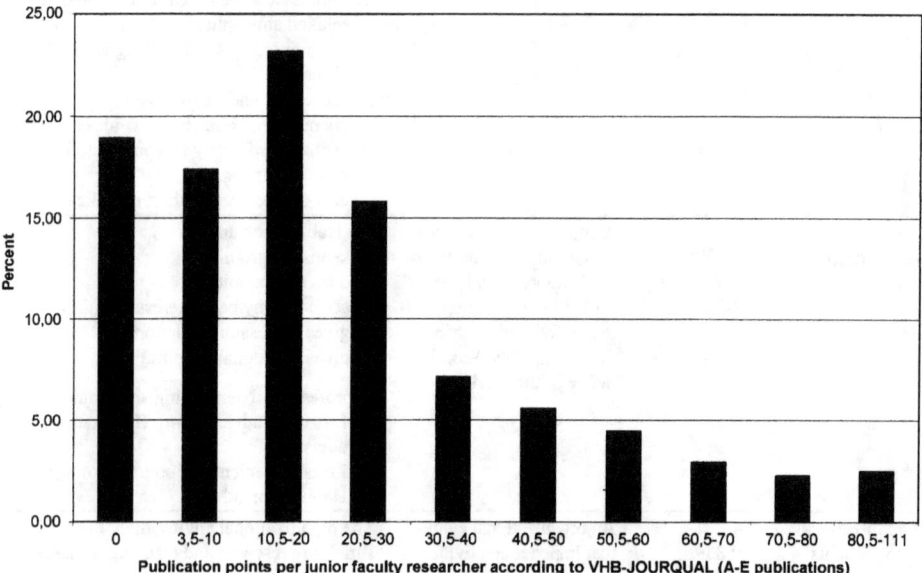

Fig. 3. Publication productivity of junior faculty researchers in the field of management in Germany, Austria and Switzerland according to VHB-JOURQUAL weighting means (N=449)

Results indicate that almost 19 percent of all junior faculty researchers in our sample have no journal publications. 17 percent of the junior faculty researchers have a publication productivity between 3.5 and 10 points according to the VHB-JOURQUAL which corresponds to approximately one B-publication. 23 percent of all junior faculty researchers have a journal publication count of 10.5-20 publication points and only 17 percent of all junior faculty researchers have more than 40 publication points according to VHB-JOURQUAL.

Tab. 2. Mean values for the variables of work environment

	Organizational Encouragement	Supervisory Encouragement	Organizational Impediments	Workload Pressure
Banking/Finance	56.1 (13.9)	37.2 (7.5)	9.9 (5.3)	16.1 (4.9)
Taxes	54.7 (14.3)	39.5 (4.7)	8.5 (6.6)	14.5 (4.4)
Entrepreneurship	61.3 (5.4)	36.0 (8.5)	10.0 (1.7)	18.2 (4.4)
University Management	49.3 (31.2)	34.3 (13.0)	13.5 (10.8)	19.8 (5.4)
International Management	58.5 (26.2)	36.8 (15.7)	12.1 (6.6)	12.0 (4.0)
Logistics	62.9 (14.7)	36.3 (11.8)	9.5 (5.7)	16.8 (6.4)
Marketing	54.4 (17.2)	33.9 (9.8)	9.6 (4.7)	17.4 (4.9)
Public Management	49.2 (11.3)	36.0 6.0)	14.2 (5.6)	19.5 (4.6)
Operations Research	72.5 (9.9)	42.0 (8.1)	5.8 (2.1)	13.3 (3.3)
Organisation	52.4 (21.4)	34.0 (10.5)	12.6 (6.3)	15.4 (6.0)
HR Management	57.4 (16.7)	36.3 (5.0)	10.6 (5.9)	17.1 (4.1)
Production Management	56.5 (18.3)	34.4 (9.9)	8.9 (4.0)	16.0 (4.8)
Controlling	54.2 (15.6)	33.8 (8.4)	10.0 (4.0)	17.5 (4.4)
Strategic Management	51.3 (19.3)	33.4 (10.6)	10.8 (6.0)	14.6 (3.7)
Technology and Innovation Management	58.8 (18.5)	33.3 (10.9)	10.4 (7.5)	18.2 (4.6)
Environment Management	60.5 (13.9)	37.0 (5.2)	8.0 (4.0)	17.2 (5.5)
MIS	56.1 (16.9)	34.1 (9.0)	11.0 (5.6)	17.7 (5.0)
Mean (σ)	55.7 (17.1)	35.1 (9.2)	10.4 (5.6)	16.7 (5.0)
Median	58	37	9	16
Min-Max	13-84	7-49	4-28	5-28

The numbers in parentheses in columns 2-5 show standard deviations. All items are measured on 1-7 rating scales.

Our hypotheses were tested using logistic (satisfaction and confidence) and linear regression analyses (publication productivity). Hypothesis 1a is supported: organizational encouragement has a strong positive effect on job satisfaction ($p < 0.05$). Hypotheses 1b and 1c are also supported: organizational encouragement also has a significant positive effect on self-confidence ($p < .01$) and on publication productivity ($p < 0.05$). Contrary to the prediction made in H2b and H2c, the regression results show that supervisory encouragement is not significantly associated with self-confidence and publication productivity. Thus, H2b and H2c are not supported. However, support for hypothesis 2a was found: supervisory encouragement is positively associated with job satisfaction ($p < 0.05$).

Furthermore, we find no support for hypotheses 3a, 3b and 3c: organizational impediments are not significantly associated with job satisfaction, self-confidence nor publication productivity. However, the effects of workload pressure on job satisfaction, self-confidence, and publication productivity are negative and significant, confirming hypotheses 4a, 4b, and 4c.

From the control variables, only career age and three of the academic division variables (operations research, accounting and organization) are significantly related to job

Tab. 3. Hypotheses tests[2]

	Job satisfaction Hypotheses (a)		Self-Confidence Hypotheses (b)		Publication Productivity Hypotheses (c)	
	Standardized β	Sig.[1]	Standardized β	Sig.[1]	Standardized β	Sig.[1]
H1 Organizational Encouragement	0,79	*	1,17	**	0,19	*
H2: Supervisory Encouragement	0,89	*	0,13		-0,07	
H3: Organizational Impediments	-0,06		0,38		-0,04	
H4: Workload Pressure	-0,83	**	-1,04	***	-0,14	*
Career Age	-0,15	**	-0,04		0,14	*
Gender	0,19		0,15		-0,15	*
Banking/Finance	1,42		0,04		0,09	
Bus. Taxation	-1,53		-22,13		0,05	
University management	-0,71		-0,20		0,03	
International Management	-0,97		-0,27		0,10	
Logistics	1,53		0,67		0,06	
Marketing	-0,69		0,20		-0,01	
Public Management	-0,08		22,05		0,11	
Operations Research	-3,20	**	-0,25		0,08	
Organization	4,89	**	0,51		0,11	
Human Resources	-0,61		0,61		0,03	
Production Management	-1,42		0,77		0,17	
Accountancy	4,99	*	-0,64		0,03	
Technology and Innovation management	0,94		-0,76		0,08	
Environmental economics	-0,50		-0,21		-0,12	
Computer studies in economics	2,15		0,32		-0,06	*
Theory	0,39		-0,32		F-value	3,12***
	Cox & Snell R^2	0,27	Cox & Snell R^2	0,18	R^2	0,23
	Nagelkerkes-R^2	0,36	Nagelkerkes-R^2	0,23	Adjusted R^2	0,15
	Percentage of forecasts	71,02	Percentage of forecasts	68,16		

[1] Standardized regression coefficients are shown; † p ≤ .10, * p ≤ .05, ** p ≤ .01, *** p ≤ .001; p values are for two-tailed tests; OLS-Regression was used to regress on publication productivity and logistic regression models were employed to regress on job satisfaction and self-confidence

satisfaction. None of the control variables are significantly related to self-confidence and career age and gender as well as the academic divisions of accountancy and computer studies in management are significantly related to publication productivity.

E. Discussion and Conclusion

This study set out to assess the relation between a creativity stimulating work environment and job satisfaction, self-confidence, and publication productivity of junior faculty members in German-speaking Europe. We argued that the intensity of organizational encouragement and supervisory engagement would be positively related to job satisfaction, self-confidence, and publication productivity, whereas organizational impediments and workload pressure would be negatively related. As the hypotheses tests reveal, a total of seven of the twelve hypotheses were confirmed. The results of the study as a whole demonstrate that the independent variables have a distinct influence on the emergence of job satisfaction and self-confidence, as well as on publication productivity.

According to this study, organizational encouragement is positively associated with the emergence of job satisfaction, self-confidence, and publication productivity, whereas workload pressure is negatively associated. However, the empirical analysis did not find the expected relationships between organizational impediments and job satisfaction, self-confidence, and publication productivity or between supervisory encouragement, self-confidence, and publication productivity. The results of this study also emphasize the role of the working environment in respect of both job satisfaction and work productivity, thereby confirming earlier studies that ascertained this relationship in the context of knowledge-intensive organizations (Abele, Cohrs, and Dette, forthcoming).

Overall, the results of this study demonstrate that junior faculty members' working environment with regard to creativity can actually be differentiated into four dimensions: organizational encouragement, supervisory encouragement, organizational impediments and workload pressure. Although the independent variables are moderately related, they have different predictive power and unique patterns of association with all three dependent variables. The results specifically state that while all four dimensions are indeed related, they are autonomous and independent constructs. This becomes clear from the moderate correlation between the four variables. Of all the independent variables, organizational encouragement and supervisory encouragement share the greatest variance between them. However, even the 33% common variance between organizational encouragement and supervisory encouragement demonstrates that they are not identical but autonomous constructs. This insight also provides evidence that the respondents were able to differentiate between the different dimensions of the creativity-related aspects of their work environment.

Consequently, these findings are also relevant in respect of the often-discussed theoretical and conceptual differentiation between different dimensions of the creative working environment. These insights confirm earlier studies on creativity dimensions that found that they are independent of each other (Amabile et al., 1996), as well as contributing to the creation of greater conceptual clarity regarding the various forms of working environment as also postulated by Amabile et al. (1996) and Ekvall and Ryhammer (1998).

On the whole, the results reveal that in line with empirical studies to date, a thoroughly detailed view of creativity-enhancing conditions is imperative in the context of knowledge-intensive organizations (e.g., Amabile et al. 2005). The differences in relationship patterns between types of creative work environments emphasize the need to examine the different aspects and their effects, as well as their level. The differentiation of the respective dimensions of the creative work environment – organizational encouragement, supervisory encouragement, organizational impediments, and workload pressure – makes understanding and deconstructing work productivity and work attitude in the university context and in similar contexts possible.

This study aims to contribute to the literature in several ways. First, the results improve the standard of knowledge on creativity-friendly work environment as an influencing factor on important variables in the university context, i.e. job satisfaction, self-confidence and publication productivity. Second, this study examines and compares different dimensions of a creativity-enhancing work environment from junior faculty members' perspective. Third, it is a first account of junior faculty's working conditions in German-speaking Europe. Furthermore, it introduces the creativity-enhancing work environment as a unit of analysis to the field of research on academic productivity. By simultaneously measuring positive and negative aspects of the work environment, our research is able to separately assess the influence of these work conditions on job satisfaction, self-confidence and professional productivity. In addition, by studying the effects of a creative work environment on job satisfaction and job performance, this study addresses research questions that have not as yet been explored, and for which for example Ai (1999) has called. In conclusion, the study examines the effects of creativity-enhancing working conditions on a highly specialized, specific context characterized by high autonomy, knowledge intensity, and performance pressure. Consequently, beyond the direct university context, the results are also significant for similar contexts, such as specialists or entrepreneurs working within corporations.

This study also has implications for practice. First, junior and senior faculty should be aware of the importance of the creative work environment for job satisfaction, self-confidence and publication productivity. Second, our study demonstrates that workload pressure is actually detrimental to job satisfaction, self-confidence and publication output, and should thus be avoided. Junior faculty who experience significant workload pressure in their working environment for a longer period of time might want to consider changing their environment to one that exerts less pressure on them. From our results, senior faculty advising junior faculty can deduce that the creation of pressure does not contribute to increased productivity and should therefore avoid it. Third, both organizational and supervisory encouragement can help junior faculty to increase their job satisfaction and work output, thus helping their academic careers. Finally, in order to foster junior researchers' job satisfaction, self-confidence, and publication productivity, advisors should abstain from expecting unrealistic research productivity and try to avoid too many distractions from research. They should rather opt for an organizational culture that encourages innovative steps through the fair, constructive judgment of ideas, and rewards and recognizes creative work. It should furthermore have mechanisms for developing new ideas, encourage an active flow of ideas, and have a shared vision of what the organization is trying to do.

Like others, this study has some limitations that have to be taken into account with regard to the interpretation and generalizability of the results. The restrictions of the chosen questionnaire survey method have already been discussed in section C. III. Since many publications of the junior faculty were already published before the time of the first survey in which we assessed the working environment (April 2005). A one-year time lag between the survey and the collection of the publication data is a short amount of time in order to measure a significant impact of the work environment on the publications[3]. We acknowledge this limitation of our study, however, we think that our analysis are still valuable for studying the influence of working conditions on performance for several reasons:

First, our study design constitutes an improvement over purely cross-sectional data. Many studies to date look at questions related to the effects of the work environment using cross-sectional data sets. Even though we agree with the reviewer that one year is a short time lag to observe strong effects of the work environment on the publication productivity, it is an improvement over the use of simple cross-sectional data.

Second, our research design enables us to avoid Common Method Bias. Since we collected our independent and dependent data from different sources and at different times, we are able to avoid Common Method Bias in our analysis (Podsakoff et al., 2003). We have asked junior faculty about their work environment and we have collect data on junior faculty's publication productivity through secondary sources (e.g. data bases). Thus, we can eliminate the possibility that the answers which junior faculty members have given with regard to their working environment have influenced the dependent variable (i.e. publication productivity).

Common Method Bias is considered one of the main impediments to causal interpretation of the data. In our research we can exclude the possibility that our data are distorted due to the use of the survey instrument. What we cannot exclude completely is the possibility that junior researchers that already published successfully (dependent variable) might report less workload pressure and stress in the survey because of their success rather than because of "objective" characteristics of their working environment. (e.g. I have been successful, thus my working environment must be such and such..."). The same reasoning would apply to job satisfaction and self-confidence: Those that are satisfied with their publication performance (e.g. because they already published many papers and are confident to receive a tenure position) might probably report in the survey more often that the workload is not too high and that they receive supervisory encouragement. To address these causality issues, future studies might want to include an objective and exogenous measure for the quality of the work environment (or a proxy for it).

Third, our measure of the work environment in T_4 can serve as a proxy for the work environment in T_0. In an ideal research world (which hardly ever exists) we would have collected data on the work environment at T_0 and would have waited for 5-6 years until we measured the publication productivity of the junior faculty members at T_6 to analyse the effects of the working environment. What we have done in our study is that we have collected data on the work environment at T_4 and measured the publication productivity of the junior faculty members at T_5.

We argue that the working environment in T_4 can serve as an appropriate proxy for the working environment of the junior faculty members in T_0, T_1, T_2, T_3.

Our data show that junior faculty members tend to stay at the same institution for many years. In addition, when asked about their work environment, junior faculty members will likely have taken into account the history of the work environment and its development rather than a one-day snapshot.

We are planning and would certainly encourage other scholars to design and conduct a longitudinal study on the relationship between work environment and publication productivity. We will repeat our analyses in the coming years and test whether our results hold true. We believe that not waiting for more years to pass and to instead publish our results now (despite the acknowledged limitations) also offers advantages with regard to theoretical and practical implications, as the topic of university reforms is a very current affair today and our results therefore likely to be of interest to both management institutions, junior and senior faculty, as well as public policy makers alike.

The fact that the sample, on which this study is based, is limited to a university context can also be regarded as one of this study's strengths: first of all, this allows a context-specific view of organization-theoretical processes as repeatedly called for by other scientists (Johns, 2001; Rousseau and Fried, 2001). Some researchers argue that in respect of research on creativity, it is important to include external, situational, and social aspects instead of regarding creativity as individual behavior or an element of personality (Baer, 1998). According to Amabile et al. (2005), creativity is a psychological concept based on social interactions in the environment in which interactions emerge. If the context is omitted, this inevitably causes a simplifying reduction that does not enable one to comprehend the actual elements of the creativity process (Lewis and Weigert, 1985). Furthermore, the limitation of the sample acts as an additional check of the respondent and organization conditions, thus contributing to the homogenization of the sample through which potential distortions can be prevented (Baum, Calabrese, and Silverman, 2000).

Earlier studies in the field of job satisfaction also drew attention to the context's importance and warned against an underestimation of the external factors (e.g., Doorman and Zapf, 2001; Hulin and Judge, 2003). More accurately, this study's focus on the university context enables research on the emergence of creativity in an environment characterized by high autonomy and high knowledge intensity, in which creativity is a central requirement for job performance.

The results of this study need to be viewed in the light of its limitations. These limitations, along with the study's findings, suggest directions for further research, which may build on this study's results in a number of ways. First, this study found that organizational encouragement is associated with greater job satisfaction, self-confidence, and publication productivity. However, consistent with the arguments presented in the methodology section, it may be important to consider in future studies whether job satisfaction can actually influence publication productivity. Second, from the point of view of junior faculty, research could consider the antecedents of creative working conditions, for example the role of affect (e.g. Amabile et al., 2005). Organizational encouragement and workload pressure have, for example, different predictors. Current research studies point out that creativity can have negative and positive consequences, and can at times be counterproductive in organizational settings (Ai, 1999). Consequently, future studies could examine the working environment's costs and benefits in respect of organizational performance. It is also conceivable that working environment dimensions are subject to different moderating influences, such as preoccupation (Fiedler and Welpe, 2007) or research skills (Ai, 1999).

This study only considered the effects of the work environment in the university context. The application of this study's model to other contexts, such as technology ventures or the service industry would be an interesting and fertile research field. In this study, the predictors for job satisfaction arise from the creative work environment. Many other variables, especially, for example, the similarity between junior faculty member and senior faculty members, the communication structures, junior faculty's motivation and efforts, and the type and number of occurring conflicts between junior and senior faculty, could influence or relate to job satisfaction and self-confidence. In conclusion, the results of this study provide answers to the questions about the effects of junior faculty members' working conditions on their job satisfaction and research output, thus complementing earlier research studies on creativity (Basadur et al., 1982; Amabile, 1998; Baer, 1998; Ai, 1999; Amabile et al., 2005), job satisfaction (Downey et al., 1975; Locke, 1976; Cohrs and Abele, 2005), and publication productivity (Williamson and Cable, 2003; Fiedler and Welpe, 2007).

On the whole, this study constitutes one of the first attempts to study creative work environments in the context of universities. Having shown that different dimensions of the creative work environment influence the emergence of job satisfaction, self-confidence, and productivity, this study also meets previous research's demands for an explanation of the work environment's role in respect of job performance, with a specific focus on creativity.

Acknowledgments

The authors would like to thank Sabine Aschmutat, Michael Beckmann, Susanne Blaszejewski, Julia Brandl, Lars Fend, Egon Franck, Nikolaus Franke, Gunther Friedl, Dietmar Griechnik, Marc Gruber, Wolfgang Güttel, Svenja Hagenhoff, Dietmar Harhoff, Silvia Heer, Joachim Henkel, Thomas Hess, Andreas Klein, Markus Klein, Carmen Kobe, Christine Legner, Christian Lüthje, Kathrin Möslein, Rahild Neuburger, Siegfried Numberger, Burkhard Pedell, Andreas Richter, Manfred Schwaiger, Karin Stenke, Tina Syring, Daniel Veit, Birgit Verworn, Iwan von Wartburg, Wolfgang Weber, and Robert Wilken for their valuable comments and suggestions.

We are also indebted to Oliver Fabel for his valuable guidance and suggestions. We also thank all survey participants for their time and effort. We are grateful for the continous support of and cooperation with the German Association of Management Professors in this project. We thank Ilse Evertse for her help in editing the manuscript. We would like to thank two anonymous referees for their constructive comments.

Endnotes

* The order of authors is alphabetical. All authors contributed equally to this work and should be considered co-first authors.
1 According to literature we use the terms publication output and publication productivity as synonyms.
2 When it was not clear whether an academic career was being pursued and/or when the Habilitation supervisor was not known, the academic was contacted by e-mail and asked to provide details for clarification.
3 We thank an anonymous reviewer for pointing out this limitation of our study.

References

Abele, A.E./Cohrs, J.C./Dette, D.E. (forthcoming): Arbeitszufriedenheit – Person oder Situation? In: Fischer, L. (Eds.) Arbeitszufriedenheit, Hogrefe, Göttingen.
Ai, X. (1999): Creativity and academic achievement: An investigation of gender differences, in: Creativity Research Journal, Vol. 12, No. 4, pp. 329–337.
Amabile, T.M./Conti, R./Coon, H./Lazenby, J./Herron, M. (1996): Assessing the Work Environment for Creativity, in: Academy of Management Journal, Vol. 39, No.5, pp. 1154–1184.
Amabile, T.M. (1997): Motivating Creativity in Organizations: On doing what you love and loving what you do, in: California Management Review, Vol. 40, pp. 39–58.
Amabile, T.M. (1998): How to kill creativity, in: Harvard Business Review, September-October, pp. 77–87.
Amabile, T.M./Conti, R. (1999): Changes in the Work Environment for Creativity during Downsizing, in: Academy of Management Journal, Vol. 42, pp. 630–640.
Amabile, T.M./Hadley, C.N./Kramer, S.J. (2002): Creativity under the gun, in: Harvard Business Review, pp. 52–61.
Amabile, T.M./Barsade, S.G./Mueller, J.S./Staw, B.M. (2005): Affect and Creativity at Work, in: Administrative Science Quarterly, Vol. 50, pp. 367–403.
American Psychological Association. (2001). Publication manual of the American Psychological Association (5th ed.). Washington, DC.
Armstrong, J.S./Overton, T.S. (1977): Estimating non-response bias in mail surveys, in: Journal of Marketing Research, Vol. 16(August), pp. 396–402.
Aycan, Z. (2004): Key success factors for women in management in turkey, in: Applied Psychology: an international Review, Vol. 53, No. 3, pp. 453–477.
Backes-Gellner, U./Schlinghoff, A. (2004): Careers, Incentives, and Publication Patterns of US and German (Business) Economists. Retrieved August 3rd 2006 from: http://ssrn.com/abstract=616822.
Baer, J. (1998): Point – Counterpoint: The Case for Domain specificity of creativity, in: Creativity Research Journal, Vol. 11, No. 2, pp. 173–177.
Barnard, C.I. (1938): Functions of the Executive, Harvard University Press: Cambridge, MA.
Barron, F./Harrington, D.M. (1981): Creativity, Intelligence, and Personality, in: Annual Review of Psychology, Vol. 32, pp. 439–476.
Basadur, M./Grae, G./Green, S. (1982): Training in creative problem solving: Effects on education and problem finding and solving in an industrial research organization, in: Organizational Behaviour and Human Performance, Vol. 30, pp. 41–70.
Bass BM. (1990): From transactional to transformational leadership: learning to share the vision, in: Organizational Dynamics, Vol. 18, No. 3, pp. 19–31.
Baum, J./Calabrese, T./Silverman, B. (2000): Don't go it alone: alliance network composition and startups' performance in Canadian biotechnology, in: Strategic Management Journal, Vol. 21, No. 3, pp. 267–294.
Baumgartner, C./Udris, I. (2005): Das „Zürcher Modell" der Arbeitszufriedenheit – 30 Jahre „still going strong", in: Fischer, L. (Ed.) Arbeitszufriedenheit II, Verlag für Angewandte Psychologie, Stuttgart.
Biddle B.J./Marlin M.M. (1987): Casualty, confirmation, credulity and structural equation modeling, in: Child Development, Vol. 58, pp. 4–17.
Bortz, J./Döring, N. (1995): Forschungsmethoden und Evaluation. 2nd ed., Springer, Berlin.
Cliff, N. (1983): Some cautions concerning the application of casual modeling methods, in: Multivariate Behavioral Research, Vol. 18, pp. 115–126.
Cohrs, J.C./Abele, A.E. (2005): Einflüsse von Zielerreichung und Arbeitsplatzmerkmalen auf die Arbeitszufriedenheit: Ein Vergleich verschiedener Berufsgruppen, in: Wirtschaftspsychologie; Vol. 1/2005, pp. 21–34.

Cole, J.R./Zuckerman, H (1991): Marriage, motherhood, and research performance in science, in: Zuckerman, H./Cole, J.R./Bruer, J.T. (Eds.) The outer circle: Women in the scientific community, pp. 157–170, W. W. Norton and Company, New York.
Crane, D. (1965): Scientists at major and minor universities: a study of productivity and recognition, in: American Sociological Review, Vol. 30, pp. 699–714.
Dess, G.G./Robinson Jr., R.B. (1984): Measuring organizational performance in the absence of objective measures: The case of the privately-held firm and conglomerate business unit, in: Strategic Management Journal, Vol. 5, pp. 265–273.
Dillman, D.A. (1978): Mail and Telephone Surveys: The Total Design Method, John Wiley & Sons, New York, NY.
Dormann C./Zapf, D. (2001): Job satisfaction: a meta-analysis of stabilities, in: Journal of Organizational Behavior, Vol. 22, pp. 483–504.
Downey, H.K./Hellriegel, D./Slocum, J.W., Jr. (1975): Congruence between individual needs, organizational climate, job satisfaction and performance, in: The Academy of Management Journal, Vol. 18, No. 1, pp. 149–155.
Ekvall, G./Ryhammer, L. (1998): Leadership Style, Social Climate And Organizational Outcomes: A study of a Swedish University College, in: Creativity and Innovation Management, Vol. 7, No. 3, pp. 126–130.
Ernst, H. (2003): Ursachen eines Informant Bias und dessen Auswirkung auf die Validität empirischer betriebswirtschaftlicher Forschung, in: Zeitschrift für Betriebswirtschaft, Vol. 73, No. 12, pp. 1249–1275.
Eysenck, H.J. (1983): The roots of creativity: Cognitive ability or personality trait? In: Roeper Review, Vol. 5, pp. 10–12.
Eysenck, H.J. (1993): Creativity and personality: Suggestions for a theory, in: Psychological Inquiry, Vol. 4, pp. 147–178.
Fedor, D./Davis, W./Maslyn, J./Mathieson, K. (2001): Performance improvement efforts in response to negative feedback: The roles of source power and recipient self-esteem, in: Journal of Management, Vol. 27, pp. 79 97.
Fiedler, M./Welpe, I./Lindlbauer, K./Sattler, K. (2007): Denn wer da hat, dem wird gegeben – Einflussfaktoren auf die Publikationsproduktivität des BWL-Hochschullehrer-nachwuchses und deren wissenschaftlicher Betreuer – eine Sekundärdatenanalyse. Working Paper.
Fiedler, M. & Welpe, I. (2007): Is it is Better to Travel a Thousand Miles Than to Read a Thousand Books? Institutional and Cognitive Antecedents of Junior Faculty's Publication Productivity. Working Paper.
Fiedler, M./Welpe, I. (forthcoming): Individual and Institutional Influencing Factors on the Appointment Preferences of Management Professors, in: Schmalenbach Business Review, forthcoming.
Fiedler, M./Welpe, I./Picot, A. (2006): Terra Incognita – Forschungsleistungen und Qualifizierungswege des deutschsprachigen Hochschullehrernachwuchses für Betriebswirtschaftslehre, in: Die Betriebswirtschaft, Vol. 66, No.4, pp. 464–486.
Fischer, L./Fischer, O. (2005): Arbeitszufriedenheit: Neue Stärken und alte Risiken eines zentralen Konzepts der Organisationspsychologie, in: Wirtschaftspsychologie, Vol. 1/2005, pp. 5–20.
Graaf-Zijl, M. (2005): The economic and social consequences of temporary employment: a review of the literature, Discussion Paper No. 47, University of Amsterdam.
Hair, J.F./Anderson, R.E./Tatham, R.L./Black, W.C. (1998): Multivariate Data Analysis, Prentice Hall, Upper Saddle River, NJ.
Hiller, N.J./Hambrick, D.C. (2005): Conceptualizing executive hubris: the role of (hyper-) core self-evaluations in strategic decision-making, in: Strategic Management Journal, Vol. 26, No. 4, pp. 297–319.
Huber, G.P./Power, D.J. (1985): Retrospective reports of strategic managers: guidelines for increasing their accuracy, in: Strategic Management Journal, Vol. 6, No. 171–180.
Hulin, C.L./Judge, T.A. (2003) Job attitudes, in: Borman, W.C./Ilgen, D.R./Klimoski, R.J. (Eds.) Handbook of Psychology, Vol. 12, pp.255–276, John Wiley & Sons, Hoboken.
Johns, G. (2001): In praise of context, in: Journal of Organizational Behavior, Vol. 22, pp. 31–42.
Judge, T.A./Bono, J.E./Erez, A./Locke, E.A. (2005): Core Self-Evaluations and Job and Life Satisfaction: The Role of Self-Concordance and Goal Attainment, in: Journal of Applied Psychology, Vol. 90, No. 2, pp. 257–268.
Kaya, M. (2006): Verfahren der Datenerhebung, in: Albers, S./Klapper, D./Konradt, U./Walter, W./Wolf, J. (Eds.) Methoden der empirischen Forschung, pp. 55–72, Gabler, Wiesbaden.
Keegan, J. (1987): The Mask of Command, Penguin: New York.

Kieser, A. (2004): The Americanization of academic management education in Germany, in: Journal of Management Inquiry, Vol. 13, No. 2, pp. 90–97.
Kincaid, H.V./Bright, M. (1957): Interviewing the business elites, in: American Journal of Sociology, Vol. 63, No. 3, pp. 304–311.
Kohn, M.L./Schooler, C. (1978): The reciprocal effects of the substantive complexity of work and intellectual flexibility: A longitudinal assessment, in: American Journal of Sociology, Vol. 84, pp. 25–53.
Kumar, N./Stern, L./Anderson, J. (1993): Conducting interorganizational research using key informants, in: Academy of Management Journal, Vol. 36, pp. 1633–1651.
Lewis, J.D./Weigert, A. (1985): Trust as a social reality, in: Social Forces, Vol. 63, No. 4, pp. 967–985.
Locke, E.A. (1965): The relationship of task success to task liking and satisfaction, in: Journal of Applied Psychology, Vol. 49, pp. 379–385.
Locke, E.A. (1976): The nature and causes of job satisfaction, in: Dunnette, M. (Ed.) Handbook of Industrial and Organizational Psychology, Rand McNally, Chicago.
Locke, E.A./Latham, G.P. (1990): Work motivation and satisfaction: Light at the End of the Tunnel, in: Psychological Science, Vol. 1, No. 4, pp. 240–246.
Morgenstern, R.D./Barrett, N.S. (1974): The Retrospective Bias in Unemployment Reporting by Sex, Race and Age, in: Journal of the American Statistical Association, Vol. 69, No. 346, pp. 355–357.
Müller-Camen, M./Salzgeber, S. (2005): Changes in academic work and the chair regime: The case of German business administration academics, in: Organization Studies, Vol. 26, No. 2, pp. 271–290.
North, D.C. (1990): Institutions, Institutional Change and Economic Performance, Cambridge University Press, New York, NY.
Podsakoff, P.M./Organ, D.W. (1986): Self-reports in organizational research: Problems and prospects, in: Journal of Management, Vol. 12, No. 4, pp. 69–82.
Podsakoff, P.M./MacKenzie, S.B./Lee, J.-Y./Podsakoff, N.P. (2003): Common method biases in behavioral research: a critical review of the literature and recommended remedies, in: Journal of Applied Psychology, Vol. 88, No. 5, pp. 879–903.
Polanyi, M. (1966): The tacit dimension. Doubleday, Garden City, NY.
Pomaki, G./Maes, S./ter Doest, L. (2004): Work conditions and employees' self-set goals: Goal processes enhance prediction of psychological distress and well-being, in: Personality and Social Psychology Bulletin, Vol. 30, pp. 685–694.
Price, J.L. (1997): Handbook of organizational measurement, in: International Journal of Manpower, Vol. 18, No. 4/5/6, pp. 303–435.
Rogelberg, S.G./Fisher, G.G./Maynard, D.C./Hakel, M.D./Horvath, M., (2001): Attitudes Toward Surveys: Development of a Measure and its Relationship to Respondent Behavior, in: Organizational Research Methods, Vol. 4, pp. 3–25.
Rousseau, D.M./Fried, Y. (2001): Location, location, location: Contextualizing organisational research, in: Journal of Organizational Behavior, Vol. 22, pp. 1–13.
Saari, L.M./Judge, T.A. (2004): Employment Attitudes and Job Satisfaction, in: Human Resource Management, Vol. 43, No. 4, pp. 395–407.
Seidler, J. (1974): On using informant's: A technique for collecting quantitative data and controlling for measurement error in organizational analysis, in: American Sociological Review, Vol. 39, pp. 816–831.
Staw, B.M. (1984): Organizational Behavior: A review and reformulation of the Field's outcome variables, in: Annual Review of Psychology, Vol. 35, pp. 627–666.
Stephan, P. (1998): Gender differences in the rewards to publishing in Academe: Science in the 70's, in: SEX Roles, Vol. 38, pp. 11–12.
Tirole, J. (2002): Rational irrationality, in: European Economic Review, Vol. 46, No. 4-5/2002, pp. 633–655.
Tushman, M., (1977): Communication across organizational boundaries. Special boundary roles in the innovation process, in: Administration Science Quarterly, Vol. 22, pp. 587–605.
Warr, P./Cook, J./Wall, T. (1979): Scales for the measurement of some work attitudes and aspects of psychological well-being, in: Journal of Occupational Psychology, Vol. 52, pp. 129–148.
Williamson, I.O./Cable, D.M. (2003): Predicting early career research productivity: The case of management faculty, in: Journal of Organizational Behavior, Vol. 24, pp. 25–44.

Young Researchers in the Field of Management: Assessing the Relation between the Work Environment for Creativity and Job Satisfaction, Self-Confidence, and Publication Productivity

Summary

This study assesses different dimensions of the work environment (i.e. organizational encouragement, supervisory encouragement, organizational impediments and workload pressure) with its relation to job satisfaction, self-confidence, and publication productivity of junior faculty in the field of management. We use pre-tested scales from creativity research that have acceptable factor structures, internal consistencies, and test-retest reliabilities to test our hypotheses with logistic (satisfaction and confidence) and linear regression analyses (publication productivity). The results indicate that organizational encouragement has a strong positive influence and workload pressure a strong negative influence on job satisfaction, self-confidence, and publication productivity. We believe that the paper can provide two important contributions: First, it offers a first account of the working conditions of junior faculty in the field of management in German-speaking Europe. Second, it introduces creativity-enhancing work environment as unit of analysis to the field of research on job satisfaction, self-confidence, and academic productivity. By simultaneously measuring both positive and negative dimensions of the work environment in respect of creativity, our research aims at separately assessing these working conditions' influence on job satisfaction, self-confidence, and professional productivity – three variables that are considered highly relevant for a successful research career.

Betriebswirtschaftlicher Hochschullehrernachwuchs: Wie hängen Kreativität fördernde Rahmenbedingungen mit Arbeitszufriedenheit, Zuversicht und Publikationsproduktivität zusammen?

Zusammenfassung

Dieser Beitrag untersucht die Bedeutung verschiedener Eigenschaften eines Kreativität stimulierenden Umfelds für Arbeitszufriedenheit, Zuversicht und Publikationsproduktivität des wissenschaftlichen Nachwuchses im deutschsprachigen Europa. Wir verwenden etablierte Skalen aus der Kreativitätsforschung, welche akzeptable Werte für die Faktorenstrukturen, die interne Konsistenz und die Test-Retest Reliabilitäten aufweisen und testen unsere Hypothesen mit logistischen (Zufriedenheit und Zuversicht) und linearen Regressionsanalysen (Publikationsproduktivität). Unsere Ergebnisse zeigen, dass organisatorische Unterstützung einen starken positiven Einfluss und der empfundene Druck der Arbeitsbelastung einen stark negativen Einfluss auf die Arbeitszufriedenheit, die Zuversicht und die Publikationsproduktivität haben. Wir glauben, dass unsere Arbeit die folgenden Beiträge leistet:

Erstens liefert sie einen Statusbericht zu den Arbeitsbedingungen deutschsprachiger Nachwuchswissenschaftler in der Betriebswirtschaftslehre. Zweitens führt sie Kreativität als Analyseeinheit in das Forschungsfeld zu Arbeitszufriedenheit, Zuversicht und Publikationsproduktivität ein. Indem wir gleichzeitig sowohl negative als auch positive Dimensionen des Arbeitsumfelds im Bezug zu Kreativität messen, können wir ihre jeweiligen Einflüsse auf Arbeitszufriedenheit, Zuversicht und Publikationsproduktivität, welche als zentrale Variablen einer erfolgreichen Forschungskarriere gelten, beurteilen.

WWW.GABLER.DE

Strategy concepts and their implementation in practice

Joachim Zentes | Dirk Morschett | Hanna Hanna Schramm-Klein
Strategic Retail Management
Text and International Cases
2007. VIII, 366 pp., 90 Fig., 34 Tab. Softc. EUR 29,90
ISBN 978-3-8349-0287-0

The author develops an evolutionary theory of the globalisation of firms using a thorough historical analysis to identify the basic globalisation processes. The identification of the underlying mechanisms allows managers to perceive these mechanisms in their influence on the evolutionary dynamics of the firms and to use these dynamics actively.

The Authors
Joachim Zentes is Professor of Marketing and Management at the Saarland University, Saarbrücken, Germany. He is Director of the Institute for Commerce & International Marketing (H.I.MA.) and Director of the Europa-Institut at Saarland University. He holds a chair in Business Adminstration, with a focus on Foreign Trade and International Management. Joachim Zentes is also a member of various boards of directors and advisory boards in Germany and abroad.
Dirk Morschett is Assistant Professor of Marketing and Management at the Institute for Commerce & International Marketing (H.I.MA.), Saarland University, Saarbrücken.
Hanna Schramm-Klein is Assistant Professor of Marketing and Management at the Institute for Commerce & International Marketing (H.I.MA.), Saarland University, Saarbrücken.

Order your copy now: kerstin.kuchta@gwv-fachverlage.de
Telefon +49(0)611. 7878-626

KOMPETENZ IN SACHEN WIRTSCHAFT

Further Education: The Role of School Type

Klaus Harney, Susanne Warning*

Abstract

- Using an educational economics framework this paper examines performance differences between day schools and evening schools for adult education.
- Perceived performance differences are proposed to be caused by student ability differences at the two school types which is in line with theoretical reasoning from signaling theory: high ability students in equilibrium credibly signal their type to employers by choosing day schools while low ability students choose to attend evening schools.
- Applying Data Envelopment Analysis based on data of schools for adults in the German state Hessen we reveal differences in this multidimensional performance measure between day schools and evening schools.
- Regression analyses detect further factors influencing the DEA scores. Not only the dummy variable indicating school type but also environmental and school specific factors show significant impact on the performance of schools for adults.

Keywords Adult education · school organization · performance · signaling

JEL: I21, I28

Prof. Dr. Klaus Harney (✉)
is full professor at the Ruhr-Universität Bochum. Research interests: empirical and theoretical research of educational organizations especially for adult education; history of vocational education. Ruhr-Universität Bochum, Lehrstuhl für Berufs- und Wirtschaftspädagogik, Arbeitsstelle für berufliche Aus- und Weiterbildung, 44780 Bochum, Germany; E-mail: klaus.harney@ruhr-uni-bochum.de

Dr. Susanne Warning (✉)
is researcher at the IAAEG, Universität Trier. Research interests: economics of education, theoretical and empirical analysis of organizations. Institut für Arbeitsrecht und Arbeitsbeziehungen in der Europäischen Gemeinschaft (IAAEG), Universität Trier, 54286 Trier, Germany; E-mail: warning@iaaeg.de

A. Introduction

"Adult learning has taken on a much higher profile in the last decade, as OECD economies and ageing societies are increasingly knowledge-based. High unemployment rates among the unskilled, the increased and recognised importance of human capital for economic growth – together with public interest in improving social and personal development – make it necessary to increase learning opportunities for adults within the wider context of lifelong learning." (OECD 2003, p. 3).

Along with the increasing importance of education in general also further education gained more and more attention: A greater number of young, highly qualified school leavers enter the labor market which in turn leads to pressure for less qualified people to improve their situation on the labor market by investing in education at a later stage of life. While supplementary education has played only a minor role for a long time, nowadays there are significantly many (i.e., up to 30 percent; cf. Konsortium Bildungsberichterstattung 2006, Hillmert 2004) young people aiming for supplementary education, and even among those aged around their fifties between 14 and 16 percent participate in these programs (Henz 1997, p. 228).

Important institutions for providing further education, especially supplementary education, are the public schools for adults. These schools include *Abendhauptschulen*, *Abendrealschulen*, *Abendgymnasien* and *Kollegs*. In Germany, the total number of students attending schools for adults was about 56,700 in 2003 (BMBF 2005), the final year covered by our data in the empirical analyses.

Given scare public resources, also in state ministries which are responsible for schools for adults in Germany, and growing interest in evaluations of publicly run institutions – often measured in terms of efficiency – the organization of schools for adults has come into the focus of politicians. As there are two school types, *Abendgymnasium* and *Kolleg*, that from a legal perspective offer identical services but differ in their organizational form, we take advantage of this fact and analyze the impact of school type on performance. The main separating criterion between the *Abendgymnasium* and the *Kolleg* is that the first one is an evening school and the second one is a day school. While day schools imply full time students, the students of evening schools typically are in regular jobs during daytime. The *Kolleg*, the day school type attended by 16,500 students, and the *Abendgymnasium*, attended by 19,700 students, both offer the general qualification for university entrance (*Allgemeine Hochschulreife*) and the advanced technical college entrance qualification (*Fachhochschulreife*).

An ongoing discussion points to differences across these school types, and a number of potential explanations can be imagined for such differences. One that immediately springs to one's mind are institutional differences concerning quality of teachers, resources, teaching and learning methods, organization etc. We, however, suggest another explanation for performance differences between evening schools and day schools as we do not have any indications about systematic differences in input factors for the two school types. We argue that there are high and low ability students, and depending on his or her type a student decides to go to day school (the high ability students, in our reasoning) or to evening school (the low ability students) in order to signal ability, i.e., productivity, to potential employers. This self selection of students leads to perceived performance differences across school types and makes day schools appear to be more productive than evening schools.

Our empirical results are based on data from schools for adults in Hessen (*Abendgymnasium* and *Hessenkolleg*). As it is difficult to find generally accepted performance indicators for schools, we apply two measures to ensure a sufficient level of robustness of our results: First, we apply Data Envelopment Analysis to measure efficiency in a multidimensional way, and second, we incorporate the composition of certificates provided by the schools. We do not interpret the resulting performance measures themselves. Instead, we interpret the difference of performance across schools as aggregated productivity difference between students at the different school types. It turns out that day schools show constantly higher values than evening schools in both performance measures which hints at aggregated productivity differences of students across school types. This finding holds even after controlling for regional and school-specific factors and thus is consistent with our theoretical argument.

Evaluations of educational institutions have gained increased attention and interest which led to a considerable number of contributions in this area, for example the evaluation of schools (Primont/Domazlicky 2006; Waldo 2007; Afonso/St. Aubyn 2006) and universities (Fandel 2007; Flegg/Allen 2007; Luptacik 2003). However, to the best of our knowledge, there is no study evaluating schools for adults or even different types of schools for adults applying various multidimensional performance measures which is our main focus. Of course, there are also various models and variants dealing with signaling ability through education (e.g., Chan et al. 2007; Kim 2007; Albrecht/van Ours 2006), however, we are not aware of one in the context of schools for adult education. Thus we aim to combine these two strands of the literature and offer an explanation of perceived performance differences across types of schools for adults by tracing back performance differences of schools to productivity differences of students.

The structure of the paper is as follows: Section B provides some information on schools for adults and develops the hypothesis. Research design and empirical results are presented in Sections C and D. Finally, Section E summarizes and discusses the results and suggests some policy implications.

B. Day Schools versus Evening Schools in Further Education

Schools for adults exist in two variants: as day schools and as evening schools. To contribute to the discussion that day schools and evening schools for adults differ in performance, we start with providing some information on school types and on their students before we motivate our empirical analysis and its results. Both school types, day schools and evening schools, offer the same services in the sense of conferring the *Allgemeine Hochschulreife* and the *Fachhochschulreife* to successful graduates. Completing the *Allgemeine Hochschulreife* takes six semesters, whereas the *Fachhochschulreife* takes only four semesters which holds for day and for evening schools likewise. However, the number of hours taught is about ten to 20 percent lower at evening schools than at day schools.

Unsurprisingly, students of these two school types differ in self-confidence, motivation, and risk perception among others (Baumgart 2003). While students of a day school usually are younger and primarily concentrate on studying and taking courses, students at an evening school attend courses in the evening – which makes students much more flexible – in addition to their regular (work) life. In Hessen, about 76 percent of the students at an evening school work at least part time whereas the number of students working at day schools is only about 40 percent (Harney et al. 2005). Also, financial support for students differs across school types. There is financial support for students of day schools for the entire period of six semesters, even if this support of course does not cover opportunity costs. Students at evening schools can only apply for financial support during the last year of their further education.

The current discussion and our empirical results for the state of Hessen suggest that day schools and evening schools differ in performance. There are at least two potential explanations for such performance differences: a first one is the organization itself that could matter which would correspond to quality differences in equipment, staff or teaching methods that cause differences between day schools and evening schools. However, to the best of our knowledge there are no reasons to suspect the existence of such ex ante differences as both school types are run and financed by the same Ministry of Education under the identical objective of providing entrance qualifications for higher education. Furthermore, given that both day and evening schools offer the same certificates which are perceived as equivalent, systematic ex ante differences would suggest that one school type was strictly dominant, calling in question the rationale for existence of the other type.

Therefore, we offer, in a very stylized way, another explanation for performance variation across school types, a reasoning suggesting a selection process of students to different school types that are perceived to be different. We suggest an argument similar to the classical signaling model of Spence (1973). In Spence's framework there are two types of workers with high and low productivity who may invest in a signal called "education" to indicate high productivity and earn a wage above the average afterwards. In the model those workers decide to invest in education who bear a lower cost of producing the signal which are the high productivity workers. They find it easier, i.e., less costly, to pass exams and get the final certificate. For low productivity workers investment in education does not make sense as the costs for acquiring the signal are too high. If the spread in costs for generating the signal, i.e., getting the certificate, between high and low productivity types is great enough, then the two groups of workers will be credibly be identified by having or not having the education signal, and type-specific wages at the level of marginal productivities can be paid.

Our argument follows the basic idea of Spence, even if in our framework both groups invest in education so that learning costs finally, play only a minor rule. We argue that students signal quality, i.e., their ability before entering school, by selecting a school type depending on the relation of the value of the signal and the expected failing costs going along with the two different school types.

To set up our framework we assume two types of students: one high ability group and one low ability group. Information on a student's ability is private. Both types invest in schooling (day school or evening school) to signal future employers their ability, i.e., productivity (perhaps students are not always perfectly aware of this rationale).

Even if day and evening schools in a legal sense offer the same certificates, we assume their signals are perceived differently. Suppose employers take certificates as a signal for ability. Productivity increases generated by education are the same for both school types and for both types of students. We postulate that ability of students at day schools is higher, i.e., the high productivity type chooses to get the signal from a day school, because it is more costly to produce. We posit that deciding to go to a day school coincides with a high confidence for being successful and thus of high ability, and with a high motivation for studying, expressed e.g. by the decision to quit a former job and completely focus on school. Thus firms believe better students decide to attend a day school instead of an evening school.

We have three cost components associated with school choice in mind: First, consider the direct costs of studying for attending school successfully. They are smaller for high ability students than for low ability students but are the same at both school types and therefore play no further role in our considerations. Second, opportunity costs consist of the income loss while attending school which is higher for high ability students than for low ability students, but the difference between opportunity costs at day and at evening schools is identical for both ability groups. Therefore, they can also be ignored when thinking about signaling through school choice. As an alternative reason for excluding direct learning and opportunity costs from the analysis, imagine that higher learning costs for the low ability group are compensated by lower opportunity costs, and vice versa for the high ability group. Finally, the costs of failing and not getting a certificate matter, and thus influence students' choices of the school type. We find it plausible to assume that costs arising from failing or quitting are higher at day schools than at evening schools, given the nature of the two school types. Quitting or failing at evening school just means to continue life as usual, including continuing in the job held during studying at school. By contrast, quitting or failing at day school results in a period of unemployment. To distinguish the level of expected failing costs between high and low ability students our arguments are twofold. First, high ability students have a better chance of finding a job after quitting day school. Second, the probability of failing is smaller for them. Combining both assumptions leads to lower expected failing costs of the high ability students at day schools while they are the same for both ability groups at evening schools.

From these assumptions and considerations about costs for school and student types we conclude that only the value of the signals and the expected failing costs matter for the choices made. As long as the difference of the value of the signals between day and evening schools is greater than the expected difference of failing costs, students go to day school. Because this relation can only hold for the high ability group and not for the low ability group, only high ability students decide to go to day school.

Thus, high ability students rationally choose to produce the more costly signal, which low ability students have no incentive to choose, and employers find their prior belief that high ability students present certificates from day schools confirmed. This equilibrium in turn has an impact on the perceived performance of school types. As the more able students choose the day schools, these schools can be expected to perform better in the sense of graduating a higher percentage of their student population, even if there are no institutional or organizational differences between evening schools and day schools. Therefore, our theoretical considerations, which we developed for the case of two student types but could be extended to a continuum of types, indeed motivate performance differences. Thus, we hypothesize that there are performance differences between day schools and evening schools for adults.

There are clear signs in the data for schools for adults in Hessen that point to the relevance of our theoretical motivation of performance differences: Take the observation that in Hessen about 76 percent of students at day schools have completed an apprenticeship before entering school while this is the case only for about 60 percent of students at evening schools (Harney et al. 2005). If an apprenticeship on the one hand offers better job opportunities and on the other hand indicates higher ability, then the selection process above for signaling ability seems to be consistent with the situation at the schools for adults under consideration.[1]

Without doubt, there are further factors that influence the performance of schools which are essential for our empirical analysis. An important determinant is the area in which a school is located. Individual characteristics of students carry the social structure of the district into the institution and thus influence teaching and learning success in an indirect way. Literature shows that regional variables capture an environmental effect of schools quite well and show significant influence on school performance. Applying a matching approach, Charlot et al. (2005) reveal that higher employment rates in a district serve as incentive to attend school. Similarly, Canton/Jong (2005) show for Dutch universities that the number of beginners at universities does not directly depend on unemployment rates, but on the alternative wage students could earn instead of studying. Not only these factors directly related to the labor market are expected to influence school performance, but also size of the region where potential students come from can be shown to have an impact (Heinessen 2005). Another factor capturing the family background of students is whether students are eligible for free school meals which serves as a proxy for financial background of the family. Bradley/Taylor (1998) find evidence for a negative correlation with individual test results.

Apart from environmental factors school characteristics also influence the performance of schools. Bradley/Taylor (1998) show for UK secondary schools that larger student numbers lead to better individual results. The same is true for selectivity in the admission process. Higher selectivity at a school goes along with more successful students. Studies based on the PISA data exhibit lower educational achievement of immigrant students in school results (Schnepf 2007) which hints at disadvantages for pupils with migration background. Combining these arguments our study considers a number of environmental and school-specific variables to explain performance differences across school types in further education.

C. Research Design

The theoretically proposed argument states performance differences between day schools and evening schools as a result of students self selection. To reveal these differences in performance of school types we apply data of 13 public schools for adults for 1990 to 2003 in the state of Hessen. Our analysis proceeds in two steps: First, we construct a multidimensional efficiency index applying Data Envelopment Analysis (DEA) and we take the composition of certificates awarded as performance measures for each school. Performance differences, especially in DEA scores, across school types are interpreted as differences in the students' productivities. Second we show that differences across school types remain significant even after controlling for environmental variables. Descriptive statistics on the data and methodological background are provided in this section.

I. Performance Measurement

A multidimensional efficiency measure generated by applying Data Envelopment Analysis (DEA) measures the performance of schools for adults. Assuming a production process for schools, DEA considers multiple inputs and multiple outputs simultaneously. To evaluate this production process the weighted sum of outputs is related to the weighted sum of inputs. Higher values of this ratio indicate higher efficiency levels. Input and output amounts of schools are known, the multipliers for aggregation to these weighted sums are to be derived. Thus, DEA does not require any *a priori* multipliers for the input and output factors; an optimization program determines them endogenously. Due to a lack of generally accepted aggregation multipliers in educational production processes, prominent applications of DEA among others refer to schools (e.g., Ruggiero et al. 2002) and universities (e.g., Abbott/Doucouliagos 2002; Thursby 2000).

For each school the DEA computes a performance measure which reveals the efficiency level of the school compared to all other schools considered in the analysis. It thus can be interpreted as relative efficiency. In a non-technical way, the DEA follows two steps: First a best practice production function is determined and schools on the frontier are called efficient. This efficient frontier envelops all other schools which are inefficient. In a second step DEA measures the distance of each inefficient school from the efficient frontier. Depending on this distance, DEA calculates a score for each school which indicates its level of efficiency. All schools on the frontier receive the maximum score of 1, while the inefficient schools receive a score from the interval (0, 1). As there is a number of excellent textbooks introducing the technical features of DEA in detail (e.g., Cooper et al. 2006), we only present the models finally used here.

As the Ministry of Education lays down budgets of schools for a longer time period, we assume that input quantities of schools are fixed. Thus, schools have to improve their output levels to receive a higher efficiency score. Given this assumption, an output oriented DEA model is appropriate. Starting with the baseline model a DEA with constant returns to scale yields:

(1)
$$\max_{\phi^k,\lambda} \phi^k$$

unter den NB: $\sum_{j=1}^{n} y_{rj}\lambda_j \geq \phi^k y_{rk}$ $\quad (r = 1,...,s)$

$\sum_{j=1}^{n} x_{ij}\lambda_j \leq x_{ik}$ $\quad (i = 1,...,m)$

$\lambda_j \geq 0$ $\quad (j = 1,...,n)$

There are n schools and each of them uses m inputs to produce s outputs. School j consumes x_{ij} of input i to produce y_{rj} units of output r. Now assume school k is to be evaluated. Then ϕ^k is the factor which indicates how much all outputs of school k could be proportionally increased while all constraints continue to hold. The restrictions ensure that a linear combination of all schools produces at least as many units of each output as the evaluated school while not using more of the input factors. Thereby, the weights λ_j highlight the importance of the reference schools on the efficient frontier for the evaluated school k. The efficiency score for school k is derived as $1/\phi^{k*}$. To generate such a score for each school, the above program has to be solved n times, once for each school.

To ensure robustness of the results, we run not only a model with constant returns to scale but also one with variable returns to scale. Technically, it evolves from the model presented above just by adding the convexity constraint $\sum_{j=1}^{n} \lambda_j$.

In the production process of schools we consider the number of beginners in year t (consisting of the sum of the participants of the first two pre-semesters, *Einführungsphase 1* and *Einführungsphase 2*) and the hours taught over a three year average (t, t+1, t+2) as input factors. This latter average seems to be appropriate because usually students attend school for three years. In a first specification the numbers of school leavers with different certificates serve as output factors and consist of the *Allgemeine Hochschulreife* and the *Fachhochschulreife*. To take into account that beginners in year t only can leave school successfully three (respectively two) years after entering school, we lag these output factors correspondingly so that we consider the *Allgemeine Hochschulreife* in year t+3 and the *Fachhochschulreife* in year t+2. In a second specification we check the robustness of our results and include the inverse of the average grade of the *Allgemeine Hochschulreife* of schools as additional output factor into the DEA.[2] The inverse of grades is used because in the German grading system grades get better when their value gets smaller, and the DEA program in (1) augments outputs to optimize the goal score. All input and output data for the DEA originate from the State Ministry of Education Hessen (Kultusministerium Hessen 2005). Table 1 presents the descriptive statistics for the input and output factors, also split up for day schools and evening schools.

The dataset consists of the nine public evening schools and the four public day schools for 12 years where input factors are from 1990 to 2001 and output factors are from 1992 to 2004. For conducting a DEA this number of observations is sufficient given that we assume that there are no technological changes over our 12 year period. On average about 81 students begin studying every year at an evening school while the number of beginners at a day school amounts only to 62 on average. The other input factor, the three year average of hours taught, also differs across school types (420 at evening schools and 333 at day schools) with a similar relation. Two years after entering school about 35 students from an evening school receive the certificate of an *Allgemeine Hochschulreife* with an average grade of 2.2 and about 15 students receive the certificate of a *Fachhochschulreife*. The corresponding values for the day schools are 35 (with an average grade of 2.4) and eight.

Based on data from Table 1 we run various DEA models. First, we identify efficiency levels for day schools and evening schools separately to consider potential institution specific differences. Second, we assume a similar technology of production with constant returns to scale for both school types and run a model for evening and day schools together. Thus schools from both types are compared directly. And third, we conduct the corresponding analysis for variable returns to scale where we lose discriminatory power but gain an additional robustness check.

Tab. 1. Descriptive statistics of input and output factors for the DEA

	N	T	OBS	MEAN	STD. DEV.	MIN	MAX
Evening Schools							
Beginners in t	9	12	104	81.288	37.111	17.000	185.000
Average hours taught (t, t+1, t+2)	9	12	104	420.518	163.901	151.000	736.330
Fachhochschulreife in t+2	9	12	104	15.240	9.856	1.000	55.000
Allgemeine Hochschulreife in t+3	9	12	104	34.644	20.861	0.000	93.000
Grade *Allgemeine Hochschulreife* in t+3	9	10	88	2.217	0.214	1.665	2.620
Day Schools							
Beginners in t	4	12	43	62.233	17.412	0.000	89.000
Average hours taught (t, t+1, t+2)	4	12	43	333.008	73.692	201.000	427.667
Fachhochschulreife in t+2	4	12	43	7.814	4.119	1.000	19.000
Allgemeine Hochschulreife in t+3	4	12	43	34.512	16.987	0.000	68.000
Grade *Allgemeine Hochschulreife* in t+3	4	10	39	2.423	0.219	2.150	2.710
Overall							
Beginners in t	13	12	147	75.714	33.682	0.000	185.000
Average hours taught (t, t+1, t+2)	13	12	147	394.920	148.693	151.000	736.330
Fachhochschulreife in t+2	13	12	147	13.068	9.214	1.000	55.000
Allgemeine Hochschulreife in t+3	13	12	147	34.605	19.749	0.000	93.000
Grade *Allgemeine Hochschulreife* in t+3	13	10	127	2.280	0.219	1.665	2.710

As an alternative performance measure we use the composition of certificates provided by the schools. Both school types offer the same certificates, the *Allgemeine Hochschulreife* and the *Fachhochschulreife*. Suppose it is more difficult to succeed in acquiring the three year certificate (*Allgemeine Hochschulreife*) than in acquiring the two year certificate (*Fachhochschulreife*). Then schools with a higher fraction of high ability students show greater values in this performance measure.

II. The Role of School Type

To explain performance differences across evening and day schools, our variable of main interest is the dummy variable indicating whether the school belongs to the group of evening schools (1) or to the group of day schools (0). For both groups we compare performance levels measured in terms of the multidimensional efficiency index and the ratio of certificates. Analyzing performance levels of different types of schools provides a first insight in the importance of organizational structure of schools.

However, to take factors other than organizational structure into consideration that also influence performance of schools we apply regression analyses where the performance measures serve as endogenous variables. As exogenous variables the regression contains those factors that are mainly beyond the control of the school management (see Lovell, 1993): A set of environmental variables is used to capture the effect of school environment and social background of the students on performance. Thus we include the unemployment rate in the county (Bundesagentur für Arbeit 2006) and the number of inhabitants in the region (Eurostat 2006) in our analysis. The number of public schools for adults in the re-

Tab. 2. Descriptive statistics of the exogenous variables

Variable	OBS	MEAN	STD. DEV.	MIN	MAX
Evening school	182	0.692	0.463	0	1
Total number of students	182	238.681	115.824	77.000	578.000
Fraction of non-German students	177	0.152	0.114	0.000	0.535
Unemployment rate	133	6.495	2.203	3.000	13.600
Inhabitants (in 1000)	179	339.677	176.576	138.740	663.952
Number of competing schools	182	5.418	1.995	1.000	7.000

gion (Bezirk) captures the degree of competition among schools as well as the impact schools for adults have in the corresponding area. Suggested by the studies evaluating PISA results (Schnepf 2007) we include the fraction of non-German students (Kultusministerium Hessen 2005) to capture potential language skills or disadvantages (see also HKM 2006). School size is mapped by the total number of students (Kultusministerium Hessen 2005). Table 2 displays the descriptive statistics of the exogenous variables.

Although we are aware of the potential small sample problem for a regression analysis, we apply this technique to detect the impact of multiple influence factors on performance of schools. To validate estimations we run several models that may lend confidence to the results. First, we analyze a model with the ordinary least square estimator for pooled data. Second, to make use of the panel structure of the data, we perform a Hausman test (Greene 2003, p. 301f.) which indicates that the random effects estimator is not unbiased, leading us to use the fixed effects estimator. Considering school fixed effects we capture those school effects that are not covered by our exogenous variables.

Unfortunately, an ordinary fixed effects model does not allow including time-invariant variables. As our variable of main interest which is the dummy indicating school type, however, is time-invariant, we finally apply a modified fixed effects estimator that overcomes this problem: the fixed effects model with vector decomposition which combines the fixed effects estimator and the ordinary least square techniques (Plümper/Troeger 2007). This estimator considers time-invariant variables and then also provides coefficients for them. Basically, the estimation procedure which has been developed in the political sciences follows three steps. First, a fixed-effects model is run excluding the time-invariant variables from the analysis. Then, in the second stage, the unit-effects vector is decomposed into an error term and into a term explained by the time-invariant variables. Finally, the first stage of the analysis is re-estimated using pooled OLS and considering the time-invariant variables after adding the error term of the second stage of the analysis.

The fixed effects estimator with vector decomposition turns out to be superior to pooled OLS, random effects, and the Hausman-Taylor procedure in models with rarely changing and/or time-invariant variables in which time-varying variables are correlated with unobserved unit effects (Plümper/Troeger 2007). Applying this new estimation technique not only provides us with a coefficient for our central and time-invariant variable, the school type dummy, and for the second time-invariant variable, the number of schools in a district, something the fixed effects specification does not allow. The procedure also accounts for the unobserved unit heterogeneity, which the random effects model does not.

Finally, the fixed effects estimator with vector decomposition model is more efficient than the Hausman-Taylor procedure. Using Monte Carlo simulations Plümper/Troeger (2007) demonstrate that under conditions present in our data set their modified fixed-effects estimator leads to better results, i.e., lower root mean squared errors, than any alternative estimator. We employ the model with robust standard errors.

D. Empirical Results

To examine the relation of performance and school type, especially of schools for adults, we start highlighting the differences in performance across day and evening schools in a descriptive way. The multidimensional efficiency score from DEA and the composition of certificates awarded measure the performance of schools. For revealing the determinants of these performance measures we apply a multivariate analysis in the second step.

I. Results of Performance Measurement

Performance of schools in a multi-dimensional framework is computed by applying various DEA models for which we report the results below. The first model assumes constant returns to scale (CRS) and consists of two separate calculations (SEP) for the two different school types which afterwards are combined to the DEA-CRS-SEP score. The second model differs from the first one only in pooling the data and calculating scores from the entire sample, labeling results as DEA-CRS. Finally, the third model assumes variable returns to scale for the entire sample of schools (DEA-VRS). To show the robustness of the DEA results these three models are run for both input-output specifications; models get the additional name "graduate" (if only number of graduates are applied as outputs) or "grade" (if additionally the inverse grade is included as output variable).

Table 3 reports the results of the multidimensional performance measure and indicates robustness of the DEA results. The average level of efficiency for evening schools ranges between 63.043 and 72.550 percent for the graduate model and between 68.890 and 87.207 for the grade model; whereas the corresponding efficiency scores for day schools on average vary between 70.378 and 77.942 percent for the graduate models and 74.356 and 83.984 for the grade model.

As Table 3 suggests different results for the two school types, we run t-tests to reveal whether these differences are significant. It turns out that for the separate model the average performance of day schools with 77.942 is significantly higher than average success of evening schools showing a value of 71.799. The corresponding difference for the grade models is also statistically significant.

To prove robustness of the results we look at the results of the combined model with constant returns to scale (DEA-CRS) and find that the performance difference between day schools and evening schools remains not only significant and stable but becomes even greater for both input-output specifications. Thus, the performance difference between the two types of organization seems to be systematic. However, skipping the assumption of constant returns to scale and turning to the graduate model with variable returns to scale (DEA-VRS), performance differences across school types are not significant any-

Tab. 3. Descriptive statistics of the DEA-scores

	OBS	EFF. SCHOOLS	MEAN	STD. DEV.	MIN	MAX
Evening school						
DEA-CRS-SEP graduate	104	6	71.799	15.824	25.180	100.000
DEA-CRS graduate	104	1	63.043	14.617	19.480	100.000
DEA-VRS graduate	104	11	72.550	17.929	31.580	100.000
DEA-CRS-SEP grade	88	9	75.561	14.280	43.630	100.000
DEA-CRS grade	88	4	68.890	14.186	39.440	100.000
DEA-VRS grade	88	17	87.207	9.525	64.500	100.000
Day school						
DEA-CRS-SEP graduate	43	6	77.942	14.544	47.410	100.000
DEA-CRS graduate	43	2	70.378	15.637	32.510	100.000
DEA-VRS graduate	43	4	73.117	15.840	33.960	100.000
DEA-CRS-SEP grade	39	7	83.984	10.026	67.060	100.000
DEA-CRS grade	39	3	74.356	12.959	45.480	100.000
DEA-VRS grade	39	3	83.738	8.220	69.830	100.000
Overall						
DEA-CRS-SEP graduate	147	12	73.596	15.664	25.180	100.000
DEA-CRS graduate	147	3	65.189	15.241	19.480	100.000
DEA-VRS graduate	147	15	72.716	17.292	31.580	100.000
DEA-CRS-SEP grade	127	16	78.147	13.648	43.630	100.000
DEA-CRS grade	127	7	70.569	14.000	39.440	100.000
DEA-VRS grade	127	20	86.142	9.252	64.500	100.000

more, which indicates scale economies in production. For the grade model, it even turns out that the DEA scores are significantly greater for the day school than for the evening school. However, results will turn to the opposite when we consider further variables in the multivariate analysis.

To focus on the relation of the DEA scores from various models we study the correlations and the distribution of the scores for all three models. The correlation between the DEA-CRS model and the VRS-CRS model is 0.8464 (0.7081 for the grade specification). In line with this high degree of correlation, the value for the DEA-CRS-SEP and the DEA-CRS model is 0.8606 (0.8599 for the grade specification) and for the DEA-CRS-SEP and the DEA-VRS model it is 0.7867 (0.6158 for the grade specification). Again, these high coefficients in combination with correlations from 0.6983 to 0.7953 across specifications indicate a high level of robustness of the multidimensional performance measurement across schools.

Referring to the distribution of the DEA scores Figure 1 displays the kernel density estimates for the three models for the graduate specification[3]. They provide similar results as a histogram, but they do not depend on the end point of the bin and smooth out the contribution of each observed data point over a local environment of that data point. Even if all of our DEA efficiency scores are almost symmetrically distributed, the graphs show small differences. The estimates for the combined models show a slightly higher mean. However, the graphical presentation of the DEA scores supports the robustness of the

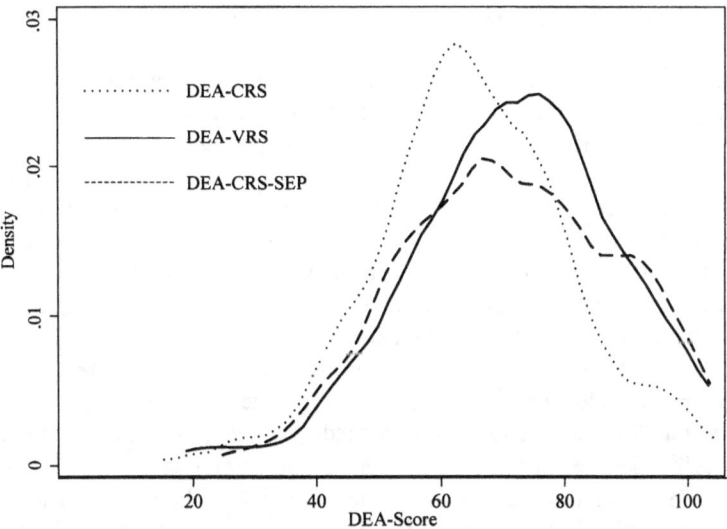

Fig. 1. Kernel density estimation (Epanechnikov) of the DEA scores for the graduate model

multidimensional performance measurement of schools. An approximately normal distribution seems to be a reasonable assumption based on this analysis.

To examine the question of differences in certificates awarded by the different school types, we concentrate on the ratio of *Allgemeine Hochschulreife* to *Fachhochschulreife*. Table 4 displays the descriptive statistics of the alternative performance measure which takes higher values when the school awards more certificates of *Allgemeine Hochschulreife* compared to *Fachhochschulreife*.

Tab. 4. Descriptive statistics of the certificate ratios

	OBS	n	T	MEAN	STD. DEV.	MIN	MAX
Evening schools	125	9	14	3.493	2.663	0.571	23.000
Day schools	54	4	14	8.278	10.181	0.000	65.000
Overall	179	13	14	4.936	6.376	0.000	65.000

The ratio of *Allgemeine Hochschulreife* to *Fachhochschule* at day schools is about eight, which implies that eight students receive the *Allgemeine Hochschulreife* per one student receiving the *Fachhochschulreife*. Testing for the difference in this alternative measure, we again apply a t-test which confirms the results of variation across school types from above. Day schools have a significantly higher ratio than evening schools.

In summary, the descriptive analysis shows that there are not only differences in the multidimensional efficiency, but there are also differences in the composition of certificates granted across day and evening schools. However, several other factors may influence the performance of schools, thus those variables will be incorporated as exogenous variables into the regression analysis in the next subsection.

II. Determinants of Performance

Evening and day schools seem to differ in performance, in the multidimensional DEA scores as well as in the composition of certificates awarded. To detect influence factors on performance that are not captured in the production process, we include environmental factors as exogenous variables in a regression analysis: first, the multidimensional DEA score in the variants from above serves as endogenous variable; second, the ratio of shares of certificates operates as endogenous variable. Table 5 presents the regression results with the different DEA scores from the graduate specification (DEA-CRS, constant returns to scale; DEA-VRS variable returns to scale; DEA-CRS-SEP, constant returns to scale, separate models) serving as endogenous variables.

To demonstrate the approach the first three regressions apply the DEA score from the constant returns to scale model and the graduate specification as endogenous variable and show the results for different regression procedures: pooled OLS, fixed effects, and the modified fixed effects estimator with vector decomposition which overcomes the problem of time invariant variables in fixed effects models. While the coefficients for the time-variant variables in the ordinary fixed effects model and the fixed effects vector decomposition model are the same, standard errors are different. Therefore, in the sequel the results of the most reliable estimation procedure (fixed effects vector decomposition, see Section C) are presented.

The dummy variable indicating school type, which is one if the school is an evening school and zero if the school is a day school decreases performance significantly in all estimation approaches even after controlling for school size, student background,

Tab. 5. Determinants of the DEA scores under graduate specification

	Pooled OLS	Fixed effects	Fixed effects regression with vector decomposition		
	DEA-CRS	DEA-CRS	DEA-CRS	DEA-VRS	DEA-CRS-SEP
Evening school	-9.711*** (3.02)	–	-56.171*** (5.63)	-41.385*** (5.84)	-30.028*** (5.08)
Total no students (ln)	14.032*** (5.09)	10.480 (1.29)	10.480*** (3.82)	11.788*** (3.98)	13.152*** (4.68)
Fraction of Non-German students	-36.237** (2.61)	-23.493 (1.33)	-23.493* (1.73)	-31.911** (2.13)	-53.801*** (3.80)
Unemployment	-0.849** (2.04)	-0.271 (0.35)	-0.271 (0.65)	-0.505 (1.12)	-0.308 (0.71)
Inhabitants (ln)	-0.489 (0.14)	-227.102** (2.33)	-227.102*** (4.90)	-173.862*** (5.92)	-119.140*** (4.82)
No competing schools	0.791 (0.80)	–	55.017*** (4.95)	43.918*** (6.28)	29.177*** (4.92)
Constant	9.263 (0.29)	1766.863** (2.29)	1529.032*** (4.90)	1167.705*** (5.99)	806.689*** (4.88)
Adj R-squared	0.3215	0.3854	0.3757	0.4073	0.3411
F-Value	$F_{(6,138)}$ = 12.37	$F_{(4,128)}$ = 13.48	$F_{(8,126)}$ = 14.95	$F_{(8,126)}$ = 16.71	$F_{(8,126)}$ = 13.22

t-values in brackets; *, **, *** indicates significance on the 10%, 5%, 1% level.

unemployment rate, town size, and for the number of competing schools in the area. This effect turns out to be robust for all DEA specifications and for both econometric models. Although, the econometric analysis might suffer from a low number of observations, it supports the result from the descriptive analysis which exhibited significantly lower DEA scores for evening schools than for day schools. Thus, even after controlling for environmental factors the performance difference across school types stays significant.

As to the control variables our model delivers the expected signs: larger schools show significantly higher performance levels probably due to economies of scale; schools with relatively more students showing a migration background have lower DEA scores. Schools located in larger cities exhibit lower multidimensional performance. Finally, a larger number of competing schools in the district improves performance.

To further explore the robustness of our results, we also present the corresponding estimations for the DEA specification considering the inverse grade as additional output factor, again, presenting results for the different DEA model assumptions. Table 6 displays these results.

Tab. 6. Results for the fixed effects vector decomposition model for the grade specification

	DEA-CRS	DEA-VRS	DEA-CRS-SEP
Evening school	-49.059*** (6.00)	-40.233*** (8.14)	-24.849*** (6.10)
Total no students (ln)	-5.039* (1.82)	2.508 (1.64)	-5.305** (2.18)
Fraction of non-German students	-20.997 (1.57)	-14.062* (1.85)	-47.205*** (3.89)
Unemployment	-0.544 (1.39)	0.316 (1.27)	-0.594* (1.70)
Inhabitants (ln)	-215.090*** (6.00)	-202.375*** (8.95)	-106.685*** (7.00)
No competing schools	51.085*** (6.26)	48.138*** (9.21)	25.799*** (7.35)
Constant	1546.094*** (6.51)	1421.832*** (9.39)	832.258*** (8.00)
Adj R-squared	0.4071	0.5668	0.4927
F value	$F(8,107) = 14.83$	$F(8,107) = 25.94$	$F(8,107) = 19.917$

t-values in brackets; *, **, *** indicates significance on the 10%, 5%, 1% level.

Also for the second DEA specification considering the inverse grade as additional output factor, the results, especially for our main variable the dummy indicating school type, remain stable. Schools teaching in the evening, show lower performance levels than schools operating during daytime. Environmental variables and school characteristics are significant and show almost the same pattern of signs as the models in Table 5 above. Only school size seems to have a negative impact on performance in the DEA grade models which is contrary to the graduate models.

To detect not only the influence of school type on the multidimensional efficiency score but also on the ratio of *Allgemeine Hochschulreife* to *Fachhochschulreife* we apply the latter as an endogenous variable. Table 7 presents the estimation results where the exogenous variables equal those from above.

The estimation results of the regressions, again, indicate a negative effect of the dummy variable evening school on performance which supports our hypothesis that the school type matters. Evening schools show a significantly lower ratio of *Allgemeine Hochschul-*

Tab. 7. Results for the ratio *Allgemeine Hochschulreife* to *Fachhochschulreife*

	POOLED OLS	FIXED EFFECTS	FIXED EFFECTS VECTOR DECOMPOSITION
Evening school	-5.342*** (3.85)	–	-35.186*** (6.02)
Total no student (ln)	-0.510 (0.41)	-5.374* (1.83)	-5.374*** (3.57)
Fraction of non-German students	-1.787 (0.29)	0.730 (0.10)	0.730 (0.12)
Unemployment	-0.356* (1.95)	0.362 (1.09)	0.362 (1.63)
Inhabitants (ln)	-0.803 (0.56)	-138.905*** (3.89)	-138.905*** (5.26)
No competing schools	0.297 (0.74)	–	32.356*** (5.28)
Constant	19.898 (1.44)	1106.069*** (3.95)	966.429*** (5.33)
Adj R-squared	0.1273	0.2109	0.2008
F-value	$F(6,168) = 5.23$	$F(4,158) = 5.11$	$F(6,168) = 8.82$

t-values in brackets; *, **, *** indicates significance on the 10%, 5%, 1% level.

reife to *Fachhochschulreife*. Consequently, they award less degrees of *Allgemeine Hochschulreife* compared to *Fachhochschulreife*. Assuming that it is more difficult to complete the three year certificate (*Allgemeine Hochschulreife*) than the two year certificate (*Fachhochschulreife*), the empirical results support our argument from above, namely, that high ability students choose to go to a day school which in turn leads to higher performance values of the day school compared to the evening school. Survey evidence supports this conclusion as it suggests similar objectives of students at day and evening schools concerning the aspired certificate (Harney et al. 2005). This is in line with the argument of the commission of the Ministry of Education which points out that the *Fachhochschulreife* serves as a net for those who will probably face problems with passing the *Allgemeine Hochschulreife* one year later (Grundsatzkommission des Hessischen Kultusministeriums 1995). In the education literature this kind of gratification for students with low abilities is well-known as a phenomenon of cooling out (Fend 2006, p. 114). Most environmental variables remain significant which is in line with the results of the regressions where the DEA score served as endogenous variable.

Summing up, school type matters in terms of performance, measured in multiple dimensions and measured by the ratio of certificates provided. However, other variables, such as environmental factors, also influence the performance level of schools. For the performance decreasing effect of the variable evening school we propose a self-selection effect of students. In a signaling game between students and employers those students who are more confident to complete school successfully decide to go to the day school as this can be interpreted as a credible signal for high ability. If students act in this way, then performance at day schools is perceived to be higher than at evening schools and finally, in the multidimensional DEA score, it reflects student productivity. The effect is not due to organizational differences but it is an effect of student selection which makes day schools just appear to perform better.

E. Concluding Remarks

Schools for adults in the federal state of Hessen in Germany show performance differences across school types in efficiency scores and in the proportion of certificates awarded. We reveal systematic differences across day and evening schools in both dimensions even after controlling for environmental and school specific factors. It turns out that schools teaching during daytime show higher efficiency values than schools teaching in the evening and that the relation of degrees of *Allgemeine Hochschulreife* to *Fachhochschulreife* is significantly higher at evening schools compared to day schools.

Although several explanations for this observation can be imagined, we offer one in the tradition of signaling theory which we can support by a number of stylized facts. It states that high ability students on average go to day schools, while low ability students on average choose to attend evening schools. Thus ability differences of students feed into performance differences across school types and are perceived as such.

From a practical perspective, applying data from the state of Hessen seems to be adequate as it is – together with North Rhine Westphalia – one of the leading states in Germany in terms of adult education, both in relative numbers and in state of development in scale and scope. As adult education is an important element in the German educational system, our results could serve as starting point for other states to design or restructure their schools for adults. Consequence of our results could be equalizing entrance qualifications for both school types: At UK schools higher selectivity at a school goes along with more successful students (Bradley/Taylor (1998). For Hessen, survey evidence suggests that selectivity of day schools is greater than selectivity of evening schools (Harney et al. 2005), which again suggests that more productive students attend day schools. Furthermore, various cost components seem to be an important factor for school choice, thus the design of a grant system for students seems to matter and therefore seems to be a design parameter for the schools for adults system.

To evaluate the weight of our explanation for performance heterogeneity across school types more carefully and identify the limitations of our analysis, further data would be desirable and helpful, especially, individual data on entrance qualifications and on the motivation of students to choose the favorite school. Of course, there are a number of determinants for student productivity imaginable which we were not able to capture in our empirical analysis. These factors include among others former school certificates which predetermine success quite well (Fielding et al. 1998), duties apart from school which differ systematically across school types (Harney et al. 2005) and motives for attending a school for adults. Students at evening schools are mostly interested in receiving the certificate and not in the contents itself which is often called a utilitarian attitude towards education (Harney et al. 2007; Siara 1986; Wolf 1975).

Furthermore, the signaling value of the day school could be more directly identified either by asking potential employers or by sending out questionnaires regularly to school leavers to get information on their careers (e.g., similarly to what UK universities do). It could then be evaluated if leavers of day schools follow career paths different from those leaving evening schools. Consequently, there is a huge field for future research in applying more detailed data to put the signaling argument to a much more stringent empirical test. More detailed data, especially on students' motivation for attending either school type might be helpful to strengthen the arguments on costs going along with each school type for different student abilities. Up to this point we have to confine ourselves to suggest a plausible explanation of our empirical results which is supported by the stylized facts mentioned in the introduction.

To sum up our results, there are performance differences between day and evening schools for adults. We consider perceived differences in certificates awarded very important because they create the opportunity for heterogeneous students to credibly signal their ability by choosing a school type and thereby influencing important efficiency measures of their schools. When evaluating the efficiency of school types, this aspect should be borne in mind.

Endnotes

* *Acknowledgements.* The project benefited from financial support provided by the Ministry of Education in Hessen. This represents the authors' personal opinion and does not reflect the view of the Ministry of Education in Hessen. For helpful comments and discussions we are grateful to Beatrice Kern, Oliver Fabel, Günter Fandel, Hans-Peter Hochstätter, Sascha Koch, Thomas Plümper, Dieter Sadowski, Manfred Weiß, Markus Weischet, and Peter Welzel, to the members of the project "Bildungssteuerung", to the participants of the conference of the "Bildungsökonomischer Ausschuss" of the "Verein für Socialpolitik" in Kreuzlingen, to participants of the workshop "The Economics and Management of Education" in Konstanz, and to participants of the seminar at the Institute for Labour Law and Industrial Relations in the European Community in Trier. Finally, we are very grateful to two anonymous referees of this journal for very helpful comments which helped to improve the paper.
1 For a discussion on the relation of apprenticeship and further education, especially adult education, see Zapf (1971) and Wolf (1975).
2 Unfortunately, there is no equivalent or comparable grade for the *Fachhochschulreife* available.
3 The kernel density estimates for the grade model which are omitted to save space are similarly shaped, however, the graphs are shifted to the right and more flat.

References

Abbott, M., Doucouliagos, C. (2003): The Efficiency of Australian Universities, A Data Envelopment Analysis, in: Economics of Education Review, Volume 22(2003), No 1, p. 89–97
Afonso, A., St. Aubyn, M. (2006): Cross-Country Efficiency of Secondary Education Provision: A Semi-Parametric Analysis with Non-Discretionary Inputs, in: Economic Modelling, Volume 23(2006), No 3, p. 476–491
Albrecht, J.W., van Ours, J.C. (2006): Using Employer Hiring Behavior to Test the Educational Signaling Hypothesis, in: Scandinavian Journal of Economics, Volume 108(2006), No 3, p. 361–372
Baumgart, F. (2003): Soziale Benachteiligung im deutschen Bildungssystem, in: Jelich, F.J., Goch, S. (2003): Geschichte als Last und Chance. Festschrift für Bernd Faulenbach, Klartext, Essen 2003, p. 409–423
Bradley, S., Taylor, J. (1998): The Effect of School Size on Exam Performance in Secondary Schools, in: Oxford Bulletin of Economics and Statistics, Volume 60(1998), No 3, p. 291–324
BMBF (2005): Grund- und Strukturdaten 2005, Bundesministerium für Bildung und Forschung: Bonn/Berlin.
Bundesagentur für Arbeit (2006): Arbeitslose und Arbeitslosenquote (abh. EP) sowie ausgewählte Strukturen (Frauen, Ausländer, unter 25 Jahre, Langzeitarbeitslose, Schwerbehinderte) nach Kreisen ab Dezember 1984. Online available: http://www.pub.arbeitsamt.de/hst/services/statistik/detail/z.html (26.08.2007)
Canton, E., de Jong, F. (2005): The Demand for Higher Education in the Netherlands, 1950–1999, in: Economics of Education Review, Volume 24(2005), No 6, p. 651–663
Chan, W., Li, H., Wing, S. (2007): A Signaling Theory of Grade Inflation, in: International Economic Review, Volume 48(2007), No 3, p.1065–1090

Charlot, O., Decreuse, B., Granier, P. (2005): Adaptability, Productivity, and Educational Incentives in a Matching Model, in: European Economic Review, Volume 49(2005), No 4, p. 1007–1032
Cooper, W.W., Seiford, L.M., Tone, K. (2006): Introduction to Data Envelopment Analysis and Its Uses. With DEA-Solver Software and References, Springer, New York 2006
Eurostat (2006): General and Regional Statistics, Demographic Statistics, Annual average Population. Online available: http://www.eds-destatis.de/de/esds/esds.php (26.08.2007)
Fandel (2007): On the Performance of Universities in North Rhine-Westphalia, Germany: Government's Redistribution of Funds Judged Using DEA Efficiency Measures, in: European Journal of Operational Research, Volume 176(2007), No 1, p. 521–533
Fend, H. (2006): Neue Theorie der Schule. Einführung in das Verstehen von Bildungssystemen, Verlag für Sozialwissenschaften, Wiesbaden 2006
Fielding, A., Belfield, C.R., Thomas, H.R. (1998): The Consequences of Dropouts on the Cost Effectiveness of 16-19 Colleges, in: Oxford Review of Education, Volume 24(1998), No. 4, p. 487–511
Flegg, A.T., Allen, D.O. (2007): Does Expansion Cause Congestion? The Case of the Older British Universities, 1994-2004, in: Education Economics, Volume 15, No 1, p. 75–102
Greene, W.H. (2003): Econometric Analysis, 5th edition, Prentice Hall, New York 2003
Grundsatzkommission des Hessischen Kultusministeriums (1995): Grundsatzkommission des Hessischen Kultusministeriums Zweiter Bildungsweg/Schulen für Erwachsene. Bericht: Situation und Perspektiven der Schulen für Erwachsene in Hessen, Hessisches Kultusministerium, Wiesbaden 1995
Harney, K., Koch, S., Hochstätter, H.-P. (2007): Bildungssystem und Zweiter Bildungsweg: Formen und Motive reversibler Bildungsbeteiligung, in: Zeitschrift für Pädagogik, Volume 53(2007), No 1, p. 34–57
Harney, K., Koch, S., Weischet, M. (2005): Projekt Steuerung des Zweiten Bildungswegs Hessen. Daten der Befragung der Studierenden an Schulen für Erwachsene in Hessen 2004. Bochum 2005, Ruhr-Universität Bochum
Heinessen, E. (2005): School District Size and Student Educational Attainment: Evidence from Denmark, in: Economics of Education Review, Volume 24(2005), No 6, p. 677–689
Henz, U. (1997): Der nachgeholte Erwerb allgemeinbildender Schulabschlüsse. Analysen zur quantitativen Entwicklung und sozialen Selektivität, in: Kölner Zeitschrift für Soziologie und Sozialpsychologie, Volume 49(1997), No 2, p. 223–241
Hillmert, S. (2004): Soziale Ungleichheit im Lebensverlauf: zum Verhältnis von Bildungsinstitutionen und Entscheidungen, in: Becker, R., Lauterbach, W. (2004): Bildung als Privileg? Erklärungen und Befunde zu den Ursachen der Bildungsungleichheit, VS Verlag, Wiesbaden 2004, p. 69–97
HKM (2006): Bildungspolitik in Zahlen. Daten aus dem Schulbereich 2004, Hessisches Kultusministerium, Wiesbaden 2006
Kim, J.-Y. (2007): Multidimensional Signaling in the Labor Market, in: Manchester School, Volume 75(2007), No 1, p. 64–87
Konsortium Bildungsberichterstattung (2006): Bildung in Deutschland, Ein indikatorengestützter Bericht mit einer Analyse zu Bildung und Migration, Bertelsmann, Bielefeld 2006
Kultusministerium Hessen (2005): Data Upon Request from the section „Schulen für Erwachsene – Zweiter Bildungsweg", Wiesbaden 2005
Lovell, C.A.K. (1993): Productive Frontiers and Productive Efficiency, in: Fried, H.O., Lovell, C.A.K., Schmidt, S.S. (1993): The Measurement of Productive Efficiency, Oxford University Press, New York 1993, p. 3–67
Luptacik, M. (2003): Data Envelopment Analysis als Entscheidungshilfe für die Evaluierung von Forschungseinheiten in der Universität, in: Zeitschrift für Betriebswirtschaft, Volume 73(2003), EH 3, p. 59–74
OECD (2003): Beyond Rhetoric: Adult Learning Policies and Practices. Highlights. Online available: www.oecd.org.
Plümper, T., Troeger, V.E. (2007): Efficient Estimation of Time Invariant and Rarely Changing Variables in Panel Data Analysis with Unit Effects, in: Political Analysis, forthcoming.
Primont, D.F., Domazlicky, B. (2006): Student Achievement and Efficiency in Missouri Schools and the No Child Left Behind Act, in: Economics of Education Review, Volume 25(2006), No 1, p. 77–90
Ruggiero, J., Miner, J., Blanchard, L. (2002): Measuring Equity of Educational Outcomes in the Presence of Inefficiency, in: European Journal of Operational Research, Volume 142(2002), No 3, p. 642–652
Schnepf, S.V. (2007): Immigrants' Educational Disadvantage: An Examination across Ten Countries and Three Surveys, in: Journal of Population Economics, Volume 20(2007), No 3, p. 527–545
Siara, C. (1986): Untypische Statuspassagen. Bildungs- und Berufsfindungsprozesse im Zweiten Bildungsweg, Campus-Verlag, Frankfurt/New York 1986

Spence, M. (1973): Job Market Signaling, in: The Quarterly Journal of Economics, Volume 87(1973), No 3, p. 355–374
Thursby, J.G. (2000): What do We Say about Ourselves and What Does It Mean? Yet Another Look at Economics Department Research, in: Journal of Economic Literature, Volume 38(2000), No 2, p. 383–404
Waldo, S. (2007): Efficiency in Swedish Public Education: Competition and Voter Monitoring, in: Education Economics, Volume 15(2007), No 2, p. 231–251
Wolf, W. (1975): Selektionsprozesse im Zweiten Bildungsweg. Untersucht am Beispiel der Hessenkollegs, Scriptor, Kronberg 1975
Zapf, W. (1971): Der nachgeholte Aufstieg – Untersuchungen über Absolventen des Zweiten Bildungswegs, in: Neue Sammlung: Göttinger Zeitschrift für Erziehung und Gesellschaft, Volume 11(1971), No 3, 249–273

Further Education: The Role of School Type

Summary

Lifelong learning has gained more and more attention during recent years which led to increasing student numbers at schools for adults. To examine the influence of the organizational form of schools for adults, we distinguish two types: on the one hand day schools that teach in the morning and/or in the afternoon, and on the other hand evening schools that offer courses mainly in the evening. Both types of schools offer the same services, the general qualification for university entrance (*Allgemeine Hochschulreife*) and the advanced technical college entrance qualification (*Fachhochschulreife*). Based on data of schools of further education in a German state for 1990 to 2003 we show: i) there are performance differences across the different types of organization; schools that are teaching during daytime show higher performance than schools that are teaching in the evening. ii) The relation of degrees of *Allgemeine Hochschulreife* to *Fachhochschulreife* is significantly higher at evening schools than it is at day schools. iii) Performance differences across schools can also be explained by regional differences. Based on these results the article offers an explanation for perceived differences of schools for adults by tracing back performance differences of schools to productivity differences of students in the light of signaling.

Erwachsenenbildung: Die Rolle des Schultyps

Zusammenfassung

Lebenslanges Lernen und Weiterbildung haben in den letzten Jahren unverkennbar an Bedeutung zugenommen. Diese Entwicklung betrifft auch die Schulen für Erwachsene. Hier können Studierende die Allgemeine Hochschulreife und die Fachhochschulreife auf dem Zweiten Bildungsweg über zwei Typen von Schulen erreichen: Abendschulen und Tagesschulen. Beide bieten gleiche „Produkte" im Sinne der Schulabschlüsse an, weisen jedoch unterschiedliche Organisationsmerkmale auf. Am Beispiel der Schulen des Zweiten Bildungsweges in Hessen für die Jahre 1990-2003 zeigen wir: i) Es gibt Unterschiede im Erfolg zwischen den Organisationstypen. Die Effizienz der Hessenkollegs (Tagesschulen) nimmt höhere Werte als an Abendgymnasien (Abendschulen) an. ii) Das Verhältnis von Abschlüssen mit Allgemeiner Hochschulreife und Fachhochschulreife ist an Hessenkollegs signifikant höher als an Abendgymnasien. Und iii) Effizienzunterschiede und Unterschiede in der Zusammensetzung der Abschlüsse lassen sich über regionale Unterschiede erklären. Aufgrund dieser Ergebnisse bieten wir eine Erklärung für die wahrgenommenen Leistungsunterschiede zwischen Schultypen im Bereich der Erwachsenenbildung an, indem wir Unterschiede im Licht der Signal-Theorie mit unterschiedlichen Fähigkeiten der Studierenden erklären.

WWW.GABLER.DE

Efficient planning, implementing and controlling of trade shows, conventions and events

Manfred Kirchgeorg | Werner M. Dornscheidt | Wilhelm Giese | Norbert Stoeck (Eds.)
Trade Show Management
Planning, Implementing and Controlling of Trade Shows, Conventions and Events
2005. XXVI, 1136 pp., 164 Fig., 41 Tab. Hardc.
EUR 129,00   ISBN 978-3-409-14333-2

Extensive overview of all aspects of trade show and convention management from the perspective of scientists, operators, exhibitors, associations and service industry. The articles especially focus on strategic and operative decision making problems. The reader gains perspectives, approaches to solutions and recommendations on the whole process in decision making. The conceptualization of successful trade shows and conventions is demonstrated by numerous best practices.

The Authors
Prof. Manfred Kirchgeorg is Head of the Department of Marketing Management at the HHL Leipzig Graduate School of Management.
Werner M. Dornscheidt is CEO & President of Messe Düsseldorf Group.
Wilhelm Giese is former CEO & President of Messe Düsseldorf Group.
Dr. Norbert Stoeck is Practice Group Manager at Roland Berger Strategy Consultants.

Order your copy now: kerstin.kuchta@gwv-fachverlage.de
Telefon +49(0)611. 7878-626

KOMPETENZ IN SACHEN WIRTSCHAFT

Works Councils and the Productivity Effects of Different Continuing Training Measures

Thomas Zwick*

Abstract

- Works councils have an important influence on the types of training measures that are offered in a firm and on the selection of training participants. Firms are more inclined to offer training with specific human capital, while employees rather benefit from general human capital. Therefore it can be assumed that firms with works councils that function as mediators and voice for the staff, would offer other training measures compared to firms without works councils. It can be also implied that works councils can enhance the impact of training on productivity through better selection and motivation of the employees. This paper reviews these hypotheses on the basis of the representative IAB establishment panel and at the same time considers the endogeneity of training supply and the unobserved heterogeneity of firms.
- The empirical analysis shows that works councils promote both, external and internal training measures. They mainly have a positive impact on the especially expensive formal internal and external courses. Therefore, the long-term benefits of works councils for training efficiency are significant.

Keywords Training measures · works councils · productivity

JEL: C23, D21, J24

PD Dr. Thomas Zwick (✉)
is Senior Researcher at the Centre for European Economic Research (ZEW Mannheim) and lecturer at the University of Zurich. Main research areas: personnel management, empirical labour market research and education economics. Centre for European Economic Research (ZEW), Mannheim, L7,1, 68161 Mannheim, Germany; E-mail: zwick@zew.de

A. Introduction

Human capital is an important source for competitive advantage and, accordingly, there is a large body of empirical literature on the productivity effects of training (Dearden et al., 2006; Zwick, 2005). Research results are ambiguous, however. Most of the analyses in fact show that higher training efforts enhance productivity, however the measured effect differ widely. The most important reasons for the differences are selection biases in the decision about training and unobserved heterogeneity of firms – some contributions for example do not take into account that industrial relations as well as management have an influence on both the training decision and on productivity. Moreover, some surveys fail to recognise that training has lagged effects (Bartel, 1995). Eventually, the theoretical literature in fact argues that works councils in Germany have an impact on the supply and effectiveness of the offered training measures (Gerlach and Jirjahn, 2001), however, there is hardly any empirical support for those assumptions (Zwick, 2005). The way firms offer training is important because of a conflict between employees and employers: While employees are rather interested in courses with generally applicable contents, employers favour training with company-specific contents. Here, works councils can possibly use their influence to the employees' benefit.

This article attempts to overcome the existing shortages in the literature about the effects of training on productivity. Because of that, the unobserved heterogeneity is eliminated by calculating differences. The endogeneity of the training supply is accounted for by instrumenting the decision whether training should be offered or not. The period of measuring productivity effects lies completely outside the training period and thus biases resulting from low productivity during training are avoided. Finally, this article considers the productivity effect of a series of different training measures and explores the particular role of works councils in translating training into productivity.

The article is structured as follows. The estimation strategy is outlined and the empirical assumptions are derived. Subsequently, the productivity effects of various training measures are shown taking into account the influence of works councils. The calculations are based on the IAB establishment panel, a representative data set for the entire German economy. The last section provides some conclusions.

B. Estimation strategy

In this paper we estimate a translog production functions where we add a number of different training measures. This procedure gives us the opportunity to take account of productivity effects of different measures at the same time. Unobserved heterogeneity and selectivity are controlled for on the basis of the model by Black und Lynch (2001), also compare Zwick (2004b): In the first estimation step we estimate the time-variant fixed productivity effects based on the variable production factors labour and capital. It is not possible at that stage to integrate all explanatory variables because a series of variables such as the presence of works councils, industrial sector, industrial relations, etc., are usually constant in our short period of time observed. Therefore, these variables would be cancelled when taking time differences. Other variables, like the supply of various training measures, were accounted for only in one wave in the company panel. Thus, we cannot calculate differences here.

The estimation equation for the first step is:

(1) $\ln Y_{i,t} = A + \beta_1 \ln K_{i,t} + \beta_2 \ln K_{i,t}^2 + \beta_3 \ln L_{i,t} + \beta_4 \ln L_{i,t}^2 + \beta_5 \ln L_{i,t} K_{i,t} + v_i + \varepsilon_{i,t}.$

Here, $Y_{i,t}$ is the gross value added of company i in year t. The variable A is a technology parameter, K is the level of capital, L is the number of employees. The invariant fixed effect over the estimation period is denoted with v_i.

In the second estimation step, we explain the fixed effects by time-invariant variables:

(2) $v_i = \beta' V_i + \tau_j' D_{ij} + \zeta_i$ mit $j = 1,..,7.$

In the vector V all covariates are pooled while the dummy vector D equals one whenever one of the seven training types is offered. In detail, we have information about the following training types: Internal vs. external courses or seminars; on-the-job training; participation in presentations, conferences, and trade fairs; job-rotation; self-induced learning with the help of media; quality circles and workshops (also compare Zwick, 2004b). Research shows that firm productivity can be explained with the help of the following additional variables (Black and Lynch, 2001; Zwick, 2006): Presence of a works council, state of technical equipment, industry, validity of or orientation at collective agreements, apprenticeship training, and the shares of different qualification levels of employees. In order to avoid biased standard errors due to errors in variables in the second estimation step, we bootstrap the standard errors using 100 replications.

A Durbin-Wu-Hausman Test shows whether the company's decision to offer training or not is endogeneous, i.e. depends on unobserved factors that also influence productivity. The identification variables for the decision to train are: In the next years problems are expected with the staffing of qualified positions and a higher necessity for training and qualification is anticipated. These variables can explain, on the one hand, whether a company already offers training in the current period. If, for example, a company expects qualification bottlenecks, it can be expected that that variable correlates positively with the current decision about training. At the same time, it cannot be assumed that the expectation of qualification bottlenecks influences the future productivity: On the one hand, human resource managers can be mistaken and, on the other hand, the feared qualification bottlenecks can be avoided with the help of an increase in training efforts in time. Consequently, these variables represent good instruments for modeling the training decision. In the case of endogeneity of training, a Heckman-correction (where the probability of offering training is introduced as an additional explanatory variable) can prevent a bias of the results. The estimation equation for the fixed effects in companies with training ($I_i=1$) and without training ($I_i=0$) are as follows (where Z is the vector of the covariates X plus the instruments):

(3) $E[v_i | I_i = 0] = \beta' V_i + \sigma \dfrac{-\varphi(\gamma' Z_i)}{1 - \Phi(\gamma' Z_i)},$

(4) $$E[v_i \mid I_i = 1] = \beta'V_i + \tau'_j D_{i,j} + \sigma \frac{\varphi(\gamma' Z_i)}{\Phi(\gamma' Z_i)}.$$

A further focus of this paper is on examining the role of works councils for establishments offering various training measures and their productivity effect. From the literature we know that works councils try to enhance employees' flexibility through training (Freeman and Lazear, 1995; Sadowski, Backes-Gellner and Frick, 1995; Gerlach and Jirjahn, 2001; Hübler 2003). That improves the employability of the employees in the case of changes in production or services. Also, with appropriately trained employees, wage raises and improvements in the workload are easier to get. Ultimately, works councils can codetermine who is offered training because they have a legal voice in that matter (Gerlach and Jirjahn, 2001).

Askildsen and Ireland (1993) show that works councils support employee development through general human capital. In the selection of training measures the interests of employers and employees are in a conflict if the employer has to pay for both kinds of training: Companies try to offer little general human capital in order to avoid poaching of employees and demands for wage increases. Employees, on the contrary, are interested in an improvement of their general human capital because that increases their flexibility in the firm and their attractiveness in the labour market (Kuckulenz and Zwick, 2005). Works councils succeed in motivating firms to consider the preferences of employees. Furthermore, they reduce the risk of opportunistic behaviour of employers after investing in human capital and the risk that expensively trained employees are poached by competitors (Gerlach and Jirjahn, 2001). Thus, it can be assumed that firms with works councils are willing to offer and pay for more and especially more general training than firms without works councils. While a series of studies examine the impact of works councils on the amount and efficiency of the offered training, the effect of the type of training has not been considered yet (Zwick, 2004b). That is why we first show in a multinominal probit model whether works councils have an influence on the various training measures (Gerlach et al., 2001).

In a series of articles it has been demonstrated that the production functions of companies with and without works councils are so different that both groups of companies have to estimated separately (Zwick, 2004b). Accordingly, a Chow-Test tests if firms with works councils are sufficiently different from firms without works councils so that a switching regression model is reasonable. Due to the difficulties in modelling the decision for works councils in the model (very few establishments introduce or abandon a works council in our data set and there is no obvious instrument), we have to assume that they are exogenous here. A frequently made argument is that by the time a works council was founded there might have been unobservable factors that influence both, productivity and the presence of works councils such as distributable rents and that this generates an endogeneity problem for works councils. These factors might change however when a works council has been installed a long time ago and having a mixture of works councils with different tenure might mitigate the endogeneity problem.

In this paper, only the group of companies with more than 20 employees is observed that includes a sufficient number of companies with and without works councils (Addison and Teixeira, 2006). Among smaller companies only a few have works councils.

C. Data

The empirical analysis is based on data from the IAB establishment panel. Detailed information about that data set can be found in Bellmann et al. (2000) and Zwick (2004b). The sample of the panel encompasses all establishments with at least one employee that is subject to social insurance. The establishments are annually asked about for example their turnover, employee characteristics, staff problems, investments, innovations, and personnel measures. In irregular intervals also special topics, e.g. training (partly) paid by the establishment and the specific training forms offered, are integrated in the questionnaire.

Capital is not surveyed directly and therefore approximated by investment. Thereby, the so-called "perpetual inventory method" is used (Black and Lynch, 2001 or Zwick, 2004a). The capital basis in period t is determined by the sum of average investment growth and the average depreciation rate. The capital stock in the consequent period $t+1$ is determined by the old capital stock in the period t plus the extension investments. The logic behind that approach is that average firms depreciate and replace a fixed part of their capital. Therefore, it is implicitly assumed that the replacement investment roughly corresponds to the depreciation.

There are three indicators for "employee participation" that are closely correlated (downward relocation of responsibility, introduction of teamwork or autonomous work groups, introduction of units with own cost/benefit calculation). That is the result of a factor analysis that suggests to integrate all three indicators into a single factor, compare Zwick (2004a). The factor captures 61% of the whole variation and exhibits a Kaiser-Meyer-Olkin value of 0.70. The factor weights of the single indicators are furthermore sufficiently high (see table A2).

We exclude those establishments that are not profit-oriented and those that have outsourced or insourced other establishments. Furthermore, establishments with less than 20 employees and establishments from the agricultural sector, as well as banks and insurances are not taken into consideration in order to reduce the heterogeneity of the sample and to ensure that employees have had the opportunity to install a works council.

In order to control for the lagged effects of training on productivity, the second stage is estimated with information about training and the other covariates in the year 1997. The firm productivity is estimated in the panel of the first estimation step in the period 1998–2001.

D. Results

Works councils support, as predicted by the theoretical literature, the supply of training (Gerlach and Jirjahn, 2001; Gerlach et al., 2002; Zwick, 2004b). In table 1, establishments are separated in three distinct groups – those that do not carry out training; firms that offer external training or training that is not attended during the working hours (external courses, seminars, presentations, trade fairs, and self-induced learning); and firms that offer internal training measures (internal courses, on-the-job training, quality circles). The idea behind that separation is to examine whether works councils facilitate training and what kind of training (internal or external) is being supported. Hereby we assume that in the external training forms rather general human capital is developed, while in internal training rather firm-specific capital is introduced (Kuckulenz and Zwick, 2005). An advantage of that method is that other reasons for offering certain training measures are controlled for, e.g. firm size, industry, etc. We find, on the one hand, that works councils support the supply of both internal and external training. However, works councils make no difference in the choice of offering either merely external or merely internal training – the partial correlation coefficient of works councils is even a little higher for internal than for external training. Furthermore, it is interesting to note that large firms rarely offer only external training, while there are many large firms that offer exclusively internal training.

Tab. 1. What influence do works councils have on training types? Multinomial logit for 1997

Exogenous Variables	External Training Coefficients	t-Values	Internal Training Coefficients	t-Values
Apprenticeship training	0.393**	2.56	0.528***	4.21
Collective agreements	0.032	0.20	0.336**	2.45
Share of qualified workers	1.069***	3.76	1.324***	6.03
Export	0.055	0.23	-0.141	-0.79
Modern technical facilities	0.115	0.77	0.550***	4.55
Investment in ICT	0.198	1.18	0.455***	3.44
Works council	0.413**	2.19	0.638***	4.23
Factor employee participation	0.044	0.83	0.067*	1.65
Formally defined regulations in staffing	0.002	0.01	0.497***	3.00
Incentive wages	0.187	0.61	0.641***	2.67
Establishment size 200-499	0.168	0.59	1.297***	6.36
Establishment size 500-999	-1.419*	-1.85	1.465***	4.88
Establishment size 1000+	-0.118	-0.13	2.607***	4.34
Constant	-1.827***	-6.43	-1.477***	-6.91
13 Sector- Dummies and Dummy for East Germany	Yes		Yes	
Number of observations	2391			
Pseudo R^2	0.17			

Note: Reference category is "no training". The significance levels are reproduced with the help of asterisks: *** significantly under 1%, ** under 5%, and * under 10%.
Source: IAB establishment panel, waves 1997 – 2001, own estimation.

The implementation of the two-step estimation strategy for avoiding the unobserved heterogeneity and biases due to endogeneity of training shows that not all training types have a positive impact on productivity (see also Zwick, 2005): External training, self-induced learning, and quality circles have a positive effect, while on-the-job training, job rotation, and internal courses have no effect on productivity, see table 2.

We might assume that the production functions for firms with and without works councils differ in many respects and therefore we test this using a Chow-test. It indeed shows

Tab. 2. Influence of training type on productivity, dependent variable: average fixed effect 1998 – 2001

Exogenous Variables	OLS Regression		OLS Regression with selection correction	
	Equation (2)			
	Coefficients	t-Values	Coefficients	t-Values
External courses and seminars	0.179***	2.67	0.247**	2.50
Internal courses and seminars	0.145**	2.08	0.152**	2.13
On-the-job training	- 0.045	- 0.65	- 0.031	-0.40
Participation in presentations, conferences, trade fairs, etc.	- 0.058	- 0.89	- 0.054	-0.87
Job rotation	- 0.015	- 0.18	0.025	0.29
Self-induced learning with the help of media	0.151**	2.27	0.139**	2.01
Quality circles, workshops	0.163**	2.41	0.110	1.45
Apprenticeship training	0.095	1.54	0.055	0.84
Collective agreements	0.160**	2.48	0.160**	2.56
Share of qualified workers	0.490***	4.05	0.478***	4.25
Export	0.164**	2.37	0.117*	1.71
Modern technical facilities	0.193***	3.78	0.214***	4.55
Investment in ICT	0.042	0.78	0.049	1.00
Works council	0.456***	7.54	0.455***	7.77
Factor employee participation	- 0.003**	- 0.22	- 0.004	-0.27
Formally defined regulations in staffing	0.116	2.01	0.126**	2.25
Incentive wages	0.085	1.18	0.058	0.75
Establishment size 200-499	0.468***	6.20	0.501***	6.90
Establishment size 500-999	0.485***	3.85	0.489***	3.49
Establishment size 1000+	0.709***	5.96	0.708***	5.95
Constant	- 0.414***	- 2.72	- 0.424***	-3.08
Selection correction term			0.060	0.92
13 Sector- Dummies and Dummy for East Germany	Yes		Yes	
Number of observations	1093		1057	
Adjusted R²	0.52		0.51	

Note: The significance levels are reproduced with the help of asterisks: *** significantly under 1%, ** under 5%, and * under 10%, bootstrapped standard errors with 100 replications.
Source: IAB establishment panel, waves 1997 – 2001, own estimation.

that both production functions are significantly different and therefore should be estimated separately.[1] According to our theoretical considerations we also find that in companies with works councils the training effect is higher than in companies without works councils (see also Zwick, 2004a). The Durbin-Wu-Hausman test shows that both instruments have a significant explanatory power.[2] This means that the decision for training is endogeneous and a Heckman-correction should be implemented.

The selection term for training in the Heckman-correction is significantly positive only in firms with works councils (see table 3). A possible interpretation is that firms stimulate

Tab. 3. Influence of training type on productivity, dependent variable: average fixed effect 1998 – 2001

Exogenous Variables	Establishment without works council Equation (3)		Establishment with works council Equation (4)	
	Coefficients	t-values	Coefficients	t-values
External courses and seminars	0.087	0.63	0.465***	3.21
Internal courses and seminars	0.163	1.60	0.145*	1.68
On-the-job training	- 0.063	- 0.61	- 0.011	- 0.10
Participation in presentations, conferences, trade fairs, etc.	- 0.011	- 0.10	- 0.165*	- 1.74
Job rotation	- 0.039	- 0.23	0.031	0.36
Self-induced learning with the help of media	0.175	1.03	0.108	1.35
Quality circles, workshops	0.265	1.53	0.080	1.07
Apprenticeship training	0.052	0.63	0.092	0.92
Collective agreements	0.107	1.29	0.224**	1.98
Share of qualified workers	0.561***	2.91	0.415**	2.41
Export	0.170	1.46	0.045	0.54
Modern technical facilities	0.192**	2.43	0.254***	4.32
Investment in ICT	0.072	0.90	- 0.015	- 0.19
Factor employee participation	0.009	0.39	- 0.019	- 1.02
Formally defined regulations in staffing	0.084	0.90	0.109	1.55
Incentive wages	- 0.053	- 0.38	0.182*	1.73
Establishment size 200-499	0.524***	2.90	0.471***	4.94
Establishment size 500-999	0.740	0.97	0.472***	3.48
Establishment size 1000+	0.209	0.21	0.761***	6.53
Selection correction	- 0.042	-0.46	0.191**	2.08
Constant	- 0.361	- 1.62	- 0.039	- 0.18
15 Sector- Dummies and Dummy for East Germany	Yes		Yes	
Number of observations	505		552	
Adjusted R^2	0.25		0.44	

Note: The significance levels are reproduced with the help of asterisks: *** significantly under 1%, ** under 5%, and * under 10%, bootstrapped standard errors with 100 replications.
Source: IAB establishment panel, waves 1997 – 2001, own estimation.

training especially in firms that have a productivity disadvantage (also compare Zwick, 2006). We find that the productivity effect of internal and external courses in firms with works councils is significant, while it is not detectable in firms without works councils. If we fully interact the works council dummy with all covariates, we find that formal external training leads to a significantly higher productivity impact in establishments with works councils, while it leads to a significantly lower productivity impact of the participation at trade fairs, conferences and presentations. This implies that works councils have an impact on who is selected for the relatively expensive external courses[3] and suggest those employees who would experience a significant improvement of their qualifications and skills.

E. Conclusions

This paper shows that the supply of external and internal courses, self-induced learning, as well as quality circles, have a positive and significant effect on the gross added value in German firms. Firms that offered at least one of these training measures in 1997 were able to enhance their productivity by up to 45% for the period 1998-2001, provided these firms have works councils. Without works councils the productivity enhancement for all training measures was considerably smaller and less significant. It can be assumed that the attainable productivity effect in firms that do not offer training, would be significantly lower.

This article considers the selectivity of the decision about the supply of training measures and uses expected qualification bottlenecks as external instruments that explain the firm's training decision. The consideration of that selectivity increases the estimated productivity effect of most of the training measures. That points to the fact that establishments offer training especially in periods of a productivity deficit and on the other hand, it suggests that the instrumental variables estimation reduces the error in measurement in the training variables. The selection term is significant only in the case of establishments with works councils. Furthermore, the unobserved time-invariant heterogeneity of establishments is taken account of in a first estimation of a production function. In a second step, the fixed effects derived from the first estimation step, are explained with the help of time-invariant firm characteristics including seven training measures.

Ultimately, it is shown that the presence of a works council has a positive effect on productivity of especially expensive internal and external courses. Obviously, the long-term benefits of works councils for training efficiency are significant, i.e. in avoiding poaching, opportunistic behaviour, in mediation between training interests of employees and employers, and in the efficient selection of training participants.

Appendix

Tab. A1a. Descriptive statistics production function 1998 – 2001

Variables	1998	1999	2000	2001	Notes
Gross added value	12.85	12.92	13.07	13.14	Turnover minus input costs, in DM, in logs
Capital	12.45	12.41	12.44	12.48	Constructed with the help of the perpetual inventory method, in DM, in logs
Labour	1.95	1.92	1.96	1.97	Number of employees, in logs

Notes: Shares are calculated from the samples used in the production functions and are weighed.
Source: IAB firm panel, waves 1997 – 2001, own estimation.

Tab. A1b. Descriptive statistics covariates 1997 or 1998

Variables	1997	1998	Notes
External courses and seminars	0.66		Dummy variable. Supply in the first half-year 1997
Internal courses and seminars	0.50		
On-the-job training	0.51		
Participation in presentations, conferences, trade fairs, etc.	0.52		
Job rotation	0.12		
Self-induced learning with the help of media	0.18		
Quality circles, workshops	0.17		
Share of qualified workers	0.59		Share of employees with training qualification
Export	0.13		Firm exports. yes=1. no=0
Modern technical facilities	0.68		Technical facilities are up-to-date. yes=1. no=0
Works councils		0.20	Establishment has a works council. yes=1. no=0
Collective wage agreements	0.61		Establishment participates in collective agreements or orients itself on them. yes=1. no=0
Single company	0.36		Establishment is a single company. yes=1. no=0
Limited company	0.10		Establishment is a limited company. yes=1. no=0
Corporation	0.04		Establishment is a corporation. yes=1. no=0
Limited liability company	0.52		Establishment is a limited liability company. yes=1. no=0
Higher requirement for training and qualification (Instrument)	0.10		Establishment expects higher necessity for training and qualification in the next two years. yes=1. no=0
Expected problems in finding employees for qualified positions (Instrument)	0.35		Establishment expects problems in finding suitably skilled employees. yes=1. no=0
Apprenticeship training	0.51		Establishment employs apprentices. yes=1. no=0
Incentive payment	0.07		Establishment offers incentive payment. yes=1. no=0
Formally defined regulations in staffing	0.16		Establishment has formal regulations in staffing. yes=1. no=0

Note: Shares are calculated from the samples used in the production functions and are weighed.
Source: IAB firm panel, Waves 1997 – 2001, own estimation.

Tab. A2. Component matrix of the factor analysis

Factor	Factor value	Variables	Factor weight
Participation	1.82	Delegation of responsibility to lower hierarchies	0.81
		Introduction of teamwork / self dependent work groups	0.80
		Introduction of units with own cost/benefit calculation	0.72

Tab. A3. Fixed effects estimation of the production function, gross added 1998 – 2001, equation (1)

	Coefficients	t-values
Capital	0.227 *	1,78
Capital*Capital	- 0.017	- 1,43
Labour	0.214	1,15
Labour*Labour	0.063 *	1,80
Labour*Capital	0.007	0,42
Year Dummy 1999	0.018	1,09
Year Dummy 2000	0.078 ***	4,75
Year Dummy 2001	- 0.575 ***	- 33,27
Constant	11.602 ***	15,16
13 Sector dummies	yes	
Number of observations	10301	
Number of firms	6004	
Wald-Test for mutual significance: 374.16	p = 0.00	

Note: Heteroscedasticity-robust standard error.

Endnotes

* This paper benefitted from comments of seminar participants in Konstanz and Dresden. It won the 2006 Ernst & Young Conference Best Paper Award at the 68th annual conference of the Association of University Professors of Management (VHB). The estimations have been performed by controlled remote data access via the Forschungsdatenzentrum of the Bundesagentur für Arbeit (FDZ). I am especially grateful to two anonymous referees for helpful comments and to Dana Müller and Peter Jacobebbinghaus from the FDZ for their help in accessing the data.
1 The test value of $X^2(30)=84.65$ is significant at the 5%-level.
2 The Durbin-Wu-Hausman test value is 3.31 and significant at the 1%-level. At the same time, none of the instruments has a significant impact on the productivity equation, neither individually, nor jointly.
3 The instruments are: In the next years problems are expected with the staffing of qualified positions and a higher necessity for training and qualification is anticipated. The Durbin-Wu-Hausman test value is 3.31 and significant at the 1%-level. At the same time, none of the instruments has a significant impact on the productivity equation, neither individually, nor jointly.

References

Addison, John and Teixeira, Paulino (2006): The Effect of Worker Representation on Employment Behavior in Germany, Industrial Relations, 45 (1), 1–25.

Askildsen, Jan and Ireland, Norman (1993): Human Capital, Property Rights and Labour Managed Firms, Oxford Economic Papers, 45, 229–242.

Bartel, Ann (1995): Training, Wage Growth, and Job Performance: Evidence from a Company Database, Journal of Labor Economics, 13, 401–425.

Bellmann, Lutz, Kölling, Arnd, Kistler, Ernst, Hilpert, Markus, Heinecker, Paula and Conrads, Ralph (2000): Codebook zum IAB-Betriebspanel, Nürnberg.

Black, Sandra and Lynch, Lisa (2001): How to Compete: The Impact of Workplace Practices and Information Technology on Productivity, The Review of Economics and Statistics, 83, 434–445.

Dearden, Lorraine, Reed, Howard and Reenen, John van (2006): The Impact of Training on Productivity and Wages: Evidence from British Panel Data, Oxford Bulletin of Economics and Statistics, 68 (4), 397–421.

Freeman, Richard B. and Lazear, Edward P. (1995): An Economic Analysis of Works Councils. In: Rogers, Joel und Streeck, Wolfgang (eds.): Works Councils: Consultation, Representation, and Cooperation in Industrial Relations, Chicago: University of Chicago Press, 27–52.

Gerlach, Knut and Jirjahn, Uwe (2001): Employer Provided Further Training: Evidence from German Establishment Data, Schmollers Jahrbuch, 121 (2), 139–164.

Gerlach, Knut, Hübler, Olaf and Meyer, Wolfgang (2002): Investitionen, Weiterbildung und betriebliche Reorganisation, Mitteilungen aus der Arbeitsmarkt- und Berufsforschung, 35(4), 546–565.

Hübler, Olaf (2003): Fördern oder behindern Betriebsräte die Unternehmensentwicklung? Perspektiven der Wirtschaftspolitik, 4 (4), 379–398.

Kuckulenz, Anja and Thomas Zwick (2005): Heterogene Einkommenseffekte betrieblicher Weiterbildung, Die Betriebswirtschaft, 65 (3), 258–275.

Sadowski, Dieter, Backes-Gellner, Uschi and Frick, Bernd (1995): Betriebsräte in Deutschland: Gespaltene Rationalitäten?. In: Herder-Dornreich, Phillip, Schenk, Karl-Ernst und Schmidtchen, Dieter (Hrsg.): Jahrbuch für Neue Politische Ökonomie, Bd. 14, Tübingen, 157–181.

Zwick, Thomas (2004a): Employee Participation and Productivity, Labour Economics, 11 (6), 715–740.

Zwick, Thomas (2004b), Weiterbildungsintensität und betriebliche Produktivität, Zeitschrift für Betriebswirtschaft, 74 (7), 651–668.

Zwick, Thomas (2005): Continuing Vocational Training Forms and Establishment Productivity in Germany, German Economic Review, 6 (1), 155–184.

Zwick, Thomas (2006): The Impact of Training Intensity on Establishment Productivity, Industrial Relations, 45 (1), 26–46.

Works Councils and the Productivity Effects of Different Continuing Training Measures

Summary

Works councils have an important influence on the types of training measures that are offered in a firm and on the selection of training participants. Firms are more inclined to offer training with specific human capital, while employees rather benefit from general human capital. Therefore it can be assumed that firms with works councils that function as mediators and voice for the staff, would offer other training measures compared to firms without works councils. It can be also implied that works councils can enhance the impact of training on productivity through better selection and motivation of the employees. This paper reviews these hypotheses on the basis of the representative IAB establishment panel and at the same time considers the endogeneity of training supply and the unobserved heterogeneity of firms.

The empirical analysis shows that works councils promote both formal external and internal training measures. They mainly have a positive impact on the especially expensive internal and external courses. Therefore, the long-term benefits of works councils for training efficiency are significant.

Betriebsräte und die Produktivitätswirkungen unterschiedlicher betrieblicher Weiterbildungsarten

Zusammenfassung

Betriebsräte üben einen wichtigen Einfluss darauf aus, welche Weiterbildungsarten in einem Betrieb angeboten werden und wer Weiterbildung bekommt. Da Unternehmen eher geneigt sind, Weiterbildung mit spezifischem Humankapital anzubieten, während Beschäftigte Kurse mit eher allgemeinem Humankapital bevorzugen, kann vermutet werden, dass Betriebe mit Betriebsräten, die eine Vermittler- und Sprachrohrfunktion der Belegschaft einnehmen, andere Weiterbildungsarten anbieten als Betriebe ohne Betriebsräte. Es kann zudem vermutet werden, dass Betriebsräte die Produktivitätswirkung von Weiterbildung durch eine zielgenauere Auswahl und eine besser Motivation der Beschäftigten erhöhen. Dieses Papier überprüft diese Hypothesen auf der Basis des repräsentativen IAB Betriebspanels und berücksichtigt gleichzeitig die Endogenität des Angebots von Weiterbildung und unbeobachtete Heterogenität der Unternehmen. Die empirische Analyse demonstriert, dass Betriebsräte sowohl interne als auch externe Weiterbildung fördern und hauptsächlich die teuere formelle interne und externe Weiterbildung unterstützen. Dadurch bringen Betriebsräte langfristig signifikante Vorteile für die Weiterbildungseffizienz.

A comprehensive/extensive and up-to-date management tool box

Michael Grabinski
Management Methods and Tools
Practical Know-how for Students, Managers, and Consultants
2007. xvi, 257 pp. With 76 Fig. Softc.
EUR 29,90 ISBN 978-3-8349-0383-9

This textbook includes the most important methods and tools for managers and consultants. The author does not restrict himself to describing the scientific methods but also shows how to apply them to real-life situations. The management tools he introduces have been successfully tested during 20 years of experience. The various methods are described and analysed in detail, and many examples illustrate their application. Thus, the textbook gives a fundamental and comprehensive insight into the practice of successful management. It is clearly structured and provides essential in-depth knowledge for students as well as for managers and consultants.

The Author
Professor Dr. Michael Grabinski is professor for business administration at the University of Applied Sciences Neu-Ulm, independent management consultant, and chairman of the board of BITE AG, Filderstadt.

Content
_ Introduction
_ Business process modeling
_ Balanced scorecard
_ Controlling process
_ Organization
_ Quantitative tools
_ Operations management

Order your copy now: kerstin.kuchta@gwv-fachverlage.de Telefon +49(0)611. 7878-626

KOMPETENZ IN SACHEN WIRTSCHAFT

Public Employment Services and Employers: How Important are Networks with Firms?

Stefanie Behncke, Markus Frölich, Michael Lechner*

Abstract

- This paper examines whether contacts between caseworkers in public employment offices and employers impact on the reemployment chances of the unemployed they counsel. This analysis is made possible through a large administrative dataset on unemployed combined with an extensive survey of caseworkers' characteristics and their strategies. This data was created for evaluating public employment services in Switzerland. We use econometric techniques from the treatment evaluation literature to identify causal effects of a more intense employer focus of the caseworkers. The estimation results indicate that caseworkers who maintain direct contacts to firms achieve higher reintegration rates.

Keywords Public employment services · new public management · employer focus

JEL: J68

Stefanie Behncke (✉)
(Dipl.-Volksw., MSc) is scientific assistant at the University of St. Gallen. e-mail: Stefanie.Behncke@unisg.ch

Dr. Markus Frölich (✉)
is professor at the University of Mannheim, e-mail: Markus.Froelich@unisg.ch

Prof. Dr. Michael Lechner (✉)
is Professor of Empirical Economics and Econometrics at the University of St. Gallen. Research interests: applied labor market economics, especially evaluation of active labor market policies and training programmes, empirical health economics and microeconometrics with focus on policy evaluation.
e-mail: Michael.Lechner@unisg.ch, www.siaw.unisg.ch/lechner

A. Introduction

This paper examines whether a network between employment offices' caseworkers and employers affects the reemployment chances of the unemployed. Direct contacts to employers might provide caseworkers with additional information on vacancies, skill requirements, and current developments in the local labour market. This information and the direct relationship itself may assist the placement of the unemployed. On the other hand, employer contacts also consume a substantial share of caseworkers' time, which otherwise could have been spent on other activities. To analyse this trade-off, we examine the impact of a direct relationship between caseworkers and employers on the employment chances of their unemployed clients. We find that caseworkers who maintain such networks with firms achieve higher employment rates. In particular, the less skilled of their unemployed clients benefit most.

Public employment services are supposed to assist in the matching of unemployed to employers and thereby reduce the unemployment rate. Given the large public expenditures devoted to employment services, there is a considerable interest in enhancing their effectiveness.[2] One channel that has received public attention recently is the attitude towards *employers*. In recent years, several countries progressively entered the employers as an additional client group besides unemployed and jobseekers. Caseworkers no longer focus mainly only on counselling, job search training and other active labour market programmes, placement, verification of job search efforts and imposing sanctions if needed, but engage in direct contacts with firms. Private firms and companies are courted by caseworkers in an attempt to encourage the registration of vacancies and to brighten the image of unemployed persons. This focus on employers received increasing attention in Germany, UK, Switzerland, and other countries. In Germany, jobcentres should devote at least 20 percent of their placement capacities to employers, introduce so-called employer managers as a new staff position, and segment employers into different types of client groups (Schütz and Ochs, 2005). In the UK, the employer service directorate was set up in 2001/2002 to engage with employers in making public jobcentres the preferred recruitment channel (Bunt, McAndrew, and Kuechel, 2005). Not only are caseworkers asked to establish and maintain direct, even personal relationships with firms and their human resources departments, they are also encouraged to endorse the firms' perspective and particular needs, which may even be considered as a marketing strategy to improve the image of the public employment offices. In this paper, we examine whether a more intensive employer focus increases the employment chances of the unemployed. Due to data availability, we focus on Switzerland.

This paper also contributes to the literature on effective *organization of public institutions*, where the lack of market competition does not ensure that only the most effective organizational forms survive. Asymmetric information and conflicting goals may hinder achieving optimal organization forms in this principal-agent relationship. External evaluations may therefore be needed to provide guidance on improving organizational structures. The effectiveness of public employment services has been analyzed from a macroeconometric perspective, e.g. by estimating job-vacancy matching functions as in Berman (1997). Only little empirical research has taken a microeconometric perspective. Sheldon (2003) and Vassiliev et al. (2006), for instance, analyse the efficiency of Swiss employment offices by linking input factors such as the number of counsellors to performance measures. Although both studies find considerable inefficiencies,[3] they are not able to explain fully the differences between efficient and inefficient offices. This paper complements this type of research by analysing whether employer contacts affect efficiency by changing the reemployment chances for the unemployment.

In the next section, we describe the institutional details for Switzerland and explore reasons why the intensity and the form of the caseworker to employer interaction might be an important determinant of job finding rates. In section C, we describe the data set, which consists of administrative data linking unemployed, caseworkers, and employment offices, complemented with an extensive survey of all Swiss caseworkers asking about their characteristics and strategies. Section D provides descriptive statistics, and Section E explains the concept of causality and the identification strategy used. It also presents briefly the *propensity score matching* estimator used to disentangle causal effects from correlations. The empirical results are presented in Section F, which suggest that unemployed persons indeed benefit from a direct link between caseworkers to firms. Three appendices provide further details on the econometrics and the empirical results.

B. The Swiss public employment services

1. The Swiss unemployment insurance system

Until the recession of the early 1990s, unemployment was very low in Switzerland, a small country with 26 different administrative regions, called *cantons*. With the recession, the unemployment rate rose rapidly to more than 5% (see Figure 1). This triggered a

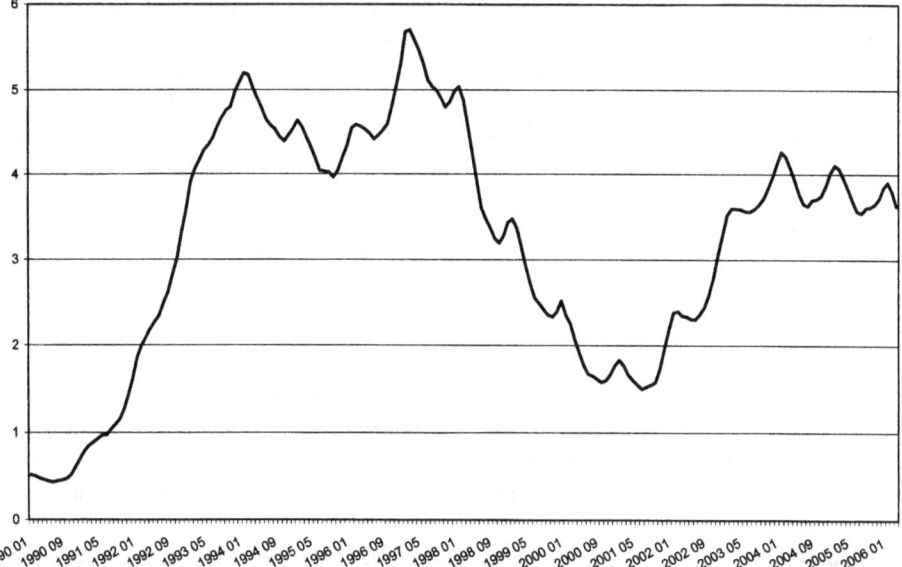

Fig. 1. Swiss unemployment rate (January 1990 - December 2006)
Note: Monthly unemployment rate. Source: Swiss national bank (Monatshefte).

comprehensive revision of the federal unemployment insurance act in 1996/1997. With this revision, the about 3000 municipal unemployment offices were consolidated to a smaller number of regional employment offices (REO). Compared to the previous municipal offices, which were largely concerned with administering unemployment benefits, these regional offices, of which there were about 110 employment offices[4] operating in 2003, aimed at providing professional services with respect to counselling, placement, activation, and training.

The federal State Secretariat for Economic Affairs (*seco*) established four targets that the employment offices should pursue with respect to 'their' unemployed clients: rapid de-registration, prevention of long-term unemployment, prevention of benefit exhaustion and prevention of re-registration. In order to achieve these targets, well-trained caseworkers provide counselling and placements services and assign active labour market programmes such as subsidized employment or training to the unemployed to qualify them for the requirements of employers. Unemployed persons are requested to accept any suitable job-offer, to participate in assigned labour market programmes, and to exhibit sufficient search effort. Otherwise, sanctions in the form of benefit cuts could be imposed. Another important activity of caseworkers is establishing and strengthening contacts to (local) employers.

2. Caseworker interactions with employers

Caseworkers vary with regard to their employer interactions in two aspects: Intensity and channels of contact. Depending on the size and organizational structure of the employment office, some caseworker have *direct*, more intensive contacts to employers, while others have rather *indirect* contacts. The latter comprehends intermediation channels such as vacancies posted in newspapers or on the Internet. It also comprehends a specialization within the employment office, where some caseworkers specialize on maintaining close contacts to employers while the other caseworkers use them as intermediaries. Caseworkers differ also in their perception of the role of employers: some caseworkers consider them as an additional client group, which should be offered good services. Others would not regard the employers as a client group by itself but rather consider employer contacts only as a means to offer better services to their unemployed.

One may ask whether a caseworker should devote a share of his time to direct employer contacts. A more intensive contact to employers could provide caseworkers with additional insights on the job market. Such an informal knowledge might assist caseworkers in matching unemployed to appropriate employers. Caseworkers might also gain some private information on job openings or receive information earlier. On the other hand, contacting employers is time consuming and thus reduces the amount of time available for counselling, consolation in case of personal problems, psychological backing, controlling, and sanctions, etc. Other sources of information, e.g. the Internet or Intranet, might be more efficient for placing unemployed or updating knowledge on the current labour market situation.

Another question concerns the optimal form of the interaction between employers and caseworkers. In Switzerland, employers are not obliged to register open vacancies with the employment offices. If the employment office aims for an active placement strategy, it is important that the potential employers consider the employment office to offer a useful placement channel. There is anecdotal evidence that at least some employment offices initially pursued a strategy that was in contrast to the employer's interests: By assigning job placements to unemployed persons frequently, they attempted to force individuals to search harder for jobs and imposed sanctions if the unemployed person did reject too many job placements. This strategy, however, increased the administrative burden on the side of the employers, which received a large number of inadequate or unmotivated unemployed. Thus, employers became reluctant to contact employment offices for filling vacancies. Over time, the annoyance of the firms reduced the leeway of the employment offices. This then induced a gradual shift of the employment offices towards a more employer friendly attitude, which, of course, in turn jeopardises the instrument of forced job placements for exerting pressure. This shift in orientation, however, was not centrally enacted. It took place in different locations at different times and different paces.[5]

We exploit these differences in the employer focus and the handling of employer contacts across employment offices in 2003 to estimate their effects on the employment chances of their unemployed until December 2006. Figure 1 showed that the unemployment rate was relatively stable in that period such that any changes in our estimated effects over time are unlikely to be a simple reflection of changes in the business cycle but rather can be interpreted as short-term versus mid-term effects of employer contacts. This sheds some light on the effects on job stability. If e.g. more employer contacts simply increased the outflow rate into low pay or unstable jobs, we would expect positive short-term effects but much smaller (or even zero) mid term effects. On the other hand, a stable unemployment rate also means that our policy conclusions are restricted to this labour market environment and may not necessarily be valid in periods of economic booms or declines.

C. Data

1. Data sources and sample selection

We conducted a detailed survey among all caseworkers to investigate the intensity and channels of employer interactions. We sent a questionnaire to them and all employment office managers who worked in an employment office between 2001 and 2003, and still worked there by the end of 2004. The questionnaire was returned by 1560 individuals, which represents a response rate of 84%. These questionnaires were then linked to data on the caseworkers' clients from the unemployment and pension registers. For each unemployed person the *first* caseworker during her unemployment spell is considered.[6] We thereby can link each unemployed person to his caseworker's activities.

The population of unemployed used for our analysis is the inflow into unemployment in the year 2003. The labour market outcomes of these unemployed persons are followed until the end of 2006. Very detailed individual information from the databases of the unemployment insurance system (AVAM/ASAL) and the social security records (AHV) are available for these individuals. These data sources contain for example socioeconomic characteristics, including nationality and type of work permit, qualification, education, language skills (mother tongue, proficiency of foreign languages), experience, profession, position and industry of last job, occupation and industry of the desired job as well as an employability rating by the caseworker. The data also contains detailed information on registration and de-registration of unemployment, benefit payments and sanctions, participation in ALMP, and the entire employment histories from January 1990 with monthly information on earnings and employment status (employed, unemployed, non-employed, self-employed).

In total 239004 persons registered as newly unemployed during the year 2003. We consider only the first registration in 2003 for each person and consider any further registrations as part of the outcome variables. In other words, the analysis is person based and not spell based. Of these individuals, 219540 persons registered in one of the 103 employment offices that are included in our study.[7] For 215251 persons the first caseworker is well defined, whereas for the other 4289 no caseworker in charge could be found. Furthermore, we exclude 1441 foreigners with less than a yearly work permit, 16481 unemployed without benefit entitlements, and 5778 individuals who either have a disability insurance claim or apply for one, since these individuals receive different services. 191551 individuals are left in our sample after this selection. We conduct most of our estimations within the subpopulation of individuals older than 24 and younger than 55.

2. Definition of outcomes: employment

To be able to use the most recent data, we rely on the information system of the unemployment insurance (AVAM/ASAL), which only provides us with information on transitions into and out of unemployment but not much information on employment spells. We have to rely on recorded destination states of the unemployed persons when leaving the unemployment register. We define an individual as employed in month t if she has deregistered at the employment office because of having found an occupation, and has not re-registered yet. She is considered as not employed if she had de-registered with a destination state other than employment or if still being unemployed. When repeated unemployment spells occur, the most recent information is used, of course. This definition may be subject to some measurement error because a de-registered individual could have left the active labour force or could have found an occupation after de-registering without claiming one. Nevertheless, we were able to compare the information from the unemployment insurance system with the employment information from the pension funds, though only for a shorter period in which both data sets overlap, and found that our measure of the employment situation is fairly reliable (see Frölich et al. 2007 for more details).

To analyse the dynamic impacts of the caseworker's employer interaction on the employment probabilities, the employment status of the unemployed person is measured month by month until the end of the observation period in December 2006. Hence, for individuals who registered in January 2003, their employment situation is observed for 47 months, whereas only 35 months are observed for those registering in December 2003. This allows us to estimate the effects of the caseworker-employer interactions not only in the short term but also in the medium term.

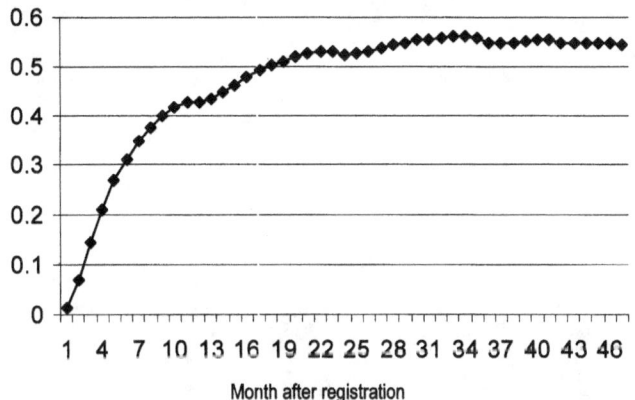

Fig. 2. Average employment rate in month t after registering as unemployed

Figure 2 shows the evolvement of the employment rate for the population of this study. It presents the employment rate in month t after registration at the employment office for the population who registered as newly unemployed during 2003. About 2% of the population de-registers one month after registering because of having found an occupation. About 10% have found a new job after two months and about 45% (55%) have found an employment one year (two and more years) after they became unemployed.

D. Descriptive analysis of contacts with employers

In order to measure the interactions between caseworker and employers we use the data on the survey questions, which had been administered to the caseworkers. As argued above, direct contacts to employers might give caseworkers crucial information for effective placement of the unemployed. The question most informative about this aspect is the following (translated):

Which source did you *mainly* use in order to obtain information regarding current labour market developments, vacancies, required skills etc? (max. 3 options)

☐₁ database of the REO (AVAM)   ☐₅ direct contact with employers
☐₂ Internet   ☐₆ other caseworkers
☐₃ newspapers   ☐₇ courses and talks
☐₄ professional journals   ☐₈ other: ....

Caseworkers could choose three out of eight options. Around 44% stated that they used direct contacts with employers as one of the three main sources of information. As Figure 3 indicates, employers are one of the major information sources of caseworkers.

We define caseworkers who chose the option "direct contact with employers" as caseworkers who have a more intensive contact with employers, whereas those who did not choose this option are regarded as having less direct and less intensive contacts. While

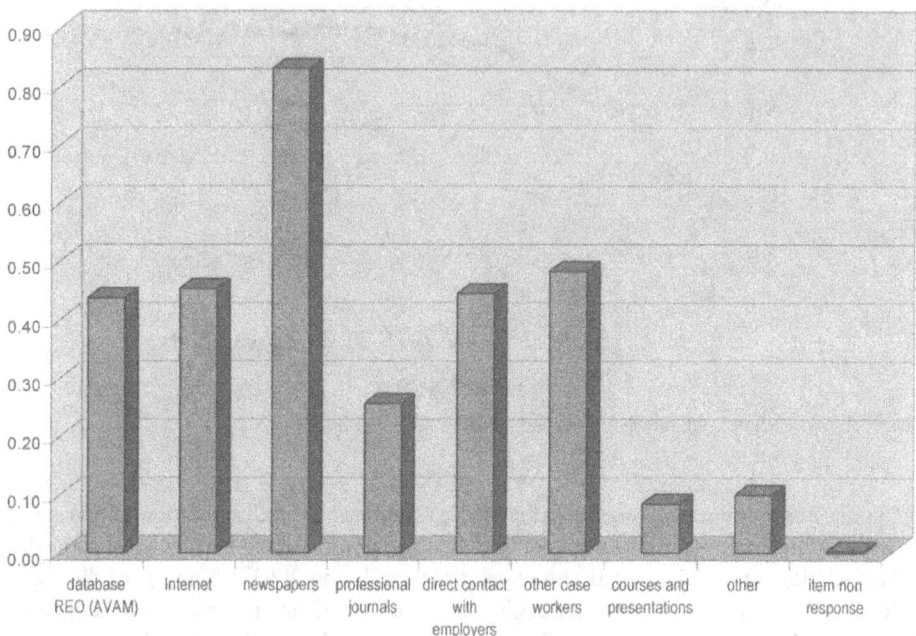

Fig. 3. Main sources of information
Note: Percentage of workers who mentioned the respective source. 1441 caseworkers.

there could be different ways to measure the intensity of a contact, e.g. number of phone calls or visits at firm, we argue that the more crucial criterion for the employment prospects of the unemployed is whether important information is actually obtained. Thus, we use *direct* and *intense* and *considering employer as important information source* as synonyms in this paper.

We aim at identifying the *causal* effect of having a caseworker with a more intensive employer contact on the employment prospects of her unemployed. A naïve estimator of this causal effect would be to compare labour market outcomes of those unemployed whose caseworkers had direct employer contacts with those whose contacts were less pronounced, as is shown in Figure 4. However, if those two groups of unemployed (and caseworkers) are different in important characteristics that influence employment chances as well, the graphs in Figure 4 partly reflect these unobserved characteristics. Suppose, for example, that caseworkers with more intensive employer contacts have longer tenure with their employment office as well. If caseworkers with longer tenure are also more able in placing their unemployed, then the comparison as in Figure 4 does not provide the ceteris paribus effect of direct employer contacts but is partly due to the differences in caseworkers' tenure. For policy implications, however, it is crucial to know whether *changing* employer interactions (holding everything else constant) improves employment prospects, or not.

In Figure 4, we note cyclicality in the employment rate among those unemployed whose caseworkers have direct contacts to employers. The employment rates decrease

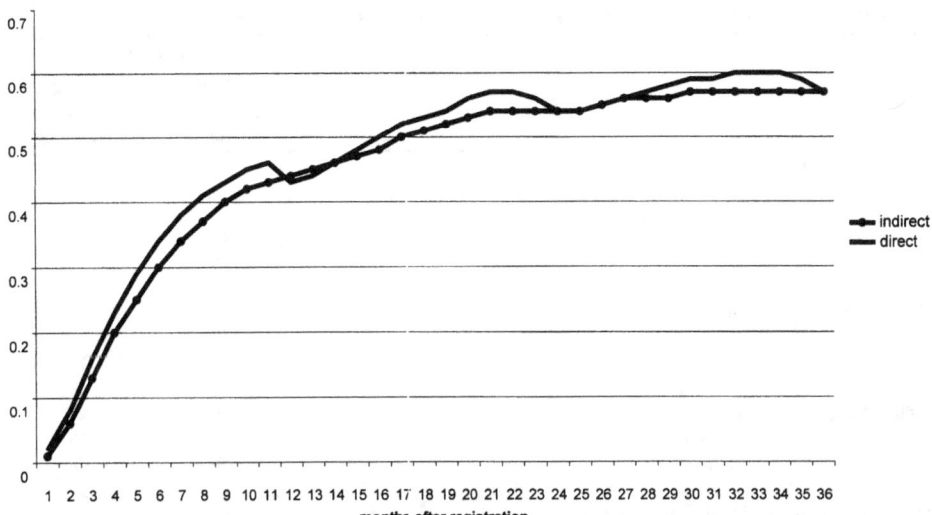

Fig. 4. Employment rates for unemployed persons by employer-contacts status of their caseworker

Note: This figure shows average employment rates for the individuals age 24 to 55 years. 44041 unemployed persons with first caseworker who used direct employer contacts as a major information source. 56211 unemployed persons with caseworker who did not use employers as a major information source.

abruptly from month 11 to 12, from 22 to 23 and 24, and from 34 to 35 and 36. In the control group, however, this pattern is not observed and the employment rate increases nearly monotonously. This cyclicality is driven by a few caseworkers with large inflows of unemployed in January, November, and December 2003 from the sectors construction, tourism and services, many of them in the canton Valais. These individuals are particularly affected by the seasonality in the construction and tourism sector with higher unemployment risk in the winter season. This leads to the cycles after 12, 24, and 36 months. If we eliminate these about 25 caseworkers, the cycles vanish but the main estimation results remain (see Appendix C).

The descriptive statistics provided in Table 1 show that the two groups differ in characteristics that are important determinants of the labour market success of the unemployed. Caseworkers who consider employers as an important information source are more likely to counsel men, foreigners and individuals who are less educated, less skilled and/or have a low employability rating. Furthermore, these caseworkers differ also in their own characteristics: gender, tenure, work experience in private placement offices, education, and vocational training (see Table 1). Not accounting for these differences may lead to biased estimates of the impact of employer contacts. Therefore, the next section discusses the selection problem and presents a flexible methodology to identify the causal effects when sufficiently informative data is available.

Tab. 1. Selected average characteristics by employer-contacts status of their caseworker

		Caseworkers having indirect employer contacts	Caseworkers having direct employer contacts
Characteristics of their unemployed clients			
Number of unemployed		56211	44041
Age in years		36.6	36.6
Female		46	42
Swiss		63	60
Civil status:	single	41	39
	married	47	50
	divorced	11	10
	widowed	1	1
Mother tongue:	German	46	40
	French	15	18
	Italian	9	9
	Not German, French or Italian	30	34
Mother tongue is equal to cantonal language		63	60
Number of foreign languages		1.8	1.6
Education:	less than eight years	3	4
	8-11 years	20	24
	secondary track	38	38
	tertiary track	13	11
Qualification level:	skilled	59	55
	semiskilled	14	18
	unskilled	22	23
Chances to find a job:	easy	12	12
	medium	73	76
	difficult	15	12
Characteristics of caseworkers			
Number of caseworkers		778	623
Age in years		44.1	44.8
Female		46	35
Tenure in years		5.6	6.1
Previous work experience in municipality office		10	8
Previous work experience in private placement office		21	27
Own experience of unemployment		63	63
Highest education level:	vocational qualification	34	28
	above vocational qualification	40	48
	tertiary track (university or polytechnic)	26	22
Special vocational training of caseworker (Eidgenössischer Fachausweis)		21	25

Note: The entries in the table are shares in %, means, or number of observations, by subgroup.

E. Econometric methodology

1. Identification problem and empirical strategy

Consider an individual i who registers as unemployed at time t_0 at his regional employment office. This person is then assigned to a caseworker of that office, who will be in charge of this individual for at least several months.[8] As discussed above, his chances of finding a job may depend on how well his caseworker is connected to local firms. Let $S_i = 1$ if his caseworker has direct employer contacts, and $S_i = 0$ otherwise.

We are interested in the impact of having a caseworker with direct employer contacts on the subsequent employment chances of this unemployed person, which is measured by the employment status Y_τ in month τ after registration. In particular, we would like to compare the employment status if the caseworker had direct employer contacts compared to the employment status if the caseworker not had direct employer contacts. We base our analysis on the prototypical model of the microeconometric evaluation literature with binary treatment (see Rubin, 1974). Let $\{Y_\tau^0, Y_\tau^1\}$ denote the potential employment outcomes for a particular unemployed person τ months after registration. Y_τ^1 would be the employment status if this unemployed person was counselled by a caseworker with direct employer contacts, whereas Y_τ^0 would be the employment status if counselled by one without. Only one of these two outcomes can be observed since each unemployed person is counselled either by a caseworker with ($S=1$) or without ($S=0$) direct employer contacts. With this notation, we define θ_τ as the average effect of having a caseworker with direct contacts for those unemployed persons who are actually in the situation of having such a caseworker:

$$\theta_\tau := E[Y_\tau^1 - Y_\tau^0 \mid S = 1].$$

This causal parameter is usually called the average treatment effect on the treated (ATET), a term borrowed from the biometrics literature, which pioneered this field of causal analysis.

Note that under suitable regularity conditions the observable outcome Y_τ can be expressed as:

$$Y_\tau = S Y_\tau^1 - (1-S) Y_\tau^0.$$

Therefore, we can rewrite the ATET in terms of the observable outcomes and the potential outcomes Y_τ^0 for the group of unemployed with $S=1$:

$$\theta_\tau := E[Y_\tau^1 \mid S=1] - E[Y_\tau^0 \mid S=1] = E[Y_\tau \mid S=1] - E[Y_\tau^0 \mid S=1].$$

$E[Y_\tau|S=1]$ can be estimated consistently by the sample mean of the observable outcomes in the subsample of those unemployed with caseworkers with direct employer contacts. However, such a simple estimator is not available for the so-called mean counterfactual outcome, $E[Y_\tau^0|S=1]$. An obvious idea would be to learn this potential outcome from those unemployed who actually experienced caseworkers with $S=0$. Although this idea is in general valid, it requires some specific adjustment (based on some untestable assumption) if the groups of unemployed (and caseworkers) with direct and less direct employer contacts differ in other dimensions that influence employment outcomes as well. Taking an unadjusted mean from this group would lead to an estimate that is subject to the so-called selection bias. However, if these other factors that influence labour market outcomes as well, are observable, they can 'be controlled' for by suitable econometric techniques, like regression-type modelling in its various forms. However, whether all relevant background factors are indeed observable (which we argue below is relatively plausible in this study), is an assumption that cannot be empirically verified without 'complete' data, which is of course never available.

This assumption is known as the *conditional independence assumption* (CIA) and is exploited in this study.[9] It implies identification of the average counterfactual outcome $E[Y_\tau^0|S=1]$:

$$E[Y_\tau^0 \mid S=1] = \underset{X|S=1}{E} E[Y_\tau^0 \mid X, S=1] = \underset{X|S=1}{E} E[Y_\tau^0 \mid X, S=0] = \underset{X|S=1}{E} E[Y_\tau \mid X, S=0].$$

The estimation technique relies on the mean of the outcome variable for a specific value of characteristics X in the subsample of unemployed with caseworkers of type $S=0$. These averages of the outcome variables for specific values of X are then weighted according to the distribution of X in the pool of participants. The identification strategy thus relies on being able to observe all these confounding variables X. For being able to do so the extremely detailed linked caseworker-client dataset is crucial, as will be argued below.

2. Selection into treatment

Plausibility of the conditional independence assumption requires that all relevant factors that jointly determine outcomes and treatment are observed in the data. This requires an understanding how the treatment is determined.

The caseworker-employer interactions as captured by the random variable S depends on four processes: First, which type of caseworkers are hired, second, how caseworkers are allocated to the unemployed, third, what kind of labour market environment they face, and fourth, what types of clients they counsel. The interaction between caseworkers and firms could be related to their general skills in finding jobs for their clients. Caseworkers with longer tenure, for instance, might be better in placing their clients due to their own experience, but may have developed a better network with firms as well. Therefore, we include caseworker characteristics such as their age, gender, education, work experience, and experience of own unemployment as covariates. In addition, we would like to observe the intrinsic working ethos of caseworkers because it could be that more motivated caseworkers are also more likely to have time-consuming contacts with firms. If more motivated workers had contacts with employers because they considered them as effective, we would overestimate the magnitude of any potential positive effects, but the sign of the effects would still be correctly estimated.

The allocation of jobseekers to caseworkers is also most likely to be a joint determinant. Caseworkers who mainly counsel unemployed from one particular industry might be more likely to develop employer contacts within this industry, but might be also more likely to place their clients effectively since they know the industry requirements better than their colleagues who are responsible for all industries. Therefore, we control for the allocation process of unemployed to caseworkers within the employment office. We know from the questionnaire how unemployed are allocated to caseworkers, e.g. by occupation, alphabet, age, and employability.

Furthermore, we need to control for the characteristics of the unemployed persons as well. On the one hand, caseworkers differ in their personalities, but they also react to the types of unemployed and the labour market environment. If vacancies are scarce, they might put more effort into contacting firms to raise the number of vacancies. Similarly, a caseworker who counsels mainly individuals with good employment prospects might consider employer contacts as more, or less, important than her colleague with clients who are more difficult to place: either she does not expect any pay-off from employer contacts since her clients find jobs anyway, or she has more time resources to satisfy the needs of her employers. Therefore, we will include in the analysis a large number of characteristics of the unemployed individuals such as their age, gender, skills, education, nationality, employment history and so on.[10]

Appendix B shows all the covariates that are included in the subsequent estimations to control for the selection into treatment. Probit estimates indicate that caseworkers have a higher probability to have direct employer contacts if they are male, have longer tenure and have worked in a private placement office before. The probability of having direct employer contacts decreases the more unemployed with low employability rating or looking for part-time jobs are counselled. If the employment office is located in a medium sized municipality, the likelihood of having direct employer contacts increases.

One might still be concerned that caseworkers who invest into employer contacts might be different in unobserved characteristics from those who do not. The fact that we later find positive effects may then partly be reflecting the higher motivation or work effort of those caseworkers. Presumably, those caseworkers however would only devote their time to employer contacts if that strategy were indeed effective. In that case, we would be overestimating the true effects but the sign of the effects would be still correct.

3. A note on estimation

The estimator used is a matching estimator as implemented in Lechner, Miquel, and Wunsch (2004). It matches unemployed individuals whose caseworker is of type $S=1$ to other unemployed whose caseworker is of type $S=0$ but have comparable characteristics X. It then compares the employment outcomes between these two groups of matched unemployed. The advantage of matching estimators is that they are essentially nonparametric and allow for arbitrary individual effect heterogeneity.[11] It is an extension of a first-nearest neighbour propensity score matching estimator in two directions: First, matching does not only proceed with respect to the propensity score but also incorporates additionally some other covariates deemed to be particularly important for outcomes and selection. Second, instead of using first-nearest neighbour matching, all neighbours within a pre-specified radius are used. Furthermore, they increase the matching quality by exploiting the fact that appropriately weighted regressions that use the sampling weights from matching have the so-called double robustness property. This property implies that the estimator remains consistent if the matching step is based on a correctly specified selection model *or* if the regression model is correctly specified (e.g. Rubin, 1979; Joffe, Ten Have, Feldman, and Kimmel, 2004). Moreover, this procedure should increase precision and may reduce small sample bias as well as asymptotic bias of matching estimators, see Abadie and Imbens (2006)[12] and thus increase robustness of the estimator in this dimension as well. Calculation of standard errors takes into account of the dependence coming from the fact that several individuals are counselled by the same caseworker. The actual matching protocol is presented in Appendix B.

F. Empirical results

As discussed above, the caseworker to employer interaction could influence employment probabilities by providing caseworkers with important insights on the current developments in the local labour market or job-openings. The estimated treatment effects are depicted in Figure 5.

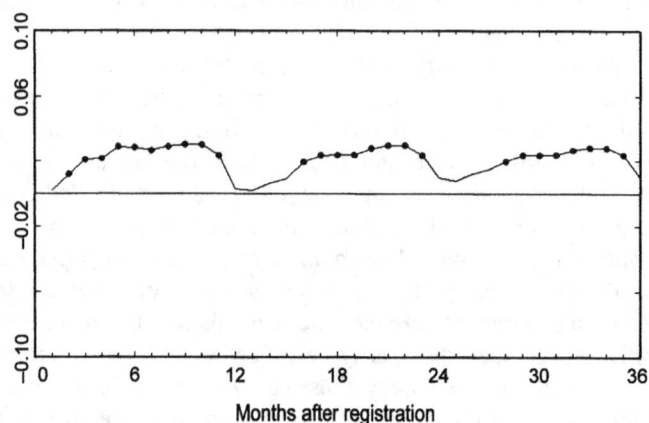

Fig. 5. Treatment effect of having a caseworker with direct employer contacts
Note: Average treatment effect on the treated (ATET) for the subsample of unemployed age 24 to 55 years. Abscissa: Months after registration of unemployment. Ordinate: Treatment effect on employment probability in percentage points. Dots indicate significance at 5% level, triangles significance at 10% level.

Point estimates above zero indicate that direct employer contacts increase employment outcomes in month τ after registration. Dots indicate a significance level below 5%, triangles below 10% (and above 5%). The graph shows that from the second month after registration, the effects are positive. Six months after registration, the employment probability of unemployed individuals whose caseworkers had direct employer contacts are on average 3%-points higher as unemployed without such caseworkers. These effects are remarkably stable over time, which suggests that maintaining a direct network with local employers can be important. They are not significant around the twelfth and twenty-fourth months after registration. This cyclical pattern, which has already been observed in Figures 2 and 4 stems from a few caseworkers with large inflows in the seasonal sectors construction and tourism. A further discussion in Appendix C shows that if we eliminate these caseworkers the cycles vanish but the main effects remain.

We also examined the effects for different subgroups to analyze possible effect heterogeneity. Figure 6 shows the employment rates for four subgroups: young unemployed (< 24 years), older unemployed (> 55 years) and unemployed with high and low qualification. The employment rates are given separately for treated and controls, analogously to Figure 4. Figure 7 below gives the estimated treatment effects.

Figure 7 indicates that unqualified unemployed persons benefited the most from having caseworkers with direct employer contacts. There is also evidence that qualified and

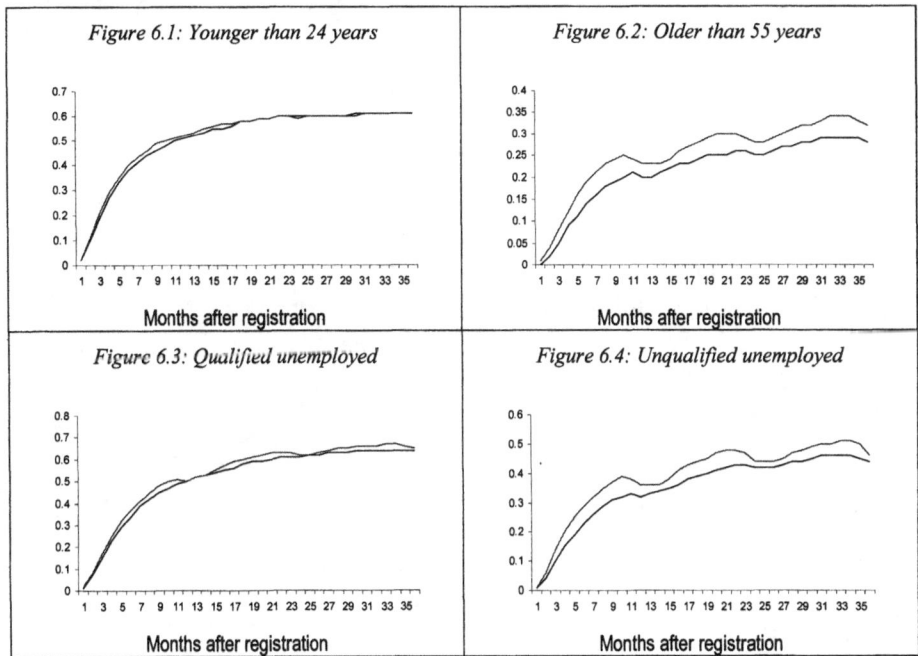

Fig. 6. Employment rates for four different subpopulations
Note: Abscissa: Months after registration of unemployment. Ordinate: Employment probabilities in percentage points.

older unemployed benefited as well. No significant effects can be found for the younger unemployed.

There is also other evidence that confirms our finding that having networks with employers increases employment chances. We asked the caseworkers how much of their time they devoted to counselling, administrative tasks, and employer contacts. Caseworkers who devoted a larger share of their resources to employers were more likely to consider employers as an important source of information.[13] Unemployed persons had higher reintegration rates if their caseworkers devoted more time to employer contacts. The estimated treatment effects are depicted in Appendix C.

We also analysed whether certain aspects of the form of the employer contacts matter, but the estimates turned out to be too imprecise to draw firm conclusions. One of these aspects was whether caseworkers tended to place unemployed via directive or whether they preferred personal contacts to the employer. Furthermore, we asked caseworkers whether they tended to aim for rather very many job placements or a few, well selected job placements. The questionnaire also asked how caseworkers maintained their networks with employers, i.e. whether they tended to expand the network by contacting additional firms to persuade them to post vacancies or whether they preferred to maintain and strengthen the network with firms that regularly had posted vacancies. Again, no firm conclusions emerged from these estimates.

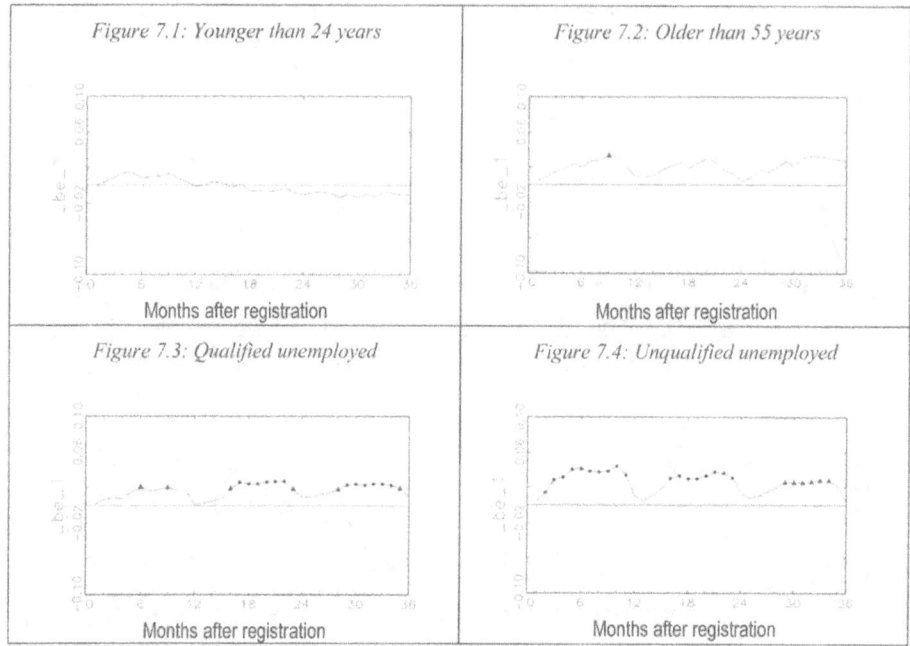

Fig. 7. Treatment effect of having a caseworker with direct employer contacts, by subgroups

Note: Average treatment effect on the treated (ATET) for the subsample of unemployed age 24 to 55 years. Abscissa: Months after registration of unemployment. Ordinate: Treatment effect on employment probability in percentage points. Dots indicate significance at 5% level, triangles significance at 10% level.

G. Conclusions

Caseworkers in regional employment offices provide several services that help to match unemployed persons to employers and thereby ease the problem of high unemployment. The effectiveness of services such as counselling and placements may depend on the existence of direct networks to local firms. Employer contacts could be relevant since they transmit informal knowledge on potential vacancies and current labour market developments. On the other hand, they consume resources that could have been used otherwise. Whether there is a pay-off to direct employer contacts in terms of reintegration rates of unemployed thus remains an empirical question. A pure descriptive or correlation analysis between groups of unemployed and caseworkers with and without more intense employer contacts does not provide sufficient insights due to the selection bias problem, i.e. the fact that these two groups differ by other characteristics that are correlated with labour market success and the intensity of employer contacts as well. Instead, we seek to estimate *causal* effects of the employer contacts on the employment outcomes of their clients. We apply microeconometric techniques from the treatment evaluation literature. In particular, we argue that we are able to observe all important variables that *jointly* influenced labour market outcomes of the unemployed and affected whether an unemployed person faced a caseworker with more or less direct contacts to employers. Using this strategy, we estimate the treatment effect of a direct employer network on employment chances of their unemployed. This identification strategy is made possible through a unique and very detailed data set collected for this study. It consists of administrative data on unemployed persons from several sources combined with caseworker characteristics retrieved from an extensive survey. These data allow us to control for characteristics of the unemployed, of the caseworker, of the employment office, as well as for local labour market conditions. We apply matching on the propensity score for estimating the causal effects of employer contacts and find positive effects: Having direct contacts to employers increases the employment probability of their unemployed individuals by about 3%-points. In particular, the subgroup of less skilled unemployed benefits most if their caseworkers have a direct network to employers. These positive effects on employment rates persist for at least three years after registering at the regional employment office and therefore do not seem to be the result of pushing unemployed into unstable jobs.

Overall, these results indicate that contacts to employers can be helpful to increase the employment chances. Due to saturation effects and crowding out of jobseekers who are not registered at an employment office (such as those who are not entitled to unemployment benefits and often not register themselves anymore), the overall effect may be smaller than 3%-points if all caseworkers were to invest into direct networks with firms. However, the effects seem to be sufficiently large and stable to encourage employment offices to let all their caseworkers engage in building direct relationships to firms.

Appendix A: Further details on the matching estimator

The following table describes some of the details for the implementation of the matching estimator. It is presented in a more general way to show the flexibility of the method for evaluating multiple treatment states. In our application the treatment variable S however takes only two different values $S \in \{0,1\}$, i.e. the caseworker has answered to have direct employer contacts or has not. The matching estimator is thus performed only for $m=1$ and $l=0$ in the subsequent notation.

Matching is done on the propensity score and additional covariates $\tilde{x}$, which are included to ensure a high match quality with respect to these critical variables suspected to have a large effect an selection and outcomes. In this application we include gender in $\tilde{x}$. The variance estimation is based on Lechner (2001) who suggests estimating the asymptotic standard errors for $\hat{\theta}_N^{m,l}$ given the estimated weights. The adjustment for clustered standard errors, i.e. for the fact that the jobseekers of the same caseworker cannot be considered independent observations, is discussed below.

Tab. 2. A matching protocol for the estimation of ATET

Step 1	Estimate a probit model to obtain the choice probabilities: $\hat{P}(X_j)$
Step 2	Restrict sample to common support: Delete all observations with probabilities larger than the smallest maximum and smaller than the largest minimum of all subsamples defined by S.
Step 3	*Estimate the respective (counterfactual) expectations of the outcome variables.* For a given value of m and l the following steps are performed: **Standard propensity score matching step (binary treatments)** a-1) Choose one observation in the subsample defined by participation in m and delete it from that pool. b-1) Find an observation in the subsample of participants in l that is as close as possible to the one chosen in step a-1) in terms of $[\hat{P}(x), \tilde{x}]$. 'Closeness' is based on the Mahalanobis distance. Do not remove that observation, so that it can be used again. c-1) Repeat a-1) and b-1) until no participant in *m* is left. **Exploit thick support of X to increase efficiency (radius matching step)** d-1) Compute the maximum distance (d) obtained for any comparison between treated and matched comparison observations. a-2) Repeat a-1). b-2) Repeat b-1). If possible, find other observations in the subsample of participants in *l* that are at least as close as R . d to the one chosen in step a-2) (to gain efficiency); we choose R to be 90%. Do not remove these observations, so that they can be used again. Compute weights for all chosen comparisons observations that are proportional to their distance (calculated in b-1). Normalise the weights such that they add to one. c-2) Repeat a-2) and b-2) until no participant in *m* is left. d-2) For any potential comparison observation, add the weights obtained in a-2) and . **Exploit double robustness properties to adjust small mismatches by regression** e) Using the weights $w(x_i)$ obtained in d-2), run a weighted linear regression of the outcome variable on the variables used to define the distance (and an intercept). f-1) Predict the potential outcome $y^l(x_i)$ of every observation in *l* and *m* using the coefficients of this regression: $\hat{y}^l(x_i)$ f-2) Estimate the bias of the matching estimator for $E(Y^l \mid S = m)$ as: $$\sum_{i=1}^{N} \frac{1(S=m)\hat{y}^l(x_i)}{N^m} - 1(S=l)w_i\hat{y}^l(x_i).$$ g) Using the weights obtained by weighted matching in d-2), compute a weighted mean of the outcome variables in *l*. Subtract the bias from this estimate. **Final estimate** h) Compute the treatment effect by subtracting the weighted mean of the outcomes in the comparison group (*l*) from the mean in the treatment group (*m*).

Since the treatment variable is measured on the level of the caseworker but the outcome variable is measured on the level of the jobseeker, for the *computation of the standard errors*, we have to take into account that the outcomes across the jobseekers counselled by the same caseworker may be correlated. The calculation of the clustered standard errors is described in the following:

The matching estimator of the potential outcome has the general form:

$$\hat{Y}^l = \sum_{i=1}^{N} 1(s_i = l) w_i^l y_i,$$

where $i = 1, \ldots, N$ indexes the jobseekers and where the sum of the weights is one:

$$\sum_{i=1}^{N} 1(s_i = 1) w_i^l = 1.$$

To introduce the cluster structure we can re-write the matching estimator using a double sum

$$\hat{Y}^l = \sum_{j=1}^{J} \sum_{i=1}^{N} 1(s_i = 1) 1(C_i = j) w_i^l y_i,$$

where i indexes jobseekers and $j = 1, \ldots, J$ indexes the J caseworkers. The variable $C_i \in \{1, \ldots, J\}$ gives the number of the caseworker who is in charge of jobseeker i. The number of clients of caseworker j is thus given as

$$N^j := \sum_{i=1}^{N} 1(s_i = 1) 1(C_i = j) w_i^l.$$

We can compute the variance allowing that the outcomes across jobseekers counselled by the same caseworker are dependent, but assume that observations across caseworkers are independent:

$$Var(\hat{Y}^l) = \sum_{j=1}^{J} Var\left[\sum_{i=1}^{N} 1(s_i = 1) 1(C_i = j) w_i^l y_i \right]$$

$$= \sum_{j=1}^{J} N^{j2} Var\left[\frac{1}{N^j} \sum_{i=1}^{N} 1(s_i = 1) 1(C_i = j) w_i^l y_i \right].$$

Hence, the variance is obtained by summing over the caseworkers the variance of the expression A_j, which is defined as

$$A_j = \frac{1}{N^j} \sum_{i=1}^{N} 1(s_i = 1) 1(C_i = j) w_i^l y_i.$$

Since the A_j are independent across the caseworkers, we can estimate $Var(A_j)$ as

$$\widehat{Var}(A) = \frac{1}{J} \sum_{j=1}^{J} \left[A_j - \frac{1}{J} \sum_{j=1}^{J} A_j \right]^2,$$

which we now plug into the formula for $Var(\hat{Y}^l)$.

Appendix B: Results of the probit estimation

Tab. 3. Probit estimates for the main population

Binary dependent variable: having direct contact to employers				
N=101304		coefficient	std error	t-stat
Constant		0.26	0.41	0.64
Characteristics of the caseworker:				
Age		0.00	0.00	0.66
Female	*	-0.16	0.08	1.89
Tenure in employment office (in years)	**	0.03	0.01	2.35
Previous experience in municipality office (dummy)		-0.17	0.15	1.14
Previous experience in private placement office (dummy)	***	0.32	0.11	3.01
Own experience of unemployment (dummy)		0.04	0.08	0.44
Indicator for missing caseworker characteristics		-0.02	0.26	0.07
Education: above vocational training		0.14	0.10	1.41
Education: tertiary track (university or polytechnic)		-0.09	0.11	0.77
Special vocational training of caseworker (Eidg. Fachaus.)	*	0.18	0.10	1.72
Allocation of unemployed to caseworkers (reference: at random):				
By industry	**	0.16	0.08	1.96
By occupation		0.00	0.08	0.02
By age		-0.08	0.26	0.31
By employability		0.22	0.17	1.28
By region	*	0.23	0.13	1.79
Other		-0.05	0.15	0.32
Characteristics of the unemployed person:				
Female		-0.03	0.02	1.38
Age/100		-0.01	0.07	0.10
Age/100 squared		0.09	0.81	0.11
Foreigner with permanent work permit		-0.02	0.03	0.61
Foreigner with yearly work permit		0.00	0.03	0.08
Male and foreigner with permanent work permit		0.00	0.03	0.13
Male and foreigner with yearly work permit		-0.04	0.03	1.36
Mother tongue French		0.02	0.06	0.27
Mother tongue Italian		0.03	0.05	0.58
Mother tongue other than German, French or Italian		0.07	0.07	0.94
Sum of foreign languages	**	-0.03	0.01	2.41
Foreign language: other Swiss language	***	-0.09	0.03	3.18
Foreign language: English, Spanish or Portuguese		-0.03	0.03	1.06
Excellent language skills in other Swiss language		0.00	0.03	0.15
Good language skills in other Swiss language		0.01	0.04	0.12
Excellent language skills in English, Spanish or Portuguese		-0.03	0.02	1.36
Good language skills in English, Spanish or Portuguese	**	-0.05	0.02	2.47
Widowed		-0.05	0.05	1.06
Divorced		-0.02	0.02	1.24
Single		0.00	0.02	0.25
Number of dependents		0.01	0.06	0.21
Earnings in last job /100		0.07	0.05	1.60
Education missing		-0.01	0.06	0.17
Education less than eight year		0.00	0.07	0.04
Education 8-11 year		0.00	0.04	0.07

Education secondary track		0.02	0.03	0.52
Qualification: unskilled		0.00	0.03	0.02
Qualification: semiskilled	***	0.09	0.04	2.69
Qualification: skilled without degree		-0.02	0.04	0.35
Employability low	***	-0.22	0.08	2.72
Employability medium		-0.05	0.06	0.83
Job position: self-employed or management		0.00	0.03	0.05
Job position: assistant		0.05	0.03	1.49
Job position: apprentice		0.07	0.06	1.15
Job position: pupil		-0.05	0.15	0.35
Job position: student	**	0.03	0.07	0.47
Part-time	***	-0.05	0.02	2.11
Number of unemployment spells in the last 2 years		0.07	0.01	5.15
Number of unemployment spells in the last 2 years missing		0.03	0.04	0.80
Number of months unemployed in last 2 years		-0.01	0.01	1.49
First month in AHV (= pension data) being nonzero		-0.07	0.04	1.49
First month in AHV interacted with being young & foreigner		0.02	0.04	0.50
First month in AHV interacted with being young		0.02	0.04	0.45
First month in AHV interacted with being old & foreigner		0.03	0.04	0.69
First month in AHV interacted with being old		0.02	0.04	0.54
Average wage in last 10 years	**	-0.08	0.03	2.43
Total number of months employed in last 10 years	**	0.10	0.05	1.99
Number of employment spells in last 5 years	**	0.13	0.06	2.11
Indicator for having been out of labour force in last 5 years		-0.01	0.02	0.34
Fraction of time employed in last years		-0.06	0.06	1.04
Fraction of time unemployed share in last years	*	0.10	0.06	1.73
Occupation (reference: other)				
Food industry	*	0.11	0.06	1.91
Wood and paper		0.03	0.06	0.53
Chemicals and metal	*	0.06	0.04	1.77
Textiles and leather		0.03	0.08	0.37
News		-0.01	0.04	0.33
Books		0.05	0.03	1.49
Health		-0.11	0.07	1.57
Construction	**	0.11	0.05	2.34
Restaurants		0.06	0.05	1.16
Office	**	-0.10	0.04	2.25
Retail trade		0.00	0.05	0.07
Entrepreneurs		-0.03	0.05	0.71
Public services		0.03	0.04	0.65
Engineering		0.07	0.06	1.35
Academics		0.01	0.05	0.21
Arts	**	0.13	0.06	2.18
Industrial sector (reference processing industry)				
Agriculture and forestry		0.06	0.07	0.79
Construction	*	0.07	0.04	1.81
Tourism		0.00	0.05	0.01
Services	*	-0.04	0.02	1.81
Public		-0.03	0.05	0.73
Other		-0.06	0.05	1.34
Dummy: Looking for the same job again		0.02	0.02	1.05
Dummy: No contribution to unemployment insurance		-0.04	0.03	1.43
Number of months contribution to unemployment insurance		-0.01	0.01	0.87
Percent of full-time equivalent in last occupation being zero	*	-0.04	0.02	1.72

Local labour market characteristics				
French speaking employment office		0.22	0.14	1.54
Italian speaking employment office		-0.06	0.21	0.27
Unemployment rate in industry		0.03	0.06	0.56
Unemployment rate of canton		-0.07	0.07	1.06
Size of municipality ≥200000 inhabitants		0.11	0.17	0.67
≥150000	***	-0.45	0.16	2.88
≥75000	***	-0.51	0.18	2.89
≥30000		-0.02	0.10	0.17
≥15000		-0.04	0.08	0.46
≥8000		-0.06	0.07	0.89
≥3000		0.02	0.06	0.27
≥2000		0.00	0.05	0.10
GDP of canton per capita		-1.08	0.68	1.58

Appendix C: Further estimation results

1. Time resources for employer contacts

To assess the reliability of our results we compare them with the results emanating from a related question of the survey, where caseworkers were asked:

How much of your working time did you devote to the following activities? (sum=100%):

    counselling: _____ %
    administrative tasks: _____ %
    contacts with employers: _____ %

1395 caseworkers answered this question. On average, they devoted 60% of their time to counselling, 32% to administrative tasks, and 8% to contacts with employers.

21.4% of the caseworkers devoted no time to employer contacts, 30.8% used between 0 and at most 5% of their time for employer contacts and 32.2% between 5 and 10% of their time. Another 10.8% of the caseworkers invested up to 20% of their time and the remaining 4.8% of caseworkers invested up to 80% of their time. Note that a staff member of the employment office who uses 100% of his time for employer contacts would not have been included in our survey since we surveyed only caseworkers who also counselled unemployed persons. Hence, the above question may not correctly capture the total resources an employment office invested into employer contacts (since staff specializing only on employer contacts would be omitted), but on a caseworker level it distinguishes between caseworkers with few or zero employer contacts and caseworkers who invest a larger share of their time to this.

The correlation between time devoted to employer contacts obtained from the above question with the binary indicator of whether direct contacts to employers have been a main source of information is 0.41. Hence, both questions are clearly related and measure aspects of the existence of a direct network to firms. Whereas the question on information sources refers more to the information actually obtained, i.e. to the benefits the caseworker derived from this investment, the question above refers more to the total time invested into employers, which would also include services provided to the employers.[14]

The following figure shows the treatment effect of having a caseworker who devotes at least 10% of his time to employer contacts compared to having a caseworker who devotes no time at all to it.[15] The estimates are based on propensity score matching with the same covariates as in Appendix B. The results suggest that job seekers enjoy higher reintegration chances if their caseworkers devote a larger share of their working time to networks with firms.

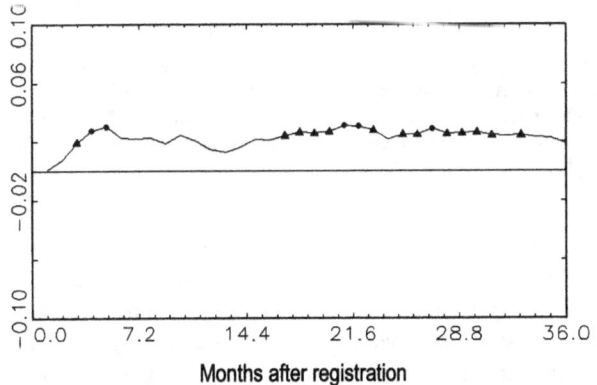

Fig. 8. Treatment effect of having a caseworker who devotes at least 10% of time to employer contacts

Note: Average treatment effect on the treated (ATET) for the subsample of unemployed age 24 to 55 years. Treatment is defined as devoting 10% or more of time to employer contacts. The non-treatment is defined as investing no time at all in employer contacts. Abscissa: Months after registration of unemployment. Ordinate: Treatment effect on employment probability in percentage points. Dots indicate significance at 5% level, triangles significance at 10% level.

2. Cyclical pattern of treatment effects

The Figures 2, 4, and 5 exhibited some cyclical patterns that were most pronounced in the treatment group. As can be seen from Figure 4, the employment rates decreased in months 12, 24, and 36 for the treatment group, whereas the employment rates increase monotonically in the control group. Some further descriptive analysis indicated that this pattern is driven by a few caseworkers who experienced large inflows of new unemployed in January, November, and December 2003 from the sectors construction, tourism, and services. Many of them were situated in the canton Valais, which has a large tourism sector. In principle, by controlling for month of registration, industry, and region, the matching estimator should take care of these differences, but in finite samples the balancing may not always be achieved in all dimensions, e.g. not for the interaction of month of registration by industry and by region. Therefore, we consider also results within subgroups defined by observed characteristics.

If we exclude the inflows of the months January and December 2003 from our sample, we obtain the estimates presented in Figure 9 that still display a cyclical pattern, which however is much less pronounced.

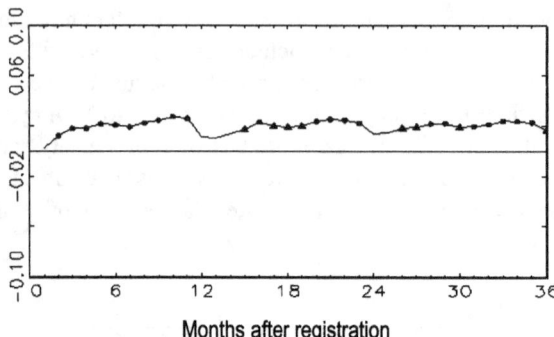

Fig. 9. Treatment effect of employer contacts (without inflows from January and December 2003)
Note: Average treatment effect on the treated (ATET) for the subsample of unemployed age 24 to 55 years without inflows from January and December 2003. Abscissa: Months after registration of unemployment. Ordinate: Treatment effect on employment probability in percentage points. Dots indicate significance at 5% level, triangles significance at 10% level.

Since the cyclical patterns in the raw data are generated by a rather small number of caseworkers, the Figures 10 show the results after dropping the outlying caseworkers. An outlier is defined as having an unusual high share of clients who are employed in the eleventh month after their registration and unemployed in the twelfth month, which is an indication of a large fraction of clients susceptible to seasonality. In the left graph we exclude the 25 caseworkers with the highest share and in the right graph we exclude 32 caseworkers who have a share of seasonal clients above 18%, which corresponds to the 97.5 quantile. The latter implies that 4268 unemployed are excluded, of whom 86% belonged to the treatment group, and 78% are from the canton Valais. The cyclical pattern vanishes, but the positive effects remain, although less precise due to a reduced sample size.

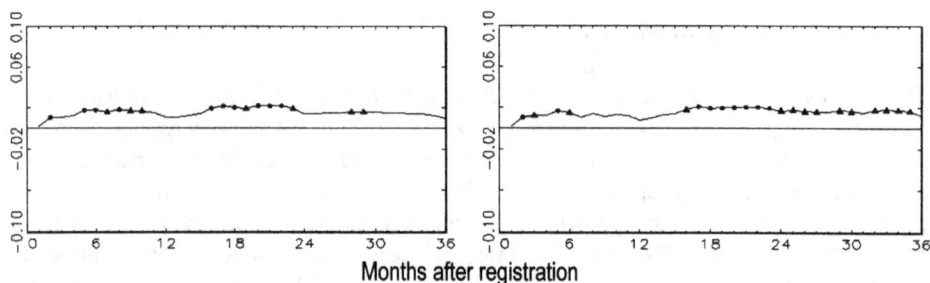

Fig. 10. Treatment effect of employer contacts (without outliers)
Note: Average treatment effect on the treated (ATET) for the subsample of unemployed age 24 to 55 years without caseworkers with large inflows of unemployed with cyclical pattern. Abscissa: Months after registration of unemployment. Ordinate: Treatment effect on employment probability in percentage points. Dots indicate significance at 5% level, triangles significance at 10% level.

Figure 11 shows the estimates excluding the canton Valais, which leads to a loss of 5760 unemployed. The cyclical pattern is less pronounced but effects are still positive, albeit less precisely estimated.

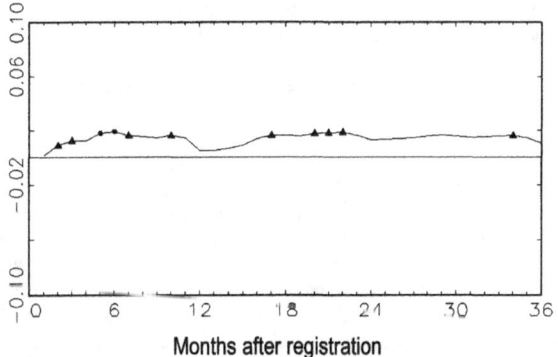

Fig. 11. Treatment effect of direct employer contacts (without the canton Valais)
Note: Average treatment effect on the treated (ATET) for the subsample of unemployed age 24 to 55 years without the canton Valais. Abscissa: Months after registration of unemployment. Ordinate: Treatment effect on employment probability in percentage points. Dots indicate significance at 5% level, triangles significance at 10% level.

Endnotes

* We are very grateful to Heidi Steiger, Stephan Hammer, Rolf Iten, Stefan Schmid, Jonathan Gast, and Thomas Ragni for collaboration at different stages of this project. We also would like to thank the editors and two anonymous referees of this journal for helpful comments. We gratefully acknowledge provision of data and financial support from the seco, Bern. The paper has been presented at the symposium on the Economics and Management of Education, Konstanz.
2 For recent studies on the effectiveness of active labour market programmes, see e.g. Wunsch and Lechner (2007) for Germany and Lechner and Wiehler (2006) for Austria.
3 Sheldon finds that placement offices reached roughly two thirds of their efficiency potential. Vassiliev et al. (2006) find a mean inefficiency on the order of 15% of best observed performance.
4 For reasons explained below, we will focus on only 103 employment offices and their caseworkers. We incorporate neither the employment offices in Geneva nor Appenzell-Innerrhoden, nor those employment offices that were newly established in early 2003.
5 The federal level of the unemployment insurance system pursues a relatively clear vision focusing on active labour market policies and rapid placement. However, in Switzerland the cantons, which enjoy financial and political autonomy in many fields, have substantial leeway in the implementation and the organization of ‚their' employment offices. Due to different philosophies and experiences with unemployment, but also due to different industry structures, the cantons have chosen different organizational structures between and within the employment offices. Since the regional employment offices existed only since about 1998, there has also been a substantial amount of experimentation with different organizational styles, visible in several re-organizations during 2001 and the first half of 2002. (Some re-organizations took place during early 2003 in some employment offices. These employment offices are excluded from the analysis.) In 1998, all cantons relied on a geographical organization where each employment office was responsible for a particular set of municipalities. Some cantons experimented then with a functional organization across employment offices, where unemployed were assigned to employment offices according to their profession/industry or their presumed difficulty in finding a job (employability). In 2003, almost all cantons organized their employment offices geographically. Exceptions are the canton Geneva and the canton Solothurn, which maintains one employment office for the difficult cases. (Solothurn further maintains two employment offices in Olten and Solothurn, respectively, organized by employability. These are located in the same buildings, so they are considered here as two sections of a single geographically organized entity in Olten and in Solothurn, respectively.)
6 For being able to link the datasets the information system of the unemployment insurance system (AVAM) was crucial, which maintains a record of all counselling meetings and contains unique personal identifiers

for each unemployed person and for each caseworker. At any point in time, each job seeker is assigned to exactly one caseworker. Using this information and having the entire population of jobseekers, we observe how many clients a caseworker counsels at any given point in time. For an unemployed person who remains unemployed for more than 6 to 8 months, the caseworker in charge is changed in some of the employment offices to initiate new dynamics in the caseworker-client relationship. By focusing on the first caseworker, we avoid the endogeneity issues of caseworker changes.
7 All these 103 employment offices were independently operating agencies responsible for a specific geographic area. We do not include the canton Geneva in our study since in Geneva the employment offices are functionally specialized according to professions and employability of the unemployed. This is in contrast to the other cantons, which largely follow a geographic structuring. We further exclude five other employment offices from the analysis, three of them as they were founded only in early 2003 so that there was no well-defined stock of unemployed in the beginning of 2003, one employment office, which specialized on the difficult cases in Solothurn, and the small employment office in Appenzell-Innerhoden.
8 A change in the caseworker usually happens only after 6 or 8 months of unsuccesful job search, if at all.
9 See Imbens (2004) for an excellent survey on this topic.
10 Note that the information available in our linked data is much richer than in other studies that rely on the conditional independence assumption (e.g. Heckman and Smith, 1999; Brodaty, Crépon, and Fougère, 2001; Larsson, 2003; Dorsett, 2005).
11 See Heckman, LaLonde and Smith (1999), for and overview over matching with a binary treatment, and Imbens (2000) and Lechner (2001) for multiple treatments. Imbens (2004) nicely summarizes that literature.
12 The results of Abadie and Imbens (2006) do not apply directly to propensity score matching, but since we also match on additional variables there are some similarities with the estimators they consider.
13 The correlation between the two answers is 41%.
14 Some employment offices have enacted the philosophy that they should serve not only the unemployed but also the firms in matters offined stock of unemployed in the beginning of 2003, one employment office, which specialized on the difficult cases in Solothurn, and the small employment office in Appenzell-Innerhoden.
15 This corresponds to a transition from the lowest to the highest quintile.

References

Abadie, A., Imbens G. W. (2006): Large Sample Properties of Matching Estimators for Average Treatment Effects, in: Econometrica, 74(1), p. 235–267
Berman, E. (1997): Help wanted, job needed: estimates of a matching function from employment service data, in: Journal of Labor Economics, 15, p. 251–292
Brodaty T., Crépon, B., Fougère, D. (2001): Using Kernel Matching Estimators to Evaluate Alternative Youth Employment Programs: Evidence from France, 1986-1988, in: M. Lechner, F. Pfeiffer (eds.): Econometric Evaluations of Labour Market Policies, Physica Verlag, Heidelberg, p. 85–124
Bunt, K., F. McAndrew, Kuechel, A. (2005): JobCentre Plus Employer (Market View) Survey 2004, Department for Work and Pensions. Research Report No 261
Dorsett, R. (2005): The New Deal for Young People: Effect on the Labour Market Status of Young Men, in: Labour Economics, forthcoming
Fischer, L. (2002): Wenn helfen krank macht, in: Der Arbeitsmarkt, November 2002
Frölich, M., Lechner, M., Behncke, S., Hammer, S., Schmidt, N., Menegale, S., Lehmann, A., Iten, R. (2007): Einfluss der Rav auf die Wiedereingliederung von Stellensuchenden, Schweizerisches Staatssekretariat für Wirtschaft (seco), SECO Publikation, Arbeitsmarktpolitik No 20 http://www.seco.admin.ch/dokumentation/publikation/00008/02015/index.html?lang=de
Heckman, J., Lalonde, R, Smith, J. (1999): The Economics and Econometrics of Active Labor Market programs, in: O. Ashenfelter, D. Card (eds.), Handbook of Labour Economics, vol. 3, p. 1865–2097
Heckman, J., Smith, J. (1999): The Pre-Program Earnings Dip and the Determinants of Participation in a Social Program: Implications for Simple Program Evaluation Strategies, in: Economic Journal, 109, p. 313–348
Imbens, G. W. (2000): The Role of the Propensity Score in Estimating Dose-Response Functions, Biometrika, 87, p. 706–710.
Imbens, G. W. (2004): Nonparametric Estimation of Average Treatment Effects under Exogeneity: A Review, in: Review of Economics and Statistics, 86(1), p. 4–29.

Joffe, M. M., T. R. Ten Have, H. I. Feldman, St. Kimmel (2004): Model Selection, Confounder Control, and Marginal Structural Models, in: The American Statistician, November, 58-4, p. 272–279.
Lechner, M. (2001): Identification and Estimation of Causal Effects of Multiple Treatments under the Conditional Independence Assumption, in: M. Lechner and F. Pfeiffer (eds.), Econometric Evaluation of Active Labour Market Policies, p. 43-58, Heidelberg: Physica
Lechner, M., Miquel, R., Wunsch, C. (2004): Long-run effects of Public Sector Sponsored Training in West Germany, Discussion Paper 2004-19, Department of Economics, Universität St.Gallen
Lechner, M., Wiehler, S. (2007): Kids or Courses? Gender differences in the Effects of Active Labour Market Policies, Discussion Paper 2007-08, Department of Economics, Universität St.Gallen
Rubin, D.B. (1974): Estimating Causal Effects of Treatments in randomized and nonrandomized Studies, in: Journal of Educational Psychology, Vol. 66, p. 688–701
Rubin, D. B. (1979): Using Multivariate Matched Sampling and Regression Adjustment to Control Bias in Observational Studies, in: Journal of the American Statistical Association, 74, p. 318–328
Schütz, H., Ochs, P. (2005): Das Neue im Alten und das Alte im Neuen - Das Kundenzentrum der Bundesagentur für Arbeit, Wissenschaftszentrum Berlin für Sozialforschung
Sheldon, G. (2003): The Efficiency of Public Employment Services: A nonparametric Matching Function Analysis for Switzerland, in: Journal of Productivity Analysis, 20, p. 49–70
Vassiliev, A., Luzzi, G., Flückinger, Y., Ramirez, J. (2006): Unemployment and employment offices' efficiency: What can be done?, in: Socio-economic Planning Sciences, 40, p. 169–186
VSAA (2002): Jahresbericht 2001/2002, Verbund Schweizerischer Arbeitsämter, www.vsaa.ch.
Wunsch, C., Lechner, M. (2007): What Did All the Money Do? On the General Ineffectiveness of Recent West German Labour Market Programmes, Discussion Paper 2007-19, Department of Economics, Universität St.Gallen

Public Employment Services and Employers:
How Important are Networks with Firms?

Summary

This paper examines whether contacts between caseworkers in public employment offices and employers impact on the reemployment chances of the unemployed they counsel. This analysis is made possible through a large administrative dataset on unemployed combined with an extensive survey of caseworkers' characteristics and their strategies. This data was created for evaluating public employment services in Switzerland. We use econometric techniques from the treatment evaluation literature to identify causal effects of a more intense employer focus of the caseworkers. The estimation results indicate that caseworkers who maintain direct contacts to firms achieve higher reintegration rates.

Erfolg der öffentlichen Arbeitsvermittlung:
Wie wichtig sind Netzwerke zu Firmen?

Zusammenfassung

Dieser Artikel untersucht die Kontakte zwischen Personalberatern in öffentlichen Arbeitsämtern und Arbeitgebern. Insbesondere wird analysiert, wie sich Kontakte mit Arbeitgebern auf die Beschäftigung der von den Personalberatenden betreuten Arbeitslosen auswirkt. Diese Analyse wird durch einen großen, sehr informativen Datensatz ermöglicht, für den administrative Informationen über die Stellensuchenden mit einer Befragung von Personalberatenden verknüpft wurden, um den Einfluss verschiedener Charakteristika der öffentlichen Arbeitsvermittlung in der Schweiz zu evaluieren. Es werden mikroökonometrische Methoden aus der Evaluationsliteratur benutzt, um kausale Auswirkungen eines Netzwerkes mit Arbeitgebern zu identifizieren. Die Ergebnisse zeigen, dass Arbeitslose, die von Personalberatenden mit direkten Kontakten zu Arbeitgebern betreut werden, höhere Wiederbeschäftigungschancen haben.

GRUNDSÄTZE UND ZIELE

Die **Zeitschrift für Betriebswirtschaft (ZfB)** ist eine der ältesten deutschen Fachzeitschriften der Betriebswirtschaftslehre. Sie wurde im Jahre 1924 von Fritz Schmidt begründet und von Wilhelm Kalveram, Erich Gutenberg und Horst Albach fortgeführt. Sie wird heute von 14 Universitätsprofessoren, die als **Department Editors** fungieren, herausgegeben. Dem **Editorial Board** gehören namhafte Persönlichkeiten aus Universität und Wirtschaftspraxis an. Die Fachvertreter stammen aus den USA, Japan und Europa.

Die ZfB verfolgt das Ziel, die **Forschung auf dem Gebiet der Betriebswirtschaftslehre** anzuregen sowie zur Verbreitung und Anwendung ihrer Ergebnisse beizutragen. Sie betont die Einheit des Faches; enger und einseitiger Spezialisierung in der Betriebswirtschaftslehre will sie entgegenwirken. Die Zeitschrift dient dem **Gedankenaustausch zwischen Wissenschaft und Unternehmenspraxis**. Sie will die betriebswirtschaftliche Forschung auf wichtige betriebswirtschaftliche Probleme in der Praxis aufmerksam machen und sie durch Anregungen aus der Unternehmenspraxis befruchten.

In der ZfB können auch englischsprachige Aufsätze veröffentlicht werden. Die Herausgeber begrüßen die Einreichung englischsprachiger Beiträge von deutschen und internationalen Wissenschaftlern. Durch die Zusammenfassungen in englischer Sprache sind die deutschsprachigen Aufsätze der ZfB auch internationalen Referatenorganen zugänglich. Im Journal of Economic Literature werden die Aufsätze der ZfB zum Beispiel laufend referiert.

Die Qualität der Aufsätze in der ZfB wird durch die Herausgeber und einen Kreis renommierter Gutachter gewährleistet. Das **Begutachtungsverfahren** ist doppelt verdeckt und wahrt damit die Anonymität von Autoren wie Gutachtern gemäß den international üblichen Standards. Jeder Beitrag wird von zwei Fachgutachtern beurteilt. Bei abweichenden Gutachten wird ein Drittgutachter bestellt. Die Department Editors entscheiden auf der Grundlage der Gutachten eigenverantwortlich über die Annahme und Ablehnung der von ihnen betreuten Manuskripte. Sie können Beiträge auch ohne Begutachtungsverfahren ablehnen, wenn diese formal oder inhaltlich von den Vorgaben der ZfB abweichen.

Die ZfB veröffentlicht im Einklang mit diesen Grundsätzen und Zielen:

- **Aufsätze** zu theoretischen und praktischen Fragen der Betriebswirtschaftslehre einschließlich von Arbeiten junger Wissenschaftler, denen sie ein Forum für die Diskussion und die Verbreitung ihrer Forschungsergebnisse eröffnet,
- **Ergebnisse der Diskussion** aktueller betriebswirtschaftlicher Themen zwischen Wissenschaftlern und Praktikern,
- **Berichte** über den Einsatz wissenschaftlicher Instrumente und Konzepte bei der Lösung von betriebswirtschaftlichen Problemen in der Praxis,
- **Schilderungen von Problemen** aus der Praxis zur Anregung der betriebswirtschaftlichen Forschung,
- „**State of the Art**"-**Artikel,** in denen Entwicklung und Stand der Betriebswirtschaftslehre eines Teilgebietes dargelegt werden.

Die ZfB informiert ihre Leser über **Neuerscheinungen** in der Betriebswirtschafslehre und der Management Literatur durch ausführliche Rezensionen und Kurzbesprechungen und berichtet in ihrem **Nachrichtenteil** regelmäßig über betriebswirtschaftliche Tagungen, Seminare und Konferenzen sowie über persönliche Veränderungen vorwiegend an den Hochschulen. Darüber hinaus werden auch Nachrichten für Studenten und Wirtschaftspraktiker veröffentlicht, die Bezug zur Hochschule haben.

MEFFERT MARKETING
DER KLASSIKER – NEU IN DER 10. AUFLAGE

WWW.GABLER.DE

Heribert Meffert | Christoph Burmann | Manfred Kirchgeorg
Marketing
Grundlagen marktorientierter Unternehmensführung
Konzepte - Instrumente - Praxisbeispiele
10., vollst. überarb. u. erw. Aufl. 2008. XX, 915 S.
Geb. EUR 39,90
ISBN 978-3-409-69018-8

Dieses bewährte Standardwerk liefert Studierenden im Bachelor- und Masterprogramm sowie Praktikern umfassende Grundlagen des Marketingmanagements aus einer entscheidungsorientierten Sicht.
Der Marketing-Klassiker erscheint in der 10. Auflage in völlig neu bearbeiteter Fassung. Alle Kapitel wurden inhaltlich und didaktisch überarbeitet, neue Entwicklungen wurden integriert. Die bewährte entscheidungsorientierte Strukturierung des Marketingmanagements wird durch markt- und kompetenzbasierte Ansätze inhaltlich erweitert. Darüber hinaus widmen sich die Autoren den heute wichtigen Fragen des Wertbeitrages des Marketing und bieten hiermit eine gelungene Synthese aus etabliertem und modernem Marketingverständnis.

Der Autor
Prof. Dr. Dr. h.c. mult. Heribert Meffert ist Professor der Betriebswirtschaftslehre, insbesondere Marketing, und emeritierter Direktor des Instituts für Marketing am Marketing Centrum Münster (MCM) der Westfälischen Wilhelms-Universität Münster.
Prof. Dr. Christoph Burmann ist Inhaber des Lehrstuhls für innovatives Markenmanagement (LiM) an der Universität Bremen.
Prof. Dr. Manfred Kirchgeorg ist Inhaber des Lehrstuhls Marketingmanagement an der HHL - Leipzig Graduate School of Management.

Einfach bestellen: kerstin.kuchta@gwv-fachverlage.de Telefon +49(0)611. 7878-626

KOMPETENZ IN SACHEN WIRTSCHAFT

HERAUSGEBER/EDITORIAL BOARD

Editor-in-Chief

Prof. Dr. Dr. h.c. Günter Fandel ist Universitätsprofessor und Inhaber des Lehrstuhls für Betriebswirtschaft, insbesondere Produktions- und Investitionstheorie an der FernUniversität in Hagen. Seine Hauptarbeitsgebiete sind Industriebetriebslehre, Produktionsmanagement und Hochschulmanagement.

Department Editors

Prof. Dr. Wolfgang Breuer ist Universitätsprofessor und Inhaber des Lehrstuhls für Betriebswirtschaftslehre, insb. Betriebliche Finanzwirtschaft, an der Rheinisch-Westfälischen Technischen Hochschule Aachen. Seine Hauptarbeitsgebiete sind Finanzierungs- und Investitionstheorie sowie Portfolio- und Risikomanagement.

Prof. Dr. Holger Ernst ist Inhaber des Lehrstuhls für Betriebswirtschaftslehre, insbesondere Technologie- und Innovationsmanagement an der Wissenschaftlichen Hochschule für Unternehmensführung – Otto-Beisheim-Hochschule – (WHU) in Vallendar.

Prof. Dr. Oliver Fabel ist Universitätsprofessor und Inhaber des Lehrstuhls für Personalwirtschaft mit Internationaler Schwerpunktsetzung am Institut für Betriebswirtschaftslehre der Universität Wien. Seine Hauptarbeitsgebiete sind Personal-, Organisations- und Bildungsökonomik.

Prof. Dr. Dr. h.c. Günter Fandel, s.o.

Prof. Dr. Armin Heinzl ist Universitätsprofessor und Inhaber des Lehrstuhls für Allgemeine Betriebswirtschaftslehre und Wirtschaftsinformatik an der Universität Mannheim. Seine Hauptarbeitsgebiete sind Wirtschaftsinformatik, Organisationslehre sowie Logistik.

Prof. Dr. Manfred Krafft ist Universitätsprofessor, Inhaber des Lehrstuhls für Allgemeine Betriebswirtschaftslehre, insbesondere Marketing und Direktor des Instituts für Marketing der Westfälischen Wilhelms-Universität Münster. Seine Hauptarbeitsgebiete sind Customer Relationship Management, Direktmarketing und Vertriebsmanagement.

Prof. Dr. Norbert Krawitz ist Universitätsprofessor und Inhaber des Lehrstuhls für Betriebswirtschaftslehre mit dem Schwerpunkt Betriebswirtschaftliche Steuerlehre und Prüfungswesen an der Universität Siegen. Seine Hauptarbeitsgebiete sind Rechnungslegung, Wirtschaftsprüfung und betriebswirtschaftliche Steuerlehre.

Prof. Dr. Dr. h.c. Hans-Ulrich Küpper ist Universitätsprofessor und Direktor des Instituts für Produktionswirtschaft und Controlling der Universität München. Seine Hauptarbeitsgebiete sind Unternehmensrechnung, Controlling und Hochschulmanagement.

Prof. Dr. Werner Pascha ist Universitätsprofessor und Inhaber des Lehrstuhls für Ostasienwirtschaft / Wirtschaftspolitik an der Universität Duisburg-Essen.

Prof. Dr. Joachim Schwalbach ist Universitätsprofessor und Inhaber des Lehrstuhls für Internationales Management an der Humboldt Universität in Berlin.

Prof. Dr. Hartmut Stadtler ist Universitätsprofessor und Inhaber des Instituts für Logistik und Transport an der Universität Hamburg. Seine Hauptarbeitsgebiete sind die Logistik, die Unternehmensplanung und die unternehmensübergreifende Planung im Rahmen des Supply Chain Management sowie deren Unterstützung durch Softwaresysteme (z.B. Advanced Planning Systeme).

Prof. Dr. Stefan Winter ist Universitätsprofessor und Inhaber des Lehrstuhls für Human Resource Management an der Ruhr-Universität in Bochum. Seine Hauptarbeitsgebiete sind die Analyse von Anreizstrukturen in Unternehmen, Gestaltung von Vergütungssystemen für Führungskräfte sowie die Institutionenökonomische Analyse von Personal- und Organisationsproblemen.

Prof. Dr. Peter Witt ist Universitätsprofessor und Inhaber des Lehrstuhls für Innovations- und Gründungsmanagement an der Universität Dortmund. Seine Hauptarbeitsgebiete sind Entrepreneurship, Gründungsfinanzierung und Familienunternehmen.

Prof. Dr. Uwe Zimmermann ist Hochschulprofessor und Leiter des Instituts für Mathematische Optimierung an der Technischen Universität Braunschweig. Seine Hauptarbeitsgebiete sind die Lineare, Kombinatorische und Diskrete Optimierung und ihre Anwendung auf komplexe Systeme in Verkehr und Logistik.

Editorial Board

Prof. (em.) Dr. Dr. h.c. mult. Horst Albach (Chairman)
Prof. Alain Burlaud
Prof. Dr. Dr. Dr. h.c. Santiago Garcia Echevarria
Prof. Dr. Lars Engwall
Dr. Dieter Heuskel
Dr. Detlef Hunsdiek
Prof. Dr. Don Jacobs
Prof. Dr. Eero Kasanen
Dr. Bernd-Albrecht v. Maltzan
Prof. Dr. Koji Okubayashi
Hans Botho von Portatius
Prof. Dr. Oleg D. Prozenko
Prof. (em.) Dr. Hermann Sabel
Prof. Dr. Adolf Stepan
Dr. med. Martin Zügel

IMPRESSUM/HINWEISE FÜR AUTOREN

Verlag

Gabler Verlag/GWV Fachverlage GmbH,
Abraham-Lincoln-Straße 46, 65189 Wiesbaden,
http://www.gabler.de
http://www.zfb-online.de
Geschäftsführer: Dr. Ralf Birkelbach, Albrecht F. Schirmacher
Programmleitung Wissenschaft: Claudia Splittgerber
Gesamtleitung Produktion: Ingo Eichel
Gesamtleitung Vertrieb: Gabriel Göttlinger

Editor-in-Chief:
Professor Dr. Dr. h.c. Günter Fandel
FernUniversität in Hagen
Fakultät für Wirtschaftswissenschaft
58084 Hagen
E-Mail: ZfB@FernUni-Hagen.de

Anfragen an den Editor-in-Chief werden per E-Mail an die Adresse ZfB@Fernuni-Hagen.de erbeten. Von Anfragen, die durch die Nutzung der Online-Suche unter http://www.zfb-online.de oder die Einsicht in die Jahresinhaltsverzeichnisse beantwortet werden können, bitten wir abzusehen.

Redaktion: Susanne Kramer, Tel.: 0611/7878-234,
E-Mail: Susanne.Kramer@Gabler.de
Annelie Meisenheimer, Tel.: 0611/7878-232, Fax: 0611/7878-411,
E-Mail: Annelie.Meisenheimer@Gabler.de

Abonnentenbetreuung: Doris Schöne, Tel.: 05241/801968,
Fax: 05241/809620

Produktmanagement: Kristiane Alesch, Tel.: 0611/7878-359,
Fax: 0611/7878-439, E-Mail: Kristiane.Alesch@Gabler.de

Anzeigenleitung: Christian Kannenberg, Tel.: 0611/7878-369,
Fax: 0611/7878-430, E-Mail: Christian.Kannenberg@gwv-fachverlage.de

Anzeigendisposition: Monika Dannenberger,
Tel.: 0611/7878-148, Fax: 0611/7878-340,
E-Mail: Monika.Dannenberger@gwv-fachverlage.de

Es gilt die Anzeigenpreisliste vom 1. 1. 2006.

Produktion/Layout: Kerstin Gollarz

Bezugsmöglichkeiten: Die Zeitschrift erscheint monatlich. Das Abonnement kann jederzeit zur nächsten erreichbaren Ausgabe schriftlich mit Nennung der Kundennummer gekündigt werden. Eine schriftliche Bestätigung erfolgt nicht. Zuviel gezahlte Beträge für nicht gelieferte Ausgaben werden zurückerstattet. Jährlich können 1 bis 6 Special Issues hinzukommen. Jedes Special Issue wird den Abonnenten mit einem Nachlass von 25% des jeweiligen Ladenpreises gegen Rechnung geliefert.

	Preise Inland	Preise Ausland
Einzelheft:	38,– Euro	44,– Euro
Studenten-*/Emeritus-Abo:	69,– Euro	88,– Euro
ausgewählte Verbände:**	168,– Euro	184,– Euro
Privat-Abo:	198,– Euro	224,– Euro
Lehrstuhl-Abo:	224,– Euro	249,– Euro
Bibliotheks-/Unternehmensabo:	388,– Euro	406,– Euro

* Studienbescheinigung
** auf Anfrage beim Verlag

© Betriebswirtschaftlicher Verlag Dr. Th. Gabler/
GWV Fachverlage GmbH, Wiesbaden 2008.

Der Gabler Verlag ist ein Unternehmen von Springer Science+Business Media.

Alle Rechte vorbehalten. Kein Teil dieser Zeitschrift darf ohne schriftliche Genehmigung des Verlages vervielfältigt oder verbreitet werden. Unter dieses Verbot fällt insbesondere die gewerbliche Vervielfältigung per Kopie, die Aufnahme in elektronische Datenbanken und die Vervielfältigung auf CD-ROM und allen anderen elektronischen Datenträgern.

Satzherstellung: Fotosatz-Service Köhler GmbH,
97084 Würzburg.
Druck und Verarbeitung: Wilhelm & Adam, 63150 Heusenstamm.

Gedruckt auf säurefreiem und chlorfrei gebleichtem Papier.

Printed in Germany   ISSN: 0044-2372

Hinweise für Autoren

1. Bitte beachten Sie die „Grundsätze und Ziele" der ZfB.

2. Die ZfB bietet ihren Autoren die Möglichkeit der Online-Einreichung ihrer Beiträge an. Manuskripte – in deutscher oder englischer Sprache – können vom Autor unter http://mc.manuscriptcentral.com/zfb direkt in das Manuskriptverwaltungssystem eingespeist werden. Hierbei ist insbesondere auf die Wahrung der Anonymität der zur Begutachtung eingereichten Vorlagen zu achten. Der Autor verpflichtet sich mit der Einsendung des Manuskripts unwiderruflich, das Manuskript bis zur Entscheidung über die Annahme nicht anderweitig zu veröffentlichen oder zur Veröffentlichung anzubieten. Diese Verpflichtung erlischt nicht durch Korrekturvorschläge im Begutachtungsverfahren.

3. Aufsätze, die im wesentlichen Ergebnisse von Dissertationen wiedergeben, werden nicht veröffentlicht. Um die Ergebnisse von Dissertationen breiter bekannt zu machen, hat die ZfB eine Rubrik „Dissertationen" im Besprechungsteil eingeführt. Hier werden vorzugsweise Erstgutachten von Dissertationen – in entsprechend gekürzter Form – abgedruckt.

4. Alle eingereichten Manuskripte werden, wie international üblich, einem doppelt verdeckten Begutachtungsverfahren unterzogen, d.h. Autoren und Gutachter erfahren ihre Identität gegenseitig nicht. Die Gutachten werden den Autoren und den Gutachtern gegenseitig in anonymisierter Form zur Kenntnis gebracht. Jeder Beitrag wird von zwei Fachgutachtern beurteilt. Bei abweichenden Gutachten wird ein dritter Gutachter bestellt. Durch dieses Verfahren soll die fachliche Qualität der Beiträge gesichert werden. Die Department Editors entscheiden auf der Grundlage der Gutachten eigenverantwortlich über die Annahme und Ablehnung der von ihnen betreuten Manuskripte. Auch haben sie das Recht, einen Beitrag direkt abzulehnen, wenn er aus formalen und/oder inhaltlichen Gründen von den Vorgaben der Zeitschrift abweicht.

5. Die Manuskripte sind in Times New Roman, 12 Punkt, 11/2zeilig mit 2,5 cm Rand zu schreiben. Sie sollten nicht länger als 25 Schreibmaschinenseiten sein. Der Titel des Beitrages und der/die Verfasser mit vollem Titel und ausgeschriebenen Vornamen sowie beruflicher Stellung sind auf der ersten Manuskriptseite aufzuführen. Dem Beitrag ist ein „Überblick" von höchstens 15 Zeilen voranzustellen, in dem das Problem, die angewandte Methodik, das Hauptergebnis in seiner Bedeutung für Wissenschaft und/oder Praxis dargestellt werden. Die Aufsätze sind einheitlich nach dem Schema A., I., 1., a) zu gliedern. Endnoten (Times New Roman, 12 pt) sind im Text fortlaufend zu numerieren und am Schluß des Aufsatzes unter „Anmerkungen" zusammenzustellen. Anmerkungen und Literatur sollen getrennt aufgeführt werden. Im Text und in den Anmerkungen soll auf das Literaturverzeichnis nach dem Schema: (Gutenberg, 1982, S. 352) verwiesen werden. Jedem Aufsatz muß eine „Summary" in englischer Sprache von nicht mehr als 15 Zeilen Länge und eine deutsche Zusammenfassung gleicher Länge angefügt werden. Für Abbildungen und Tabellen ist eine Legende vorzusehen (z.B.: Abb. 1: Kostenfunktion, bzw. Tab. 2: Rentabilitätsentwicklung). Abbildungen und Tabellen sind an der betreffenden Stelle des Manuskripts in Kopie einzufügen und im Original (reproduzierfähig) dem Manuskript beizulegen. Mathematische Formeln sind fortlaufend zu numerieren: (1), (2) usw. Sie sind so einfach wie möglich zu halten. Griechische- und Fraktur-Buchstaben sind möglichst zu vermeiden, ungewöhnliche mathematische und sonstige Zeichen für den Setzer zu erläutern. Auf mathematische Ableitungen soll im Text verzichtet werden; sie sind aber für die Begutachtung beizufügen. Mit dem Manuskript liefert der Autor ein reproduzierfähiges Brustbild (Passphoto) von sich sowie eine kurze Information (max. 7 Zeilen) zu seiner Person und seinen Arbeitsgebieten.

6. Der Autor verpflichtet sich, die Korrekturfahnen innerhalb einer Woche zu lesen und die Mehrkosten für Korrekturen, die nicht vom Verlag zu vertreten sind, sowie die Kosten für die Korrektur durch einen Korrektor bei nicht termingerechter Rücksendung der Fahnenkorrektur zu übernehmen.

7. Der Autor ist damit einverstanden, daß sein Beitrag außer in der Zeitschrift auch durch Lizenzvergabe in anderen Zeitschriften (auch übersetzt), durch Nachdruck in Sammelbänden (z.B. zu Jubiläen der Zeitschrift oder des Verlages oder in Themenbänden), durch längere Auszüge in Büchern des Verlages auch zu Werbezwecken, durch Vervielfältigung und Verbreitung auf CD-ROM oder anderen Datenträgern, durch Speicherung auf Datenbanken, deren Weitergabe und dem Abruf von solchen Datenbanken während der Dauer des Urheberrechtsschutzes an dem Beitrag im In- und Ausland vom Verlag und seinen Lizenznehmern genutzt wird.

WWW.GABLER.DE

Bachelor-Lehrbuch zum Management

MIT ZUSATZMATERIAL FÜR DOZENTEN

Georg Schreyögg | Jochen Koch
Grundlagen des Managements
Basiswissen für Studium und Praxis
2007. XIV, 461 S.
Br. EUR 24,90 ISBN 978-3-8349-0376-1

Das neue Lehrbuch von Georg Schreyögg und Jochen Koch gibt eine kompakte Darstellung der wichtigsten Inhalte des Managements. Themenauswahl und -aufbereitung sind speziell auf die Anforderungen an Studierende in Bachelor-Studiengängen zugeschnitten und das gesamte Lehrbuch ist auf ein Standardmodul in der Bachelor-Ausbildung hin konzipiert. Die einzelnen Lerneinheiten folgen dabei einem einheitlichen didaktischen Konzept: Jedes Kapitel enthält Lernziele und Schlüsselbegriffe, einen geschlossenen Lehrtext mit integrierten Informationskästen und Marginalienkommentierung, Lern- und Diskussionsfragen sowie eine abschließende Fallstudie zu Übungszwecken. Zusätzliche Service-Komponenten sollen den Einsatz als Basislehrbuch erleichtern: Alle Leserinnen und Leser können Lösungshinweise zu den Lernkontrollfragen von der Verlags-Homepage unter www.gabler.de herunterladen. Für Dozentinnen und Dozenten sind dort außerdem Zusatzmaterialien zur Unterrichtsvorbereitung hinterlegt, insbesondere Lösungshinweise für die Diskussionsfragen, Musterlösungen für die Fallstudien sowie fertige Foliensätze zur Präsentation der Lehrinhalte.

Die Autoren
Prof. Dr. Georg Schreyögg und **Dr. Jochen Koch** forschen und lehren am Institut für Management, Freie Universität Berlin.

Aus dem Inhalt
- Management: Einführung und konzeptionelle Grundlagen
- Planung und Kontrolle
- Organisation, Führung und Personaleinsatz

Einfach bestellen: kerstin.kuchta@gwv-fachverlage.de Telefon +49(0)611. 7878-626

KOMPETENZ IN SACHEN WIRTSCHAFT

jbm. Free Trial Subscription

Editorial Policy

The Journal of Business Market Management (jbm) explores all facets of business-to-business marketing, industrial market management and marketing of business services. That includes the areas of technical and commercial sales management but also industrial supply and business buying behaviour. Academics' as well as practitioners' thinking will be enriched with novel and significant ideas in terms of research approaches and results. Offering a combination of conceptual papers, empirical research analyses and case study articles the journal represents a valuable knowledge source and contributes to a better understanding of business market activities.

jbm seeks to highlight as well as to integrate various orientations of theoretical, conceptual and empirical research around the world and takes advantage of it. Thus it will provide opportunities for methodological variety as well as the enhancement of theories and theory-based empirical research. Each article must prove a challenging level of research capability and comprehensible complexity.

Response

Gabler Verlag
Subscription Department
Abraham-Lincoln-Straße 46
65189 Wiesbaden | Germany

Phone +49-0611. 7878-615
Fax +49-0611. 7878-423
Gabler@abo-service.info

jbm – Journal of Business Market Management Subscription Cheque

____ Yes, as an individual subscriber I would like to test jbm.
Please send me a copy of the next issue free of charge. If I decide to subscribe jbm at an annual rate of EUR 132,00 (approx. US $ 158,00 worldwide), I do not need to do anything – future issues will be sent automatically. If I choose to cancel, I will send a short written notice within 20 days.

____ Yes, as an institution we would like to test jbm.
Please send us a copy of the next issue free of charge. If we decide to subscribe jbm at an annual rate of EUR 414,00 (approx. US $ 494,00 worldwide), we do not need to do anything – future issues will be sent automatically. If we choose to cancel, we will send a short written notice within 20 days.

Last name | First name

University | Institute | Company | Organization

Street (no postbox, please)

City | ZIP-Code   Country

Date   Signature   311 08 100

Gabler Verlag
Abraham-Lincoln-Straße 46
65189 Wiesbaden | Germany
Geschäftsführer:
Dr. Ralf Birkelbach,
Albrecht F. Schirmacher,
AG Wiesbaden HRB 9754

KOMPETENZ IN SACHEN WIRTSCHAFT

ZfB
ZEITSCHRIFT FÜR BETRIEBSWIRTSCHAFT
Journal of Business Economics
Editor-in-Chief: Prof. Dr. Dr. h.c. G. Fandel

Home | Briefkasten | Abonnement | Mediaservice | Kontakt | Sitemap

ZfB Online
- Aktuelles Heft
- Nachrichten
- Rezensionen
- Editor-in-Chief
- Department Editors
- Editorial Board

Abovorteile

Besuchen Sie unsere Homepage:

www.zfb-online.de

Archiv
- Frühere Ausgaben
- Ergänzungshefte
- Online First

Probeabonnement
Ordern Sie hier Ihr **Go!** kostenloses zweimonatiges Probeabo!

Services
- Jahresregister
- Autorenhinweise
- Autorentracking

Online lesen:
Nutzen Sie unser ZfB-Volltextarchiv unter www.zfb-online.de. Hier können Sie alle Beiträge ab 2000 herunterladen. Für Abonnenten selbstverständlich kostenlos! Abonnenten erhalten bereits vor Drucklegung die aktuellen Beiträge.

Online schreiben:
Nutzen Sie unser Manuskripteinreichungs- und Trackingsystem „Manuscript Central™". Unter http://mc.manuscriptcentral.com/zfb können Autoren ab sofort online Beiträge einreichen.

Partner
- Gabler
- BusinessGuide
- ZFCM Online
- MIR Online
- Fuchsbriefe
- Platow Briefe
- Karriereplaner.de
- Wirtschaftsinformatik
- innovative Verwaltung
- DUV

EXTRA

ZfB-Special Issues

bestellen...

BusinessGuide

Gabler Verlag
Abraham-Lincoln-Str. 46
65189 Wiesbaden

www.gabler.de

GPSR Compliance

The European Union's (EU) General Product Safety Regulation (GPSR) is a set of rules that requires consumer products to be safe and our obligations to ensure this.

If you have any concerns about our products, you can contact us on

ProductSafety@springernature.com

In case Publisher is established outside the EU, the EU authorized representative is:

Springer Nature Customer Service Center GmbH
Europaplatz 3
69115 Heidelberg, Germany

www.ingramcontent.com/pod-product-compliance
Lightning Source LLC
LaVergne TN
LVHW020132080526
838202LV00047B/3927